A COMPILATION OF TWO

FACTORY WORKSHOP MANUALS

MANUAL No. 1:
LIGHTWEIGHT AND HEAVYWEIGHT TWIN CYLINDER MODELS 1960-1968

Originally published by Floyd Clymer, this factory manual is undated with no model years identified and no factory part number. However, on page 4 it states from '1960 onwards'. As the Atlas was the last model in this series and was manufactured through 1968 we can be sure that the manual covers the entire line of the 1960-1968 Norton 250cc to 750cc twins.

MANUAL No. 2:
750cc COMMANDO MODELS 1968-1970

Another undated factory manual, part no. 06-3062, with no model years identified. However, as it includes data relating to models after engine no. 131257 (March 1969) we can assume it was originally intended to cover the 1968-1970 Commando models equipped with the external rev-counter drive and/or the Atlas style exhaust system. In addition, while this manual includes a 1971 wiring diagram it appears to have been added as an afterthought and the later factory manuals all state 'from 1970' onwards.

© 2021 Veloce Enterprises Inc., San Antonio, Texas USA
All rights reserved. This work may not be reproduced or transmitted in any form without the express consent of the publisher

ACKNOWLEDGEMENT

We would like to take the opportunity to extend our appreciation to Norton Motorcycle Company for the publications included in this compilation. It is important to remember that the company was founded in 1898 and helped pave the way for the motorcycles we enjoy today. We are pleased to offer this reprint as a service to all Norton motorcycle owners and collectors worldwide, and we extend our thanks to the Norton Motorcycle Company for their contribution to the British motorcycle industry.

INTRODUCTION

Welcome to the world of digital publishing ~ the book you now hold in your hand was printed using the latest state of the art digital technology. The advent of print-on-demand has forever changed the publishing process, never has information been so accessible and it is our hope that this book serves your informational needs for years to come. If this is your first exposure to digital publishing, we hope that you are pleased with the results. Many more titles of interest to the classic automobile and motorcycle enthusiast, collector and restorer are available via our website at www.VelocePress.com. We hope that you find this title as interesting as we do.

NOTE FROM THE PUBLISHER

The information presented is true and complete to the best of our knowledge. All recommendations are made without any guarantees on the part of the author or the publisher, who also disclaim all liability incurred with the use of this information.

TRADEMARKS

We recognize that some words, model names and designations, for example, mentioned herein are the property of the trademark holder. We use them for identification purposes only. This is not an official publication.

INFORMATION ON THE USE OF THIS PUBLICATION

This manual is an invaluable resource for those interested in performing their own maintenance. However, in today's information age we are constantly subject to changes in common practice, new technology, availability of improved materials and increased awareness of chemical toxicity. As such, it is advised that the user consult with an experienced professional prior to undertaking any procedure described herein. While every care has been taken to ensure correctness of information, it is obviously not possible to guarantee complete freedom from errors or omissions or to accept liability arising from such errors or omissions. Therefore, any individual that uses the information contained within, or elects to perform or participate in do-it-yourself repairs or modifications acknowledges that there is a risk factor involved and that the publisher or its associates cannot be held responsible for personal injury or property damage resulting from the use of the information or the outcome of such procedures.

WARNING!

One final word of advice, this publication is intended to be used as a reference guide, and when in doubt the reader should consult with a qualified technician.

Index

	Page
Battery Lucas—All models (MLZ9E)	64
Bearing removal	23
Brake adjustment, front	47
Brake adjustment, rear	48
Brakes, dismantling and assembly	48
Brake drum, dismantling	46
Brake drum, removal	46
Camshaft bushes	33
Carburetter service	56
Chain adjustment, front	39
Chain, care of	40
Chain, primary adjustment	39-42
Chain, primary removal and refitting	43
Chain, rear adjustment	79-42
Chain removal, rear	40
Chaincase, front removal	40
Clutch	38-42
Clutch adjustment	42
Clutch assembly	42
Clutch dismantling and assembly	43
Clutch cable adjustment	39
Clutch cable removal	45
Connecting rods	24-32
Connecting rods assembling	25
Crankcase bearings	33
Crankcase bearings, fitting	26
Crankcase release valve	6
Crankcase separation	22-31
Crankshaft	23-32
Cylinder, removal	29
Cylinder, refitting	30
Cylinder barrel, removal	10
Cylinder barrel, refitting	13
Cylinder head, removal	9-11
Cylinder head, refitting	14
Decarbonising	9
Electrical service, Electra	70-73
Electrical service, Lucas	61-70
Electrical service, Wipac	57-61
Electrical wiring diagrams	74-79
Engine assembly, heavyweight	12
Engine assembly, lightweight	26-33
Engine service, heavyweight twins	9
Engine service, lightweight twins	28
Engine, removal	22
Engine removal, excluding G15 models	22
Engine, removal from frame	31
Engine and gear box removal	22
Timing chains, engine	15
Footchange assembly	45
Frame	54
Forks, front, all models except G15-CS & Jubilee	48
Forks, front, G15 CS models	51
Forks, front, Jubilee models	51
Gear box, heavyweight twins	38
Gear box, Jubilee & Navigator engines before 106838	41
Gear box, Jubilee & Navigator engines after 106838	45
Gear, Intermediate	33

	Page
Heads, refitting	30
Hub, rear, dismantling and assembling	46
Ignition timing	34
Kickstarter, dismantling	46
Lubrication	7-8
Lubrication, frames	55
Oil changing	7
Oil circulation	4
Oil filters	4
Oil pressure	6
Oil pump	4
Oil pump identification	6
Oil pump worm drive	7
Oil seal, crankcase, driving side	26
Oil seal pump	6
Oil seal pump, checking	25
Oil seal replacement	25
Oil seal, timing cover	6-30
Pistons	10
Pistons, refitting	13
Pistons, removal	12-23
Pistons, removal and fitting	30
Piston rings	30
Piston rings, fitting	12
Plug location	59
Pressure relief valve	6
Pressure relief valve, 650 SS models	4
Pressure relief valve filter	4
Regrinding details	83-85
Rocker	11
Rocker adjustment, push rod clearance	14
Rocker axles	12
Rocker ball end	11
Rockers, removal	10-31
Rocker, setting clearance	30
Roller bearings	26
Routine maintenance	7
Shaft, intermediate	25
Steering lock	50
Sump filter	4
Swinging arm, lightweight twins	55
Swinging arm, G15 CS only	54
Swinging arm, heavyweight twins, except G15 CS	54
Tappets	12
Technical data	80-82
Timing, adjustment	15
Timing cover removal	30
Timing cover, refitting	16
Timing magneto, checking	15
Transmission	38-42
Valves	10
Valves, removal	29
Valves, fitting	30
Valve grinding	30
Valve guides, removal and refitting	29
Wheel balancing	48
Wheel, front, removal and refitting	46
Wheel, rear, removal	46
Wheels and hubs, Jubilee model	53

Preface

NORTON TWIN CYLINDER MODELS

This manual has been compiled to provide in concise form, technical information, to enable competent owners also service repair staff alike, to service Norton Twin cylinder models made from 1960 onwards.

Technical details are included to show bearing dimensions, also other important details—so that a comparison can be made to check parts for wear against the tolerance allowed. Where instruments for measuring parts of this kind are available, reference should be made to the technical data, to ascertain if a replacement part is needed, or otherwise.

Maintenance instructions are also included, to enable the owner to obtain innumerable miles of trouble free running. Neglect in making essential adjustments, with indifferent attention to lubrication, can only result in unnecessary trouble—thus—nullifying the intention of the designers to produce for the owner—a trouble free machine. Without prior experience, or good workshop facilities, owners should consider having major repairs dealt with—either by the factory—or by expert repair and service staff.

Lubrication

A table of recommended lubricants—is given on page 6 the various brands have been approved and found suitable for the Norton Twin cylinder models. Where a machine is used frequently, for short journeys, and in particular during the winter months, the engine oil should be changed at frequent intervals—say every two months—in preference to a pre-arranged mileage.

A gear type oil pump is used on all Norton twin cylinder models, which are all similar in appearance, but differ dimensionally—according to the model—also engine capacity. The gears used to return oil from the sump to the oil tank—on all models—have twice the pumping capacity of the gears used on the feed—or delivery side of the system—thus keeping the sump crankcase free from excess oil content. Oil is fed by gravity through a strainer in the tank assisted by suction from the feed pump, which forces oil under pressure, via pre-determined diameter oil passages in the crankcase, lubricating the engine. Excess oil drains to the lowest portion of the crankcase to be returned to the oil tank via a close mesh metal filter. Lubrication for the rocker gear, is effected by a by-pass from the oil return pipe, which has a restricted orifice, to divert oil to the moving parts in the cylinder head.

Checking oil circulation

Provision is made to observe the oil circulation, by removing the filler cap on the oil tank, when oil can be seen emerging from the return pipe installed in the tank. A check is best made, after the engine has been stationary, when the oil return flow is positive also continuous, by reason of the surplus oil draining back to the sump. After running the engine for a short period to scavenge—the oil return will be spasmodic, due to the greater capacity of the return pump. A vent pipe—attached to the oil tank—allows pressure to escape and eliminate the possibility of an air lock.

Oil filters

Two metal type oil filters are incorporated in the oiling system for all Norton twin cylinder engines, in addition a strainer is attached to the oil feed connection in the oil tank. The wide mesh used for the strainer is intentional to avoid cavitation, or oil flow restriction, with cold oil.

The sump filter

With the exception of the lightweight twin models, the sump filter-cum-drain plug—is housed in a bronze plug, screwed into the lowest portion of the crankcase. The close mesh metal portion—is fluted in shape—of wide area.

The sump filter for the lightweight twin engines, consists of a close mesh metal sheet, covered by an alloy plate, secured to the crankcase by four studs and nuts.

To dismantle the filter for cleaning, extract with care to avoid deforming the circlip, which when removed the filter portion can be removed for cleaning.

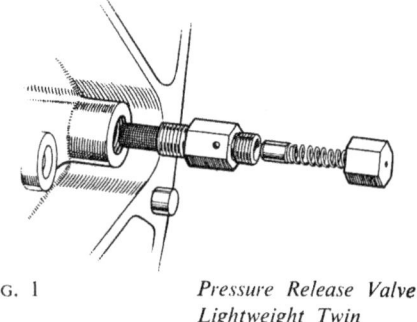

FIG. 1   *Pressure Release Valve Lightweight Twin*

Pressure relief valve filter

The plunger for pressure relief, or blow off valve, must work freely, and to guard against foreign matter affecting the free working, a cylindrical type metal gauze shielding the plunger (see figs. 1, 2) is used. Removal of the timing cover gives access to this filter, on both models.

Pressure relief valve (650 SS Models)

The filter for the above model is housed in the rear end of the timing gear cover and is accessible by unscrewing the cap nut locating the spring and filter (see fig. 2 for location).

The oil pump

An exploded view of the pump gears housed in a common pump body is shown in fig. 3. Providing clean oil is continually circulating, when the engine is running, the pump canot become deranged.

To remove the oil pump

Disconnect the Rev counter drive cable—if fitted—take off the timing gear cover (see para. timing and gears removal lightweight models) by removing ten screws. Tapping the sides of the cover with a soft faced mallet, will tend to break the joint, for easy removal. It is preferable to take off the oil pump worm drive from the crankshaft—which has a LEFT-HAND THREAD. Take off the two nuts securing the pump to the crankcase, applied leverage behind the worm drive on the pump worm can be used, if the pump resists removal.

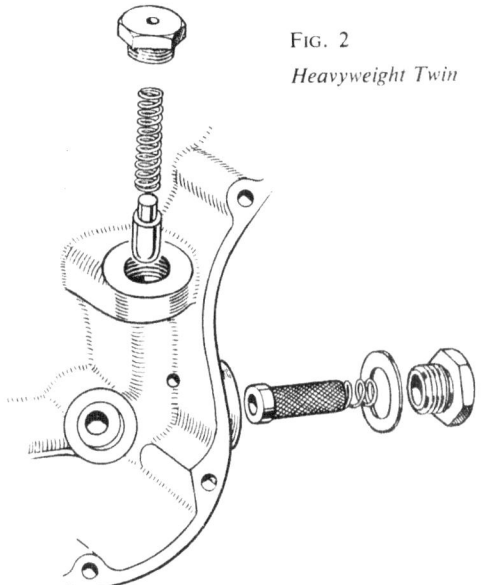

Fig. 2
Heavyweight Twin

Checking the oil pump

When rotating the pump by hand the gears should rotate without any tight places. A tendency to partially jam, suggests the presence of foreign matter, then the pump should be dismantled for cleaning, alternatively, operate the pump—immersed in a bath of suitable solvent—for cleaning.

Test for end play—by pulling and pushing on the drive spindle—end play will result in a loss of pump efficiency, under such circumstances return the pump for service. The end float should be NIL. If the volume of oil returned from the sump has decreased, or if the oil return is NIL, check the pump body face where it abuts against the crankcase, by placing a straight edge against this face, for even a slight bow —across the stud fixing holes—will allow the pump to suck air—in preference to a column of oil from the sump. If this face is not perfectly flat—it should be rubbed down on a surface plate—and ensure the pump interior is scrupulously clean afterwards.

Oil seeps into the engine

A slight oil seepage past the pump gears is inevitable, particularly when the mileage covered is considerable, If the machine is left standing for an undue length of time, it is best to drain the sump before starting the engine. Loose pump body screws will cause seepage.

Should seepage occur, when the standing is of short duration—then the pump should be checked for wear in the spindle bores.

If it is necessary to dismantle the oil pump, release the worm drive spindle nut on the pump, before the pump is removed from the crankcase on the lightweight models. This is not possible on the heavyweight models—hold the pump worm drive in a vice with copper faced clamps to prevent teeth damage during the process of releasing the fixing nut. A simple fixture to hold the pump worm drive—used in the factory—is shown in fig. 4A.

The oil pump worm drive has a parallel bore with a Woodruffe Key in the shaft, and can be removed without the aid of a pinion removal tool.

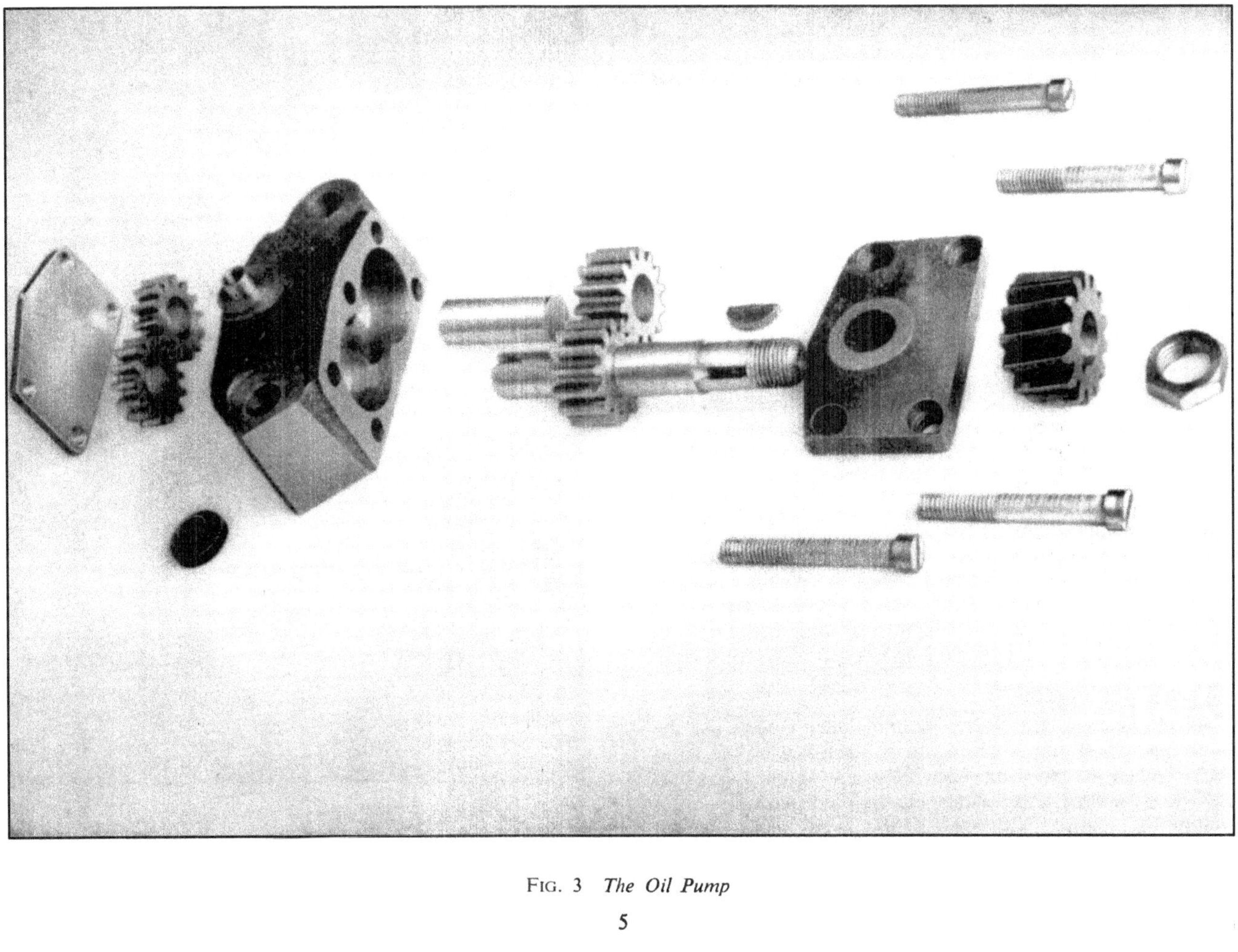

Fig. 3 *The Oil Pump*

Dismantling the pump

An examination of the pump will show that the two end plates are either flush, or slightly below the pump body. It follows that if one—or both plates are proud of the pump body after assembly—an air tight joint between the pump and the crankcase cannot be made.

With the worm drive removed (this is not essential).

Remove four pump body screws.

Remove the brass end plate.

Remove the iron plate with shaft and drive key—the drive pinion is usually a close fit on the shaft—a light tap with a brass drift will dislodge the pinion.

Remove the idler shaft from feed side.

Remove the return idler pinion.

Remove the two drive pinions.

Assemble the pump in a reverse sequence and note the small radius on the oil return gear should face the inside of the pump body.

The oil pump seal

The conical shaped oil seal (which is oil and heat resisting material) surrounds the metal nipple—the latter being a press fit into the pump body. With the pump installed and the timing cover refitted—it is patently clear that the oil seal must be under light pressure against the conical shaped seating in the timing gear cover. If the oil seal is mutilated, or without pressure—oil can leak into the timing chest instead of going to the crankshaft oil way.

When the timing gear cover is in position—the oil seal should push the cover away from the crankcase making a gap of .010″. If pressure does not exist either renew the oil seal—or use shim washers—which are supplied—between the seal and the pump body. In the event of an oil failure, this part of the system should be carefully checked.

Timing cover oil seal

Oil delivered under pressure from the feed pump, after passing through the metal nipple, which is surrounded by the conical shaped oil seal, passes through a drilled oil passage in the timing cover and breaks out, into a cavity in the cover. A super oil seal is fitted in the exit end of this cavity and engages on the plain portion of the timing side crankshaft. This oil is forced into the crankshaft oil channels to lubricate the engine. The oil pressure built up in the cavity, tends to make the seal more effective, at the same time, a damaged, or badly worn oil seal will allow leakage and curtail the oil supply to the crankshaft.

Checking oil pressure

The oil pressure can be recorded by mounting a pressure gauge as shown in fig. 4. The timing cover illustrated is used on a 650 SS. twin model. The pressure relief valve filter described elsewhere can be seen. Below this filter is a screwed plug, which can also be used as a take off point for the pressure gauge. On other twin cylinder models the timing cover is drilled and tapped central with the oil seal to accommodate the instrument depicted in fig. 4. Where extensive service work is carried out the use of a "slave" cover is a useful workshop component. The normal oil pressure is 30 to 40 lbs. per square inch at 3,000 rpm when starting from cold.

Oil pump identification

All the heavyweight Norton twin cylinder models use the same type of oil pump, which can be identified by the letter "S" stamped on the pump body. The lightweight twins also use the same type of oil pump, but have no marking—these cannot be confused with the single cylinder pumps as the drive on the latter models—is reversed.

Crankcase release valve

This valve is used on the heavyweight twins—and is located in the tunnel for the camshaft—in the driving side crankcase. The valve is intended to allow positive pressure in the crankcase—caused by the pistons descending—to escape—as this pressure is usually in the form of oil mist the discharge is taken to the oil tank—via a rubber hose. The valve consists of:

A stationary plate (below the camshaft bush) retained by a peg (T2078).

A rotary plate actuated by the camshaft (24301).

A spring to keep the rotary plate in contact with the stationary plate (T2108).

The valve is timed—also ported—to assemble insert the rotary plate face downwards—insert the spring—before fitting the camshaft.

NOTE: It is important that the rotary plate is perfectly flat, if not replace it with a new one. Wear in the driving dogs will affect the timing, and here again a new plate is needed.

The pressure relief valve

This valve—fitted in the oil feed line—is pre-set to blow off—or lift—between 40 to 50 lbs. per square inch—should some restriction, or blockage occur in the feed line, which would otherwise damage the pump gears. The valve needs no routine attention—in some cases washers are used to adjust the spring poundage—to give the right blow off value.

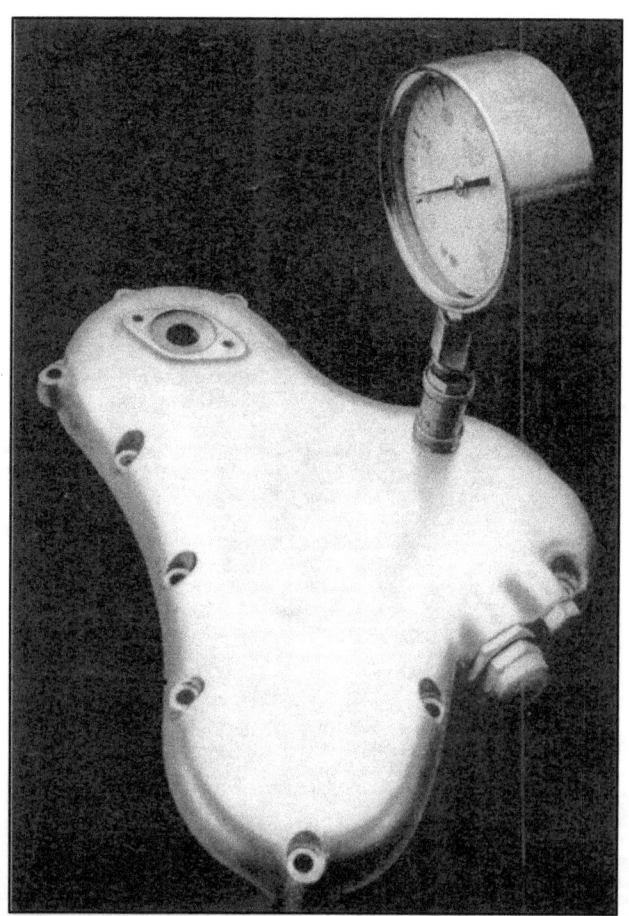

Fig. 4
Pressure Gauge Mounting

Oil pump worm drive

As there is more than one type of worm drive gear for the oil pump—and as they are not readily identified—the two types are shown in fig. 4B.

The six start worm drive is fitted to the ELECTRA model only.

Changing the oil

When a machine is new—the oil should be changed frequently—to get rid of any foreign matter the oil picks up whilst in circulation.

Routine Maintenance

Engine

The oil should be changed at the first 500 miles (800 kms.) and again at 1,000 miles (1,500 kms.). It is at this time the oil filters, described elsewhere should be cleaned. The brands of oil recommended will be found in the table of lubricants, on page 8.

It is equally important to flush out the oil tank to ensure all impurities are removed from the oiling system.

FIG. 4B

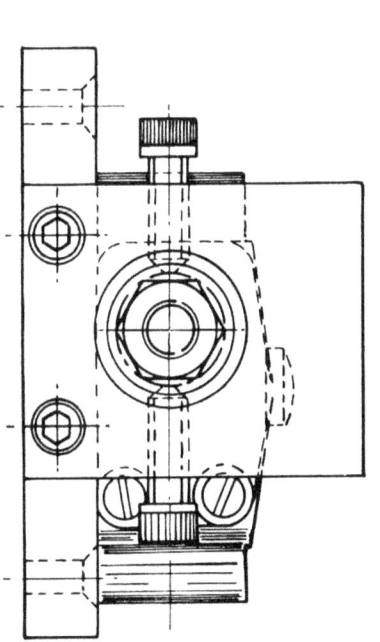

OIL PUMP WORMS

Primary drive chaincase

Drain and refill with fresh oil at the first 500 miles (800 kms.) and again at 1,000 miles (1,500 kms.) or at monthly intervals, whichever occurs first. The correct quantity to be filled can be ascertained by removing the oil level plug, in the outer portion of the chaincase, and fill until the oil seeps through the oil level hole. By periodic attention to this part of the machine, the primary chain will keep in excellent condition thus obviating the need to frequently adjust the chain, over long mileage, apart from the necessity to replace the chain, after short service.

Front forks

Drain at 1,000 miles, or earlier if so desired to get rid of impurities in the oil—see para. fork maintenance—change the oil again at 5,000 miles (8,000 kms.).

Gear box

Drain and refill with fresh oil at the first 500 miles (8,00 kms) from then on every 5,000 miles (8,000 kms.). During the latter interval check, from time to time, the level, particularly when there is evidence of oil leakage.

Rear suspension units

These are sealed units, the damper fluid filled, is sufficient to outlast the life of the unit. A little grease applied to the outside diameter of the springs—if a grating noise develops—is the only attention needed.

FIG. 4A

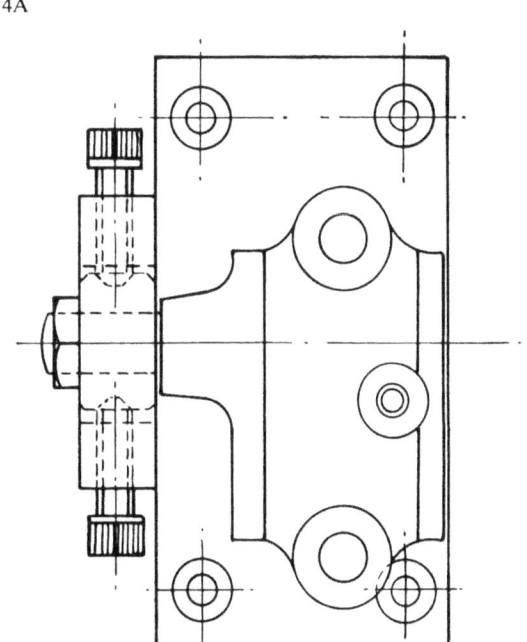

Lubrication

LUBRICANTS TO USE

Efficient lubrication is of vital importance and it is false economy to use cheap oils and grease. We recommend the following lubricants to use in machines of our make.

FOR ENGINE LUBRICATION

HOT above 50° F	COLD 32° F to 50° F	EXTREME COLD below freezing point (32° F)
SAE 50	SAE 30	SAE 20
Mobiloil D Castrol Grand Prix Energol SAE 50 Essolube 50 Shell X-100 Motor Oil 50 Regent Havoline 50	Mobiloil A Castrol XL Energol SAE 30 Essolube 30 Shell X-100 Motor Oil 30 Regent Havoline 30	Mobiloil Arctic Castrolite Energol SAE 20 Essolube 20 Shell X-100 Motor Oil 20/20W Regent Havoline 20

NOTE—For the British Isles and much of Europe the Cold and Hot recommendations approximate to Winter and Summer conditions respectively. The Extreme Cold recommendations refer to wintry conditions in parts of Northern Europe, Canada, the Baltic and Scandinavian countries, and high mountainous districts where extreme cold is the average condition.

FOR GEARBOX LUBRICATION

HOT above 50° F	COLD 32° F to 50° F	EXTREME COLD below freezing point (32° F)
SAE 50	SAE 50	SAE 30
Mobiloil D Castrol Grand Prix Energol SAE 50 Essolube 50 Shell X-100 Motor Oil 50 Regent Havoline 50	Mobiloil D Castrol Grand Prix Energol SAE 50 Essolube 50 Shell X-100 Motor Oil 50 Regent Havoline 50	Mobiloil A Castrol XL Energol SAE 30 Essolube 30 Shell X-100 Motor Oil 30 Regent Havoline 30 Energol SAE 20 Regent Havoline 20

NOTE—For the British Isles and much of Europe the Cold and Hot recommendations approximate to Winter and Summer conditions respectively. The Extreme Cold recommendations refer to wintry conditions in parts of Northern Europe, Canada, the Baltic and Scandinavian countries, and high mountainous districts where extreme cold is the average condition.

FOR HUB LUBRICATION AND ALL FRAME PARTS USING GREASE

MP Mobilgrease Regent Marfak	Castrolease Heavy Shell Retinax A or C.D.	Energrease C3

FOR TELEDRAULIC FRONT FORKS

Mobiloil Arctic (SAE-20) Essolube 20 (SAE-20)	Castrolite (SAE-20) Shell X-100 Motor Oil 20/20W (SAE-20)	Energol SAE 20

FOR REAR CHAINS

Mobilgrease No. 2 Marfak No. 2	Esso Fluid Grease Castrolease Grease Graphited Heated until just fluid	Energrease A.O.

Capacities

Oil tank—heavyweight twins—4.5 pints.
Oil tank—lightweight twins—3.5 pints.
Gear box—heavyweight twins—1 pint (560 cc.).
Gear box—lightweight twins—2.25 pints (1.25 litre).
Front forks—heavyweight twins—5 ozs. (142 cc.).
Front fork—heavyweight twins—Scrambler models 6.5 ozs. (170.4 cc.)—long fork tubes.
Front forks—Electra model—5 ozs. (142 cc.) ¼ pint.
Front forks—Navigator—5 ozs. (142 cc.).
Front forks—Jubilee model—75 cc.
Primary chaincase—Jubilee and Navigator 1/3 pint (.19 litres).
Primary chaincase—Electra—1/3 pint (200 cc.).
Primary chaincase—heavyweight twins—4.5 ozs. (130 cc.).

The oil tank level

A decal (transfer) is applied to the oil tank to indicate the recommended oil level, for the oil tank. When filling up (topping up) and, if the machine has been stationary for any length of time, it is best to run the engine for a short time to scavenge the sump. Omission to do so, will result in overfilling, with an oil discharge from the oil tank vent pipe. The oil level should be maintained to the normal level whenever possible, using the machine with a low oil level, will raise the oil temperature, due to the small amount circulating, which can have an adverse effect, on the engine.

Rocker lubrication

It is worthwhile, periodically, sealing off the oil return, to the oil tank, by placing the index finger over the spout, which returns oil to the oil tank, for a few seconds, or so. The additional pressure will tend to clear any partial obstruction in the rocker oil ways. Sealing off the oil return, for any length of time, will cause the hose attached to the metal piping in the oil line, to blow apart. This operation is also desirable when the engine is first run after being re-assembled.

Heavyweight Twins

Engine service

By reason of the similarity of design of the above models, the foregoing instructions are equally applicable to all models in this class.

There is no fixed, or known mileage, when the engine should be decarbonised, the necessity to do so, is usually indicated by a fall off in power, accompanied with an increase in petrol consumption, and possibly detonation (pinking) due to a heavy formation of carbon, on both the piston crowns also the sphere of the cylinder head.

If the performance has not deteriorated—the petrol consumption is normal—no useful purpose is served by taking the engine to pieces, the adage—"intelligent inattention is preferable to unintelligent tinkering" is a sound one. It is commonplace to receive letters in service from owners who write—"my machine was running good—until I took it apart—now it does not run so good"—hence the digression from technical matter.

When investigating a fall off in performance, the skilled operator will make a preliminary investigation, by checking rocker clearance, contact breaker gap, and ignition timing, before taking the engine apart. For example—if it is found that the rocker clearance is excessive—the reason for this can be investigated—when the engine is dismantled—thus avoiding the need to take the engine apart again at a subsequent date.

Have available a decoke gasket set—also the following tools:

A socket wrench (ring spanner) or tubular box key for ⅜" Whitworth.
A socket wrench—or tubular box key for 5/16" Whitworth.
A "C" spanner—Part Number SHU/29 (for exhaust pipe ring nuts).
A tubular box key ¼" Whitworth.
An open spanner 3/16" Whitworth.
An allen key 7/32" size.

To take off the cylinder head

Start by separating the petrol pipe from the gas tank—two spanners may be needed to hold the tap whilst releasing the pipe nut. Release the Dzus fastener at the rear of the riders seat—pull the seat backwards to clear the two pegs on the frame.

Take out the two front tank fixing bolts—watch for the rubber and steel washers. Release and remove the rubber ring at the rear end of the tank, lift the tank clear of the frame, and put it in a place safe from damage.

Remove in the following order:
Both exhaust pipes—with mufflers attached—use the "C" spanner for ring nuts.
The two spark plugs.
The cylinder head steady stay to frame.
The two banjo pins fixing the rocker box oil pipes (watch for the fibre washers.)
The air cleaner.
Using the spanners suggested, take out the five bolts from the top of the cylinder head, take off the two nuts located midway between the exhaust ports—finally the remaining three nuts below the inlet and exhaust ports.
The rocker covers.
Unscrew the ring nuts on both carburetters—pull out both throttle slides—cover them with some clean rag and tie them to the frame tube—out of harms way.

A study of the exploded drawing of the engine (page 19) will indicate the location of the four push rods, which pass though the cylinder head, also through the cylinder barrel, which prevents the head from being removed in the normal way. Lift the head as far as the frame tube will permit, gather the four push rods between the fingers of one hand (or have the aid of a second person). Raise the push rods into the head as far as they will go—until they are clear of the cylinder. The cylinder head can now be tilted and taken away from the cylinder (see fig. 6). The gasket may, or may not, adhere to the cylinder—it is of no consequence if a replacement is available. If difficulty exists in separating the head, from the cylinder, the use of a piece of wood, with one end placed under the exhaust ports (where there is most material) and the other end of the wood is given a sharp blow with a hammer, will break the joint, caused by a formation of carbon deposit. It is advisable to identify each push rod—so that they can be refitted in the same order as removed.

Decarbonising

Before attempting to remove the valves, clean—by scraping—the sphere of the cylinder head, also both valves—this will prevent carbon chippings getting into the ports, which can be difficult to remove, apart from scratching the valve seatings with the scraper.

Valve check

With the head removed, it can be decided whether the valve seatings are satisfactory, or otherwise, by: not disturbing the valves then:

Wiping the sphere of the head until it is dry.
Stand the head with the exhaust ports vertical.
Nearly fill the ports with gasoline, and leave standing for a short while.

If the seatings are sound—no leakage of fuel will occur. Do the same with the inlet port, with care to again wipe dry the sphere of the head before filling the port, or after spilling.

If the seatings are sound there is no point in disturbing the valves—other than remove carbon—from the stem—or to replace the valve springs.

Time spent in making this check—after valve grinding—when the valves are assembled—is worth while, for a slight depression in either the valve face or on the valve seat in the head does not always show a "witness" after grinding. Attention to detail of this kind, must—without doubt have a beneficial effect.

Valve springs

The valve springs do not settle down unduly, or partially collapse, unless the engine temperature has been unduly high. Heat insulating washers are used between the valve spring seat and the cylinder head, even so—the valve spring free length should be checked, when the valves are dismantled, against the dimensions given in technical data. The exhaust springs are the most likely ones to be affected. If the free length is $\frac{3}{16}''$ or more below the normal length, use new springs—if maximum r.p.m. is required. The valve springs are "rated" the two close coils go nearest to the bottom spring collar (48).

Removing the valves

To enable the inlet rockers to swing clear of the valves—take out the stud used to secure the cover for the inlet rockers.

To compress the valve springs to take out the valve keepers (collets) use a spring compressor.

Remove carbon formed on the valves with a sharp knife—use emery cloth, or abrasive strip sparingly on the stem of the valves, the abrasive should be worked up and down the stem, the way the valves work—not across the valve stem. The valve stem diameter can be checked for wear against the normal dimensions, shown in the technical data.

Should the valve face be saucer shaped—due to excessive grinding—the valve face should be machined (most dealers have suitable equipment for this work) the valve angle is 45°. Have the valve seatings in the cylinder head re-cut also, otherwise a gas seal will not be made when the valves are put back. Restrict valve grinding to a minimum, replacing the valve seatings in the cylinder head, is a major operation.

It will be noted that the valve head diameter for the inlet and exhaust valves are dissimilar, these valves can be inadvertently incorrectly assembled.

Removing the valve guides

The valve guides are a force fit in the cylinder head, an attempt to drive out the guides without pre-heating the head can cause breakage on the guide, as well as scruffing in the guide aperture in the head—the guide will then become a loose fit in the head. Use a drift made to the dimensions as shown in fig. 5. The head can be pre-heated by placing it on a hot plate, or in a domestic oven to bring the temperature up to, and not exceeding 200° centigrade. Work fast, if all the guides have to come out, before the temperature drops.

Refitting the guides

The head must be heated, as described for removing the guides. It is worthwhile using the valve as a pilot—by inserting the valve through the valve guide bore aperture—and hold it against its seat in the head—then place the guide over the valve and press it into the cylinder head as far as it will go—the guide will then be parallel with its bore in the head. Some rag between the valve head, and the fingers, during this operation will of course be necessary. Usually the valve seat in the head is recut, when a new guide is fitted, using the method described will minimise the necessity to do this.

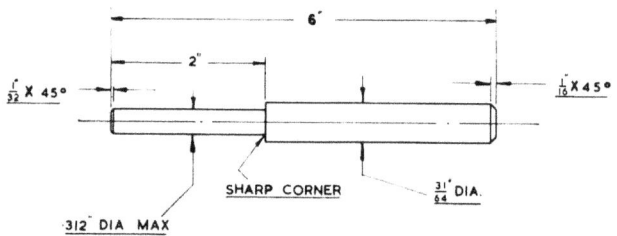

DRIFT FOR REMOVING VALVE GUIDES T 2011

MAT^L: MILD STEEL.

Fig. 5

The pistons

Unless there is good reason, the cylinder is best left undisturbed. Remove the carbon from both piston crowns with the end of a cheap six inch steel rule, or similar device. There is an annular space formed by the top land of the piston and the cylinder barrel. Carbon chippings can collect here, and unless an air line is available they are difficult to dislodge. Turn the engine until the pistons are about half an inch down the stroke, with the index finger press some clean grease into the annular space on both pistons. Turn the engine forward, past top dead centre, until the pistons are about half an inch down the opposite stroke. A ring of grease will be formed in each cylinder, with carbon chippings embedded in it, which can be removed with ease. Do this again, then for certain, no carbon can be trapped under the valves when the engine is started.

Cylinder barrel removal

Nine nuts secure the cylinder barrel to the crankcase, the tools suggested, will suffice for this work. The barrel must be raised slightly to take away the nuts under the lowest cylinder barrel fins. As a safeguard against further unwanted work—lift the barrel sufficiently to put some clean rag under the pistons in the throat of the crankcase—there may be a broken piston ring—which, for sure will drop into the crankcase, when the pistons are clear of the cylinder, the extra time is well spent.

Removing the rockers

Refer to details given for cylinder head removal on page 9 for G/15 models. The plain washer on the rocker spindle is 0.015″ thick for the heavyweight twins.

Model G15 CS

Cylinder head removal

The details given on page 9 do not apply to the above model by reason of the limited clearance between the top of the cylinder head and the frame tube.

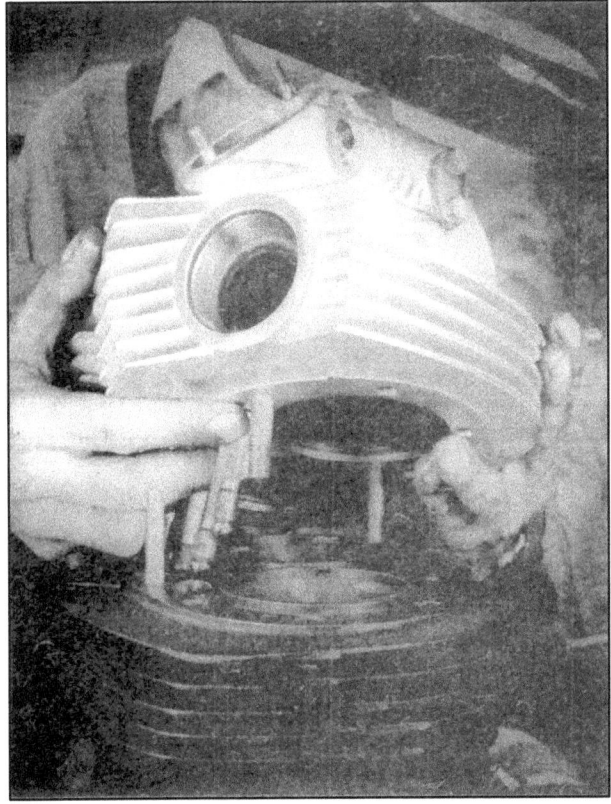

Fig. 6
G15 CS Cylinder Head Removal

To remove the cylinder head

Before the cylinder head can be taken away from the cylinder barrel, the four push rods must be extracted—to do this—the exhaust rocker spindles are removed from the cylinder head, so that the rockers can be taken out.

Have available, a bolt—about one inch long $\frac{5}{16}'' \times 26$ t.p.i. there are several bolts on the machine this size, also a short length of steel tube—to go over the bolt—the inside diameter of the tube should be just under $0.499''$—which is the size of the rocker spindle.

Start by removing the gas tank, also all the other parts attached to the cylinder head as described on page 9.

Take out bolts and nuts number five to ten (fig. 7) leave bolts one to four in position. Take off the rocker covers—for the rocker spindles (see fig. 8) and note the location of the slots in the rocker spindles—they have to go back in the same position.

Put the steel tube over the bolt—as described above—insert the bolt into the rocker spindle. The action of screwing in this bolt will extract the spindle (watch for the spindle washers) $0.015''$ thick.

Remove the cylinder head bolts one to four (fig. 7).

Raise the cylinder head at the exhaust port end as far as it will go.

Lift the four push rods as far as possible up to the top of the head—with the fingers of one hand, fix them with an elastic band or have the assistance of a second person.

Move the head towards the rear of the machine—then the push rods can be taken out, the head can now be lifted clear of the barrel.

On current engines the groove in the cylinder—where the rear stud in the cylinder head is located—has been enlarged to allow the head to be tilted further to make removal more easy. Originally this operation was confined to cylinders fitted to the G15 models only, it is now common on all 750 cylinders—so that they can be fitted to either engine.

In addition the three studs screwed into the cylinder head have been shortened by $\frac{1}{8}''$ for the same purpose. It may also be necessary—on early engines—to file a small chamfer on the edge of the inlet rocker cover *situ*—to allow the head to be tilted during removal.

The rockers

This part of the engine is not subject to premature wear—providing oil is continually circulating. End float between the rockers and the head is taken up by the spring and plain washer—the latter must be the correct thickness—viz. $0.015''$.

The rocker ball end

The ball end in each rocker, is a parallel, and interference fit in the rocker. It will be observed that there is a diagonal drilling in the rocker arm, which lines up with the flat machined on the rocker spindle. When the ball end is inserted in the rocker, this drilling is sealed off, at the outside end of the rocker arm. There is a further drilling in the ball end, which, when fitted, must line up with the drilling in the rocker, otherwise lubrication will be cut off.

To remove the ball end

Support the rocker in a suitable manner—use a flat face punch to drive out or if available use a small hand press.

To fit the ball end

Scribe a line with a pencil—along and across the oil hole—on the ball end, insert it into the rocker with the pencil line to register with the oil hole drilled in the rocker, and either press or drive home. The ball end where it makes contact with the push rod should have a mirror-like finish.

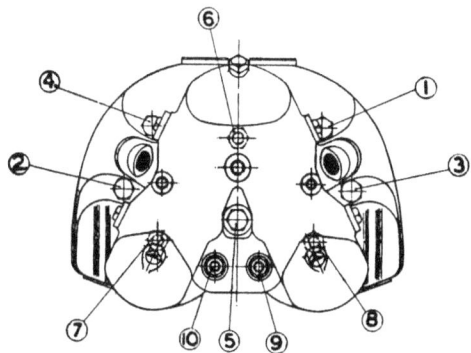

ORDER OF TIGHTENING DOWN CYLINDER HEAD NUTS & BOLTS.

Fig. 7

The rocker axles

After removing the rocker axles—as described for the scrambler models—before refitting all traces of partial seizure—or roughness on the spindle surface, must be removed with abrasive strip, remove also all traces of burnt oil or carbon from the oil grooves machined in the spindle.

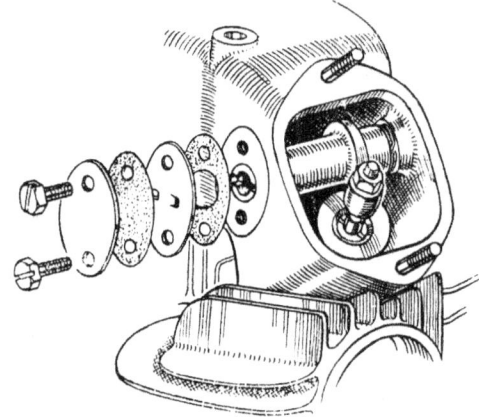

Fig. 8 *Rocker—removal*

Refitting the rockers and axle

Both rocker axles have a flat machined on one side—they are identical. These flats are for the oil pick up—and both axles must be fitted with the *flats facing inwards* (towards the centre of the head). It is worthwhile "painting" a little anti-seize compound on the axles (Molybdenum disulphide) which will give immediate lubrication, when the engine is first started—see para. on lubrication. Insert the rocker with the spring also plain washers, which usually will retain the rocker in position whilst the axle is inserted. Note carefully the location of the slot in the axle—which must register with the projection on the retaining plate (see fig. 8) the axle is a light interference fit and can be pressed home without difficulty—warming the head will provide sufficient expansion to fit the axle easily. Put back the plates and washers as depicted in the illustration.

NOTE: On the current 650 engines the clearance between the rocker and the head—when the valve is at full lift—is somewhat close. Should a replacement rocker be necessary, the dimension of the rocker on the push rod end should be similar to the rocker removed—if not, lightly grind the "fold" in the stamping—or better still use a rotary file on the head at the point of contact. Insufficient clearance at this point can cause a push rod to bend.

The tappets

These are mounted in the lower end of the cylinder barrel—retained by a separating plate—secured by four 2BA screws (two for each plate) for security these screws are linked with twisted copper wire. It is extremely rare for attention to be necessary to this part of the engine. It must be noted that the tappets are machined in pairs, so they must be put back in the same position as previously occupied, if for any reason they are removed.

NOTE: When assembled the bevelled edges are side by side facing the front of the engine—reversal will affect lubrication.

The piston rings

It is not advisable to remove the piston rings—unless there is a good reason to do so—springing the rings apart (once they have settled down) to clear the ring grooves can cause slight deformation. Providing the rings are free in the ring grooves, the carbon behind them tends to support the ring and provide a good gas seal. Should there be evidence of brown places on the ring face—this indicates gas leakage—then the ring should be replaced. The top compression ring is chromiun plated, its use, without doubt, does minimise cylinder wear. The scraper ring (oil control) is spring loaded to get a good scavenging effect.

To check the piston ring gap, insert each ring in turn into the cylinder barrel, about half an inch from the bottom, in the unworn part of the cylinder. To ensure the ring is at complete right angle to the axis of the bore, use the skirt of the piston to push the ring down the bore. The normal ring gap is given in the technical data. Fit new rings if the gap exceeds 0.028" to 0.030".

Removing the pistons

The piston crowns are stamped either left, or right hand, even so, it is worthwhile making a further mark, to avoid reversing the pistons when they are put back. The valve cut-away in the crown is dissimilar in size on the 750 engine—the crown is also marked "exhaust" for correct assembly. On the 650 and 500 engines the valve cut-away is symmetrical—it is for this reason they should be marked. For the record, the cut-aways for the inlet valve are close together—the exhaust is more widely separated, when the pistons are installed. (see fig. 9). The gudgeon (wrist) pin is a close fit in the piston, an attempt to drive out the pins, without pre-heating will tend to distort the piston skirt. Take out one of the circlips, apply some heat to the piston crown, an ordinary electric iron—or its like—can be used for this purpose if placed on the piston crown, until the applied heat is sufficient to expand the piston, to enable the pin to be pushed out. If the pin resists removal, use a sharp pointed scraper, to remove a burr or carbon alongside the recess for the pin.

Front

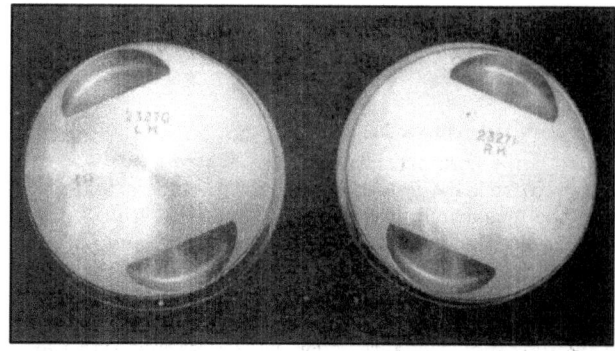

Fig. 9
Model 88 and 650 piston location

Assembling the engine

There is often a tendency—on the part of unskilled owners—to get the engine assembled in the shortest time possible. Some skilled operators are not excluded from this category, whilst this action is understandable, it is under these circumstances that things go wrong—watch a skilled race mechanic working—you will see that every part put back into the engine—is scrupulously clean—every moving part is lubricated before assembly, this together with precise also methodical working will ensure success, apart from the need to take down the engine—to make good a bad job.

Fitting new piston rings

As the design of the oil control ring is somewhat unusual, carefully consider its construction before fitting.

This ring consists of two thin rings (called rails) together with a corrugated stepped expander. A study of fig. 10, will show a step on each side of the expander—the rails are located on each side of the stepped portion of the expander.

It is vital that the ends of the expander meet each other—without overlapping—failure to do this, will make it difficult, or impossible to insert the assembled piston into the cylinder. Current issues of this ring have the ends painted green and white—these two colours should be seen when the expander is in position—if only one colour can be seen—then the expander is incorrectly fitted. It is important to remove all traces of burnt oil, or carbon from the ring grooves—particularly in the sharp corners of the ring groove, omission to do so will cause the ring to jam in its groove, and become ineffective. A broken ring—sufficiently large enough to handle—with one end filed square, is a suitable tool for this purpose.

Deal with the oil control ring first by:

Introduce one of the rails over the piston—past the lower ring groove—and let it rest on the reduced diameter of the piston (where the oil holes are drilled)—hold the piston in the right hand, with the ring grooves to the left. Put the expander into its groove—using the left hand—keep both ends of the expander together (see both colours) with the thumb nail—then move the rail already in position, into the ring groove—until it sits on the stepped part of the expander—using the right hand. Fit the second rail in a similar manner. The gaps where the rails meet, should be about one inch, each side of the expander joint. Fit the two compression rings—the top one is chromed.

Refitting the pistons

If the wrist pin (gudgeon pin) circlip is even slightly deformed—scrap it and use a new one—serious damage to the cylinder barrel will thus be avoided. Heat the piston, as described to remove it, without delay, insert the wrist pin—with some oil on it—sufficiently far enough to introduce the circlip into the piston—use a rotary motion when fitting the circlip—and insure it is snuggly in its groove, by using a pair of round nose pliers.

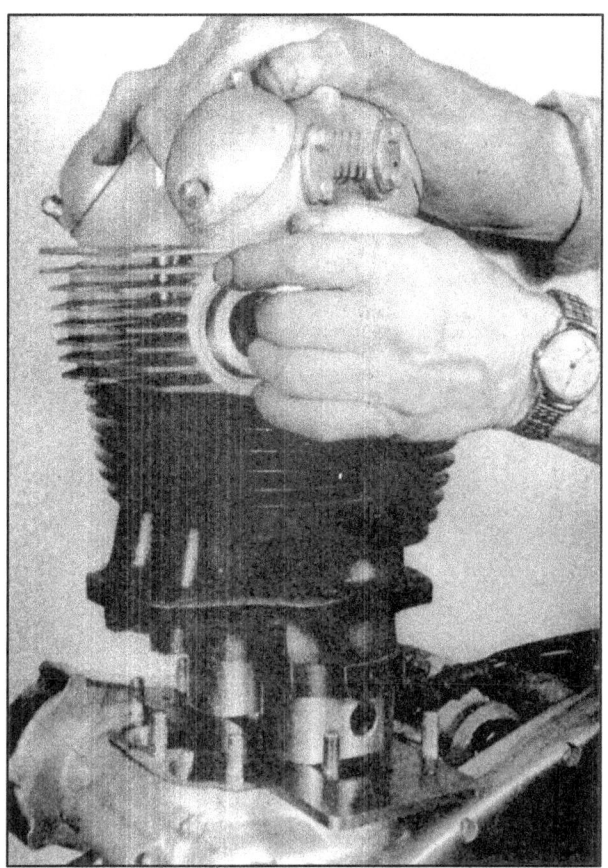

Fig. 11

Re-fitting the Cylinder assembled

oil control ring, is considered, it will be readily understood what will happen, if the leading rail does not enter the cylinder bore, during the process of fitting the cylinder, so, piston ring clamps are a must for this work, which—in use—are shown in fig. 12. These clamps are inexpensive and can be obtained from our distributors—or from any dealer in the U.K.

Refit the cylinder by:

Removing all traces of the old cylinder base gasket, clean the crankcase face.

Apply some jointing compound to the cylinder base, stick a new paper washer to it—do not use any jointing on the crankcase face of this washer.

Fit the ring clamps (as shown in fig.12) apply some clean oil to both bores.

Offer up the cylinder, engage the top lands of each piston in the bores, when a sharp push on the top of the cylinder will allow the pistons to enter the cylinder, and dislodge the ring clamps.

Refit the cylinder base nuts (slightly raise the cylinder to start the nuts where the fins are the lowest) tighten all the nuts lightly—then finally tighten these nuts in a diagonal order (not one side at a time) to complete this operation.

Refitting the cylinder barrel (Models—88—650SS—750 Atlas only)

When servicing the above models—in the factory—the cylinder head is fitted to the cylinder, before it is put back onto the crankcase, complete with the push rods assembled. (See fig. 11.) This method obviates the risk of the push rods

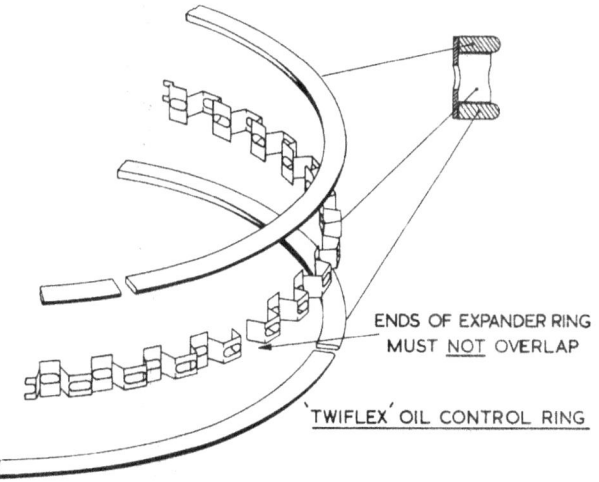

ENDS OF EXPANDER RING MUST NOT OVERLAP

'TWIFLEX' OIL CONTROL RING

Fig. 10

Refitting the cylinder barrel

If the fragile nature of the thin rings (rails) used on the

Fig. 12

Piston Ring Clamp assembled

lengthwise, between the head and the cylinder. Engage the ball ends on the rockers with the cupped portion of the push rods—a spoke—or short length of wire will assist—when it has been established that the push rods are correctly located—and not before—take out the sleeve nuts and lower the head into position. Refit the head bolts and nuts in the order removed — tighten in the order depicted in fig. 7. which is most important. Finally tighten the bolts with a torque wrench set to 25 foot lbs. Reset the rocker clearance—run the engine for a short while—then recheck the head bolts, also recheck the rocker clearance.

NOTE: the head gasket is inclined to settle down, when the engine is first run—more so on the 750 engine.

Rocker adjustment (push rod clearance)

The normal rocker clearance for the model 88SS is—inlet 0.006″—exhaust 0.008.″

For the models 650SS and all 750 models the inlet is also 0.006″—exhaust 0.008.″

To adjust the rocker, release the lock nut for the adjuster (see fig. 8) rotate the engine until the opposite rocker to the one being dealt with—is fully depressed (valve full open).

Unscrew the adjuster, about half a turn.

Place a feeler gauge of the required thickness—between the adjuster and the end of the valve stem.

Screw down the adjuster—until it just "pinches" the feeler.

Prevent the adjuster from moving—then tighten the lock nut.

Take out the feeler—pass it through the space between the adjuster and the valve to check if the clearance is correct.

Do the same thing to the rest of the rockers—by the method

not being located correctly in the tappets, also in the ball end for the rockers. To do this start by:

Fitting the head gasket, then the cylinder head to the barrel—put in the central bolt—also the rest of the head bolts lightly tightened.

Turn the cylinder barrel upside down.

Take out both tappet guide plates and tappets, as described elsewhere.

Introduce the push rods through the cylinder—the two long ones—(inlet) go in the centre, see fig. 13.

Engage the top end of the rods with the ball end on the rockers—with some oil on them.

Put back both tappets—and here again ensure the bottom end of the rods are in the cupped part.

Now follow the instructions given in the preceding paragraph for fitting the cylinder.

NOTE: The cylinder base washers, on models 88 and 650, can be reversed—check that the oil return hole registers with the washer.

Refitting the cylinder head (models—88—650SS—and Atlas only)

The cost in using a new cylinder head gasket, will amply offset the possibility of subsequent attention to the engine if the original gasket proves to be defective. Start by:-

Position the engine with both pistons on the top of the stroke—put the gasket on the cylinder.

Place the head on the cylinder—tilt it backwards—so that the push rods can be inserted into the two tunnels cast in the cylinder—the location of the push rods can be seen in the exploded drawing of the engine page 19 two push rods operate in each tunnel—the long rods are in the midway position. Lower the head, to enable the bottom end of the rods to enter the cups in both tappets. Raise the head parallel to the cylinder sufficiently to put the two sleeve head nuts

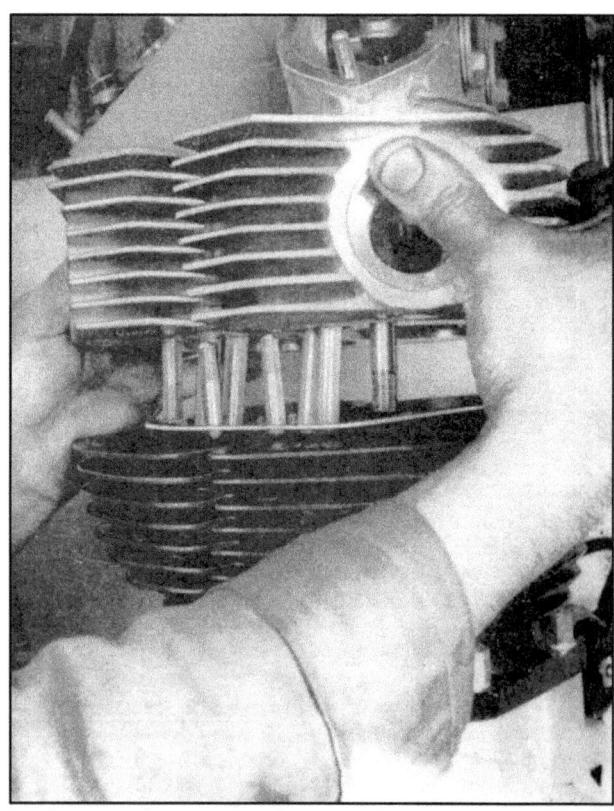

Fig. 13

Fitting the Atlas Cylinder Head

described, viz. have the opposite valve open whilst the other is being dealt with.

Engine timing chains

Both the magneto and camshaft chains have a short length, and are not affected with undue elongation. A badly slack magneto chain can affect ignition timing, its adjustment should be checked after considerable mileage. Remove the timing cover to check. The magneto is attached to the crankcase by three nuts—current models use two nuts also a bolt in the lower position—with its nut inside the timing chest. The studs also the bolt are waisted (reduced diameter) which permits limited movement of the magneto, when the fixing nuts are released. The magneto will drop slightly, when the nuts are released. To adjust the chain, use a lever to raise, and move backwards to tighten the chain. There should be $\frac{3}{16}''$ slack in the centre of the chain run, check in more than one place—the chain may have a tight place. Should the chain be unduly tight, the bearing in the magneto will be preloaded, which must be avoided, the automatic timing device will also stick.

A tension adjustment is fitted for the camshaft chain. To adjust, set the engine with one valve open (to take the load off the chain) release the two nuts securing the tension slipper, which can be moved to take up any slack in the chain. The normal adjustment is $\frac{3}{16}''$ checked in the centre of the chain run checked in more than one place. A slave cut-away timing cover (see fig. 15) is a useful device for checking also making these adjustments, which will stop any spring on the intermediate shaft.

Checking the magneto timing

The ignition timing must be set, and correctly maintained, to obtain maximum performance, also to avoid high engine temperature, apart from damage to the big ends. It is equally important that the firing point on each cylinder is identical, in terms of ignition advance. If it is found that there is a variation in the firing point on either cylinder—check the location of the contact breaker, where it is situated in the armature. A protrusion (key) is formed on the taper portion of the contact breaker, which is located in keyway in the armature. It is possible for the key portion to be incorrectly located, which would affect the angularity of the firing point. The contact breaker ramps—or cams—are ground with a makers tolerance of 0.002″ which represents approximately 0.002″ on piston travel. Before attempting to either check—or set the ignition timing—the contact breaker gap should be adjusted to have a maximum separation of 0.012″. When using a feeler gauge for this purpose, see that it is free from oil or grease, which can be deposited on the contacts, with unpleasant results. Should for any reason the cylinder head be removed, this is an opportune time to accurately measure the ignition advance, by placing a straight edge on the cylinder spigot, and use a steel rule to measure the piston travel, against the measurement given in the technical data. Use a small wood wedge to keep the automatic advance unit in the full advance position, when checking. If the cylinder head is not disturbed, the piston travel can be measured, by using a steel spoke inserted through the spark plug hole, using this method:-

Take out both spark plugs, remove the contact breaker cover.

Turn the engine in a forward direction—watching the contact breaker—until the fibre heel is about to touch the bottom ramp, or cam—which is for the left hand cylinder.

Insert the spoke through the left hand spark plug hole—hold it as vertical as possible.

Rock the engine to and fro until the piston is on the extreme top dead centre of the stroke (the rod ceases to move) make

Fig. 14 (*see page* 27)

a mark on the spoke to line up—or register with the spark plug face on the cylinder—take out the spoke.

Make a further mark on the spoke—if you are working on an Atlas—8.69 mm ($\frac{11}{32}''$) above the mark already made. Lock the automatic advance unit in the advanced position.

Put the spoke back through the spark plug hole (hold it vertical) turn the engine backwards slowly until the uppermost mark on the spoke lines up—or registers with the spark plug face. The contact points should just start to separate—use a cigarette paper between the points, when a light pull on the paper will indicate the exact point of separation.

To adjust the timing

Take off the timing cover (12 screws) disconnect rev counter drive. The fact of unscrewing the nut on the automatic timing device, will release it from the armature shaft, reposition the engine as already described (it will have moved during the process of unscrewing the self extracting nut) the contact breaker can now be turned by hand until the points are about to separate on the lower ramp—watch the wedge for the A.T.D.—it may have fallen out. A more accurate method is to use a degree plate, its application is detailed—step by step—in this subject given for the Electra also lightweight twins, on page 33.

Fig. 15

Cut-Away Timing Cover

Refitting the timing cover

Renew the gasket if the original is, even slightly mutilated, before fitting the cover after getting rid of all traces of jointing compound from the face on the crankcase, as well as broken pieces of the old gasket. Stick the new gasket to the cover by using a non flakey compound such as "Wellseal", which is first class for all engine work.

Fig. 16
Setting the Ignition

Fig. 17
Retain Valve Timing

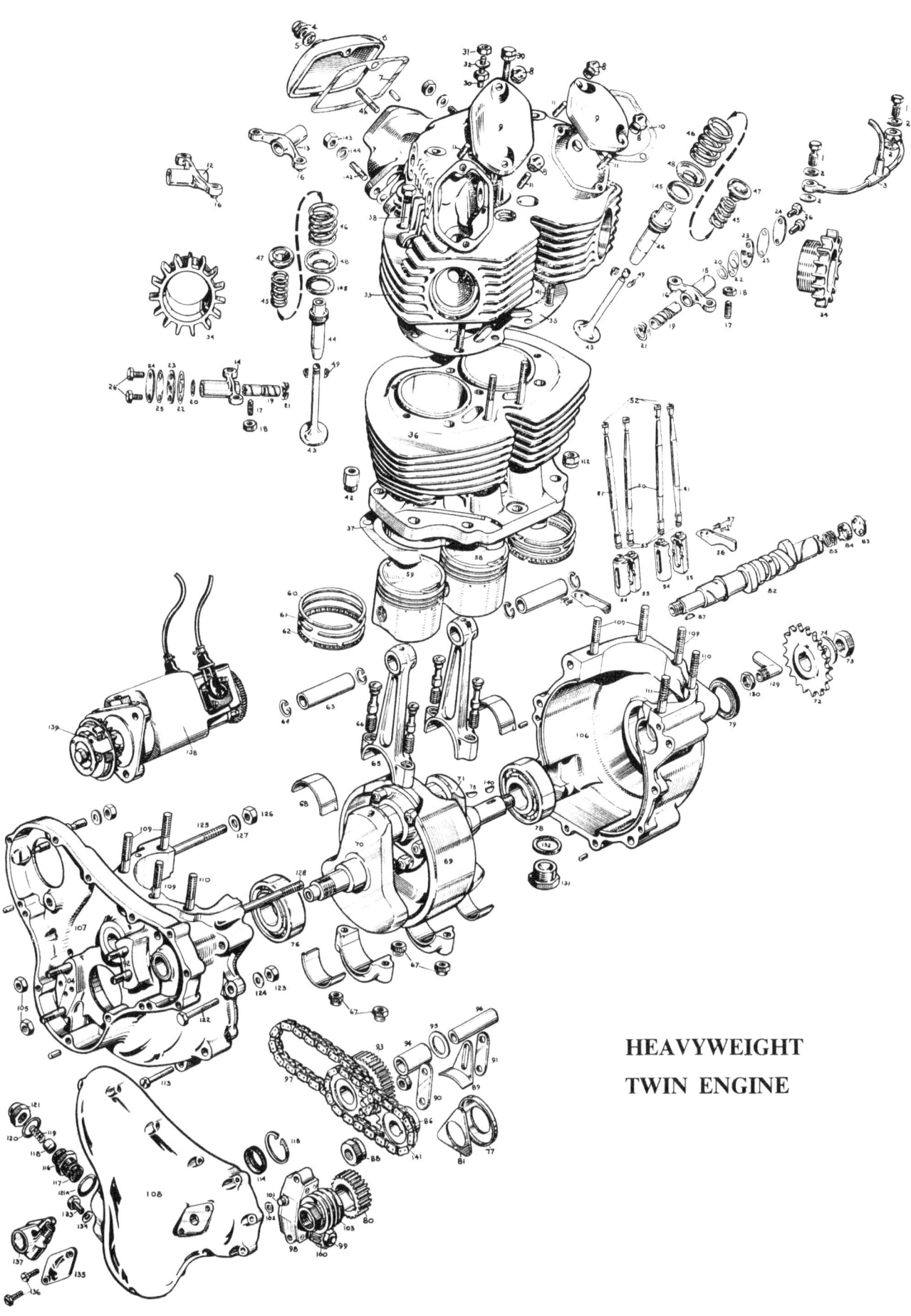

HEAVYWEIGHT TWIN ENGINE

#	Part No.	Description
1	18101	Banjo bolt for oil feed pipe.
2	T1084	Washer for banjo bolt.
3	22168	Rocker feed pipe assembly.
4	T2162	Domed nut for rear cap.
4A	18033	Stud for rear cap.
5	T2082	Washer for domed nut
6	18094	Rocker box cap (Rear)
7	T2084	Sealing washer for rear cap.
8	T2085	Nut for rocker box front cap stud.
9	18093	Rocker box cap (Front)
10	T2088	Sealing washer for front cap.
11	T2252	Stud for front cap.
12	18249	Rocker inlet, right hand.
13	18250	Rocker inlet, left hand.
14	18251	Rocker exhaust, right hand.
15	18252	Rocker exhaust, left hand.
16	T2063	Rocker ball end.
17	T2074	Rocker adjuster.
18	T232	Nut for adjuster.
19	T2237	Rocker shaft.
20	18102	Thrust washer for shaft.
21	18103	Spring washer for shaft.
22	T2083	Joint washer for shaft.
23	T2238	Locking plate for shaft.
24	T2239	Retaining plate for shaft.
25	T2240	Joint washer for plate.
26	T2256	Set pin for shaft retaining plate.
30	18032	Stud (in head) for steady plate.
31	E3224	Nut for stud.
32	E5376	Washer for stud.
33	T750/136	Cylinder head, with valve guides.
34	18092	Finned locking nut for exhaust pipe.
35	24255	Gasket cylinder head to barrel
36	24237A	Cylinder barrel.
37	24249	Washer cylinder base to Crankcase.
38	24253	Cylinder head bolt (Long).
39	T2097	Cylinder head bolt (Short).
41	24389	Stud, cylinder head to barrel.
42	24260	Nut, cylinder head to barrel stud.
43	T2204	Valve, exhaust.
44	T2011	Valve guide, inlet or exhaust.
45	22839	Valve spring, inner.
46	22838	Valve spring, outer.
47	T186	Valve spring top cap.
48	T2073	Valve spring bottom collar.
49	T187	Valve collet.
50	S650/82 in.	Push rod complete, inlet
51	S650/82 ex.	Push rod complete, exhaust.
52	T2064	Push rod top end.
53	T2182	Push rod bottom end.
54	22772	Tappet, right hand.
55	22771	Tappet, left hand.
56	T2142	Tappet location plate.
57	T2143	Screw for location plate.
58	24246	Piston complete, left hand.
59	24247	Piston complete, right hand.
60	24284	Piston ring, compression, top, chrome.
61	24285	Piston ring, compression. bottom, plain.
62	24286	Piston ring, scraper.
63	24287	Gudgeon pin.
64	23276	Circlip for gudgeon pin.
65	23297	Connecting rod.
66	23254	Big end cap bolt.
67	23253	Nut for cap bolt.
68	23255	Big end bearing.
69	24248	Flywheel.
70	23262	Crankshaft timing side
71	23261	Crankshaft driving side.
72	T2180E	Engine sprocket, 21 teeth.
73	20692	Retaining nut for rotor.
74	19147	Washer for rotor.
75	E3682	Key for engine sprocket.
76	17822	Mainshaft bearing, timing side.
77	T2008	Sealing washer timing side bearing.
78	17824	Mainshaft roller bearing, driving side.
79	T2187	Driving side shaft oil seal.
80	T2035	Half time pinion.
81	T2007	Backing plate for pinion.
82	22729	Camshaft.
83	T2078	Stationary plate, camshaft breather.
84	24301	Rotary plate, timing breather.
85	T2108	Spring for breather.
86	20829	Camshaft sprocket.
87	E3863	Key for sprocket.
88	17211	Nut for sprocket and rev-counter drive.
89	T2217	Chain tensioner slipper.
90	T2218	Plate for chain tensioner (Thick).
91	T2218A	Plate for chain tensioner (Thin).
92	T247	Stud for chain tensioner.
93	50008	Intermediate gear, with sprocket.
94	T2026	Bush for intermediate gear.
95	T2080	Washer for intermediate gear.
96	T2021	Spindle for intermediate gear.
97	18257	Driving chain for magneto.
98	23111	Oil pump assembly.
99	15511A	Nut for oil pump spindle.
100	T2077	Worm gear wheel (on pump).
101	15515	Feed bush for pump.
102	T272	Sealing washer for feed bush.
103	T2076	Pump driving worm (on mainshaft).
104	E4440	Stud, oil pump to crankcase.
105	E3231	Nut for stud.
106	24278	Crankcase, driving side only.
107	24279	Crankcase, timing side only.
108	18245RC	Timing cover, (for rev-counter fixing).
109	24251	Crankcase cylinder base stud.
110	T2209	Crankcase cylinder base stud $\frac{5}{16}''$ dia.
111	18943	Crankcase cylinder base stud $\frac{3}{8}''$ dia.
112	T2016	Nut, cylinder base stud $\frac{3}{8}''$.
113	10940	Screw, Timing to driving side crankcase sump.
114	T2124	Mainshaft oil seal, in timing cover.
115	17841	Circlip, mainshaft oil seal.
116	T2059	Pressure release body (Only).
117	T2055	Wire Gauze complete.
118	T2054	Pressure release piston.
119	T2061	Pressure release spring.
120	T2057	Pressure release union nut washer.
121	T2060	Pressure release body nut.
121A	T2058	Washer for pressure release union.
122	13870	Crankcase bolt (Short).
123	E3223	Nut, for bolt.
124	E5456	Washer for bolt.
125	T2013	Crankcase top stud (Rear).
126	E3224A	Nut, for stud.
127	E5376	Washer for stud.
128	19077	Crankcase top stud (Front)
129	24300	Elbow for Crankcase breather pipe.
130	24303	Nut, for crankcase breather elbow.
131	16945	Crankcase oil sump filter body.
132	16949	C & A washer filter body.
133	16902	Set Screw for oilway blanking.
134	T1084	Washer for pin.
135	23453	Blanking plate revolution counter drive.
136	23444	Fixing screw revolution counter drive.
137	18514	Gear box revolution counter drive.
138	42368D	Magneto (Lucas K2/FC).
139	47508D	Advance and retard unit.
140	20948	Key for alternator rotor.
141	17806	Driving chain for camshaft.
142	23563	Stud, carburetter fixing.
143	E3231	Nut for stud.
144	11796	Washer for stud.
145	23392	Heat resisting washer.

Fig. 18
Removing the G15 Engine Unit

Major Engine Overhaul

Removing the engine (excluding G15 models)

If the intention is to dismantle the engine, it is best to start by removing all the parts detailed in removing the cylinder head, the cylinder should be left in position to protect the pistons. The following tools should be available, before this work is undertaken.

Engine sprocket extractor.
Small pinion extractor (on crankshaft).
Camshaft pinion extractor.
Rocker spindle extractor (See G15 head removal).
Piston ring clamps (2).
Valve spring compressor.
Tool to stop engine moving, during engine nut removal. (See fig. 24.)
Clutch extractor (not essential)—a strong box—or stand to support the machine.

To remove the engine only

Start by draining the oil tank, also the sump—whilst this is going on:

Remove the four $\frac{1}{4}''$ bolts and nuts fixing the oil tank to the engine plates, also battery box.

Remove the left side foot peg—then the outer portion of the front chaincase.

Remove four $\frac{3}{8}''$ bolts passing through the rear engine plates (behind the gear box).

Remove the clutch pressure plate—take off the gear box mainshaft nut—fixing clutch.

Remove three nuts fixing stator—disconnect the three cable bullet terminals—pull off the stator, with care to avoid damage to the alternator wires.

Remove rotor fixing nut—take off the rotor, and spacer.

Remove the engine sprocket together with the front chain and clutch assembly in one piece.

Remove three screws fixing stator housing—also the nut on the bottom gear box pivot bolt.

Remove the nut fixing the back half chaincase to the engine plate.

Remove three allen screws fixing back half chaincase to crankcase, take off the case.

Remove oil pipe junction block from crankcase (one nut) the release valve pipe from crankcase.

Remove two studs, two bolts and nuts passing through front engine plates—why not put back on the studs and nuts the washers and nuts as they are removed—saves time putting things back.

Remove two $\frac{3}{8}''$ studs passing through the crankcase and rear engine plates.

Remove one of the $\frac{5}{16}''$ nuts on the bottom of the engine plate—lift up the engine then take out the stud from which the nut has been removed. Disconnect tacho drive.

The engine can now be lifted out of the frame.

NOTE: The cylinder head can be left on the cylinder—if so desired—it is less cumbersome with it off. Get rid of all road grit and oil from the engine—particularly from the bottom of the crankcase—to prevent fouling up the bench, for clean working.

To remove the engine and gear box—as a unit (excluding G15 models)

Strip down by removing the cylinder head, as detailed in preceding chapter.

Drain the oil tank, and sump, if the intention is to strip down the engine.

Disconnect both battery leads—take out the battery.

Remove oil junction block from crankcase (one $\frac{3}{8}''$ nut).

Remove both breather pipes from oil tank.

Remove the rectifier from back of battery box also the oil tank (two nuts at the bottom—one bolt at top).

Remove battery box—oil tank platform (four $\frac{1}{4}''$ bolts and nuts).

Remove the foot pegs, then the outer portion of the front chain case, disconnect the three alternator wires.

Remove four $\frac{3}{8}''$ nuts and bolts—uniting the rear engine plates to frame (behind the gear box).

Remove the centre stand spring from its anchorage—with the stand in the uppermost position—use a lever.

Remove the front engine plates (two studs and two bolts) also tacho drive.

Remove clutch cable—at gear box end, clip to frame all loose cables. Take out the rear chain connecting link.

The engine with its gear box can now be lifted out of the frame.

To remove engine and gear box as a unit G15 model only

Remove the gas tank, exhaust pipes, carburetters with air cleaner.

Remove tacho drive, clutch cable—gear box end, then the engine plate cover over gearbox.

Remove breather pipes, and oil lines.

Remove rear chain connecting link.

Remove right side foot peg with its rod, from the left side.

Remove all the bolts passing through the front engine plates—loosen the nuts only on the bottom one only.

Remove spring for central stand—with the stand in the up position—from its anchorage.

Remove the nuts on the left side of the rear engine plates—then take out the bolts.

Lever the engine upwards—the loose nuts on the lower bolt can be taken off, as well as the engine plates.

Move the engine forward—lift up—and out of the frame.

Separating the crankcase (see fig. 19 for fixture to support engine)

Assuming that the cylinder head has been removed—leave the cylinder on the crankcase. Take off the timing cover (12 screws), a light tap with a mallet whilst pulling on the tacho drive, will make the cover come off easily. If the sump has been drained—there should be little oil in the timing chest when the cover is taken off.

To prevent the engine turning, whilst releasing nuts such as—engine sprocket nut, camshaft nut etc. a chain bar as shown in fig. 17 is a useful tool for this purpose. This can be wrapped round the engine sprocket, the free end spragged against the bench holding the engine firmly.

Take off in the following order:-

The oil pump (two nuts) it should come away without difficulty.

The oil pump worm nut which has a **left hand thread.**

The camshaft chain tension slipper (two nuts) noting the thin plate goes onto the stud first.

The camshaft sprocket nut, intermediate gear, the small timing pinion—use a puller.

The nut securing the A.T.D. to the magneto armature—which is self extracting.

Take off together, the camshaft, intermediate sprocket, the A.T.D. together with both chains, see fig. 17.

Pinch the camshaft chain, during removal, if the camshaft sprocket is tight on the shaft, use a puller, wire the chain

Fig. 19
Bench Fixture for Engine

as shown in fig. 17, then the valve timing will not be "lost" thus saving a lot of time resetting the valve timing. It will be observed in the illustration that there are six chain link plates between the timing marks on both the camshaft also intermediate pinion.

Should a sprocket puller not be available for the camshaft sprocket, take care to avoid mutilating the crankcase face where the cover is fitted, if a lever is used.

Remove the engine sprocket nut, use the sprocket puller, by tightening the centre bolt—then a sharp blow with a hammer—on the bolt head will dislodge the sprocket from the taper on the shaft, continually tightening the tool bolt will cause damage.

Tap out the key for the sprocket from the drive side shaft.

Turn to the timing side of the engine:-

Tap out with a screwdriver and light hammer, the key in the timing side shaft, also the key in the camshaft.

Tap out the thrust washer from both the intermediate shaft also the timing side shaft—this washer is star shaped—so that the extractor tool will grip the pinion teeth in three places also the sealing washer.

Take off the magneto three nuts (late type two nuts and one bolt, with lock washer) if the magneto is left in position there is a risk of breaking the acorn nut in the H.T. brush holder with the spanner, during the process of taking off the rear cylinder holding down bolts.

Remove nuts securing cylinder to crankcase.

Turn the crankshaft until both con rods are at the bottom of the stroke—before lifting the cylinder—there is less risk in damaging the pistons when the cylinder comes away.

If the cylinder does not separate from the crankcase easily—hold the cylinder in the "crook" of the left arm—tap the cylinder fins with a soft faced mallet—and lift the cylinder at the same time. Do not use the mallet **under the fins**—use it on the edges of the fins.

Removing the pistons

Take out both outside wrist pin circlips, apply a little gentle heat to the piston crown—push out the pins. Identify the pistons for position.

Removing the bearings

Take out the bolts and nuts, holding the two crankcase halves together, also the two screws at the bottom of the crankcase.

Take hold of the crankcase with both hands—turn it so that the drive side shaft is pointing to the bench—thump the drive side shaft against the bench (a wood one of course) once or twice—when the drive side crankcase will separate, leaving the roller portion of the drive side bearing, on the drive side shaft.

Take out the camshaft, and from its housing the spring also rotary plate for the crankcase release valve.

The timing side of the crankcase will not come away so easily, as usually the shaft is a tight fit in the inner member of the bearing. A simple sleeve tool is shown in fig. 20 which is placed over the timing side shaft. To remove the remaining portion of the crankcase from the crankshaft: take hold of the crankcase with both hands—and hold it as you would a dinner plate with both hands—get a second person to give the sleeve, placed on the shaft (see Fig. 21) a few blows with a soft faced mallet, then the case will come away, leaving the bearing in the crankcase.

Removing the roller bearing

This also is a close fit on the crankshaft—to take it off use two levers between the bearing and the crankshaft. When a space between the bearing and the crankshaft is formed—a claw shaped puller will pull off the bearing from its shaft.

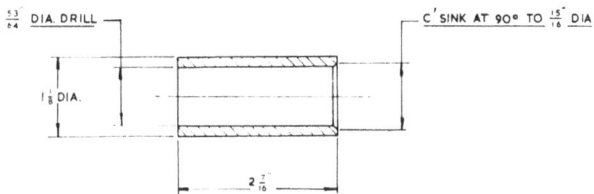

CRANKSHAFT REMOVING SLEEVE

Fig. 20

To remove the ball bearing

The crankcase must be heated for this operation, heating the case excessively will tend to loosen also the shaft for the intermediate pinion. The act of dropping the case—when it has been heated—onto a flat wood bench will cause the complete bearing to fall out of the case. Make sure that the intermediate shaft has not moved during this process. Use the same method to remove the bearing sleeve for the roller bearing.

The crankshaft

Providing there is clean oil continually circulating, whilst the engine is running, wear on the journals is extremely remote. In all probability the big end shells only will need renewal, after many, many thousands of miles. Should wear become manifest after small mileage—then for sure the oil is contaminated with abrasive, and the whole system, including the oil tank must be flushed out with solvent or gasoline.

The diameter of the journals can be checked—if suitable instruments are available—against the sizes shown in the technical data. Regrind the journals if the diameter is 0.0015" to 0.002" below the low limit.

A centrifugal sludge trap is incorporated in the centre of the crankshaft assembly, if the oil is changed at pre-arranged

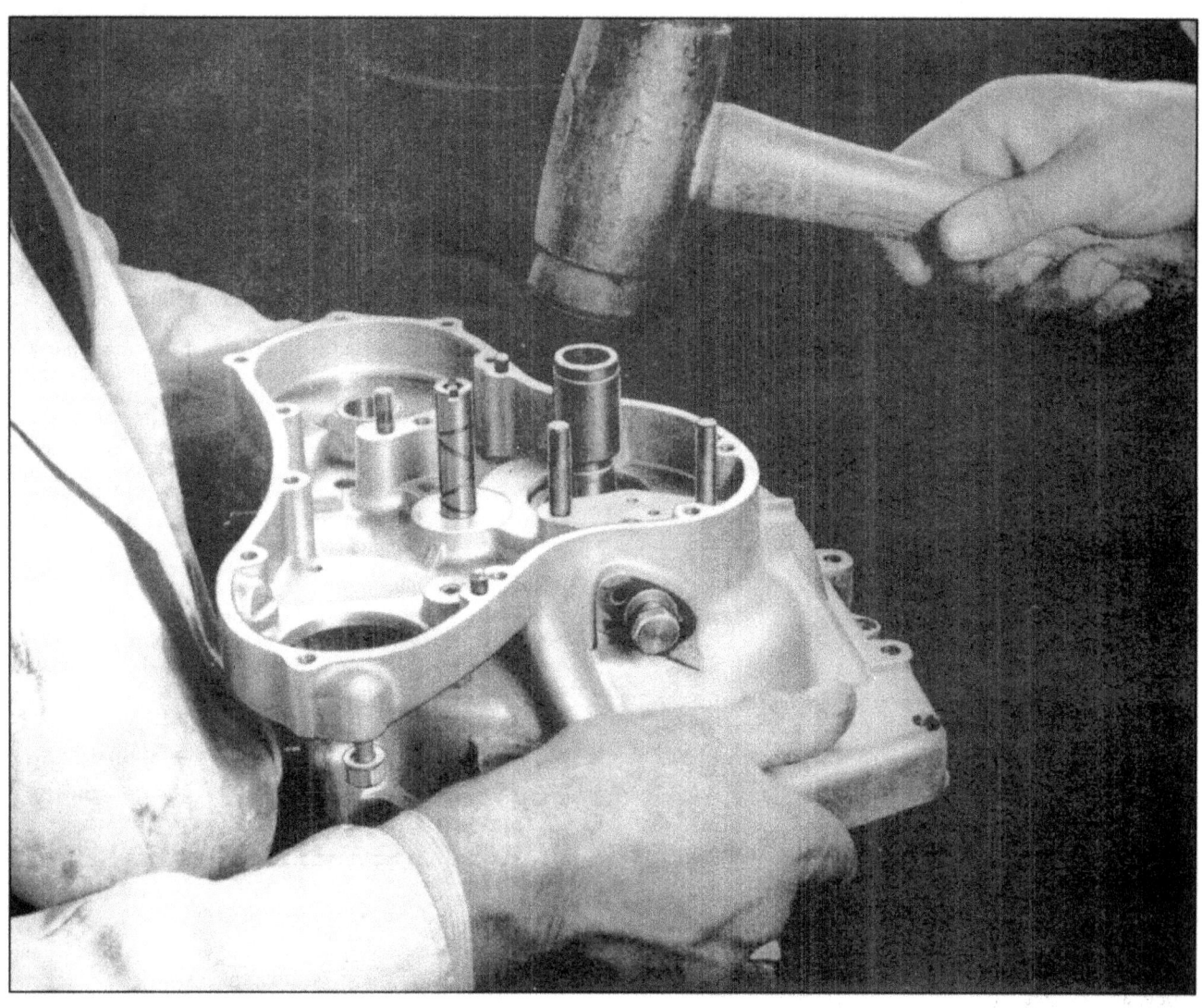

Fig. 21
Removing the Crankshaft

intervals—then there will be little sludge in the trap. Should it be necessary to strip down the crankshaft, the oil ways and sludge trap can then be cleaned. The centre flywheel is attached to both crankcheeks by four bolts and nuts also two studs with nuts.

To strip down the crankshaft

A dowel is used to correctly locate the end cheeks to the flywheel. Bend back the tab washers, take off the two stud nuts. Remove the four nuts on the bolts passing through the assembly, when the end cheeks can be detached as shown in fig. 22. Exercise extreme care to avoid bruising the machined faces of the flywheel also the crank cheeks. The oil passages as well as the sludge trap can be cleaned, and flushed out. If new big end shells are to be fitted, this is an opportune time to use superfine emery tape on the journals to produce a mirror like finish—then the oil passages can again be flushed out to get rid of any abrasive from emery tape used.

The connecting rods

Look at the con rods before taking them off the crankshaft —when it will be seen the detachable end caps are marked, either with figures, or currently with an oblique line—across the con rod also the cap thus /. The marking is made so that the caps can be fitted to the rod from which it was taken, and the same way round. Take off the two self locking nuts (and washers where fitted) give the rod a sharp jerk, away from the crankshaft, when the cap will come away from the rod. Should the cap jam—tap it back—until the stud holes are parallel with the studs, and try again. The bearing shells can be taken out without difficulty. Put back the end cap on its rod with the mark in register for attention later. On no account should either the con rod or its cap be filed (to absorb movement between the rod and the journal) if new bearing shells do not suffice—then a regrind is needed.

Assembling the crankshaft

It is of vital importance that the faces on both the crank cheeks as well as the flywheel are perfectly clean and free from bruises—for the slightest particle of foreign matter, or swarf interposed between the crank cheeks and the flywheel, will adversely affect true running of the bearing shafts.

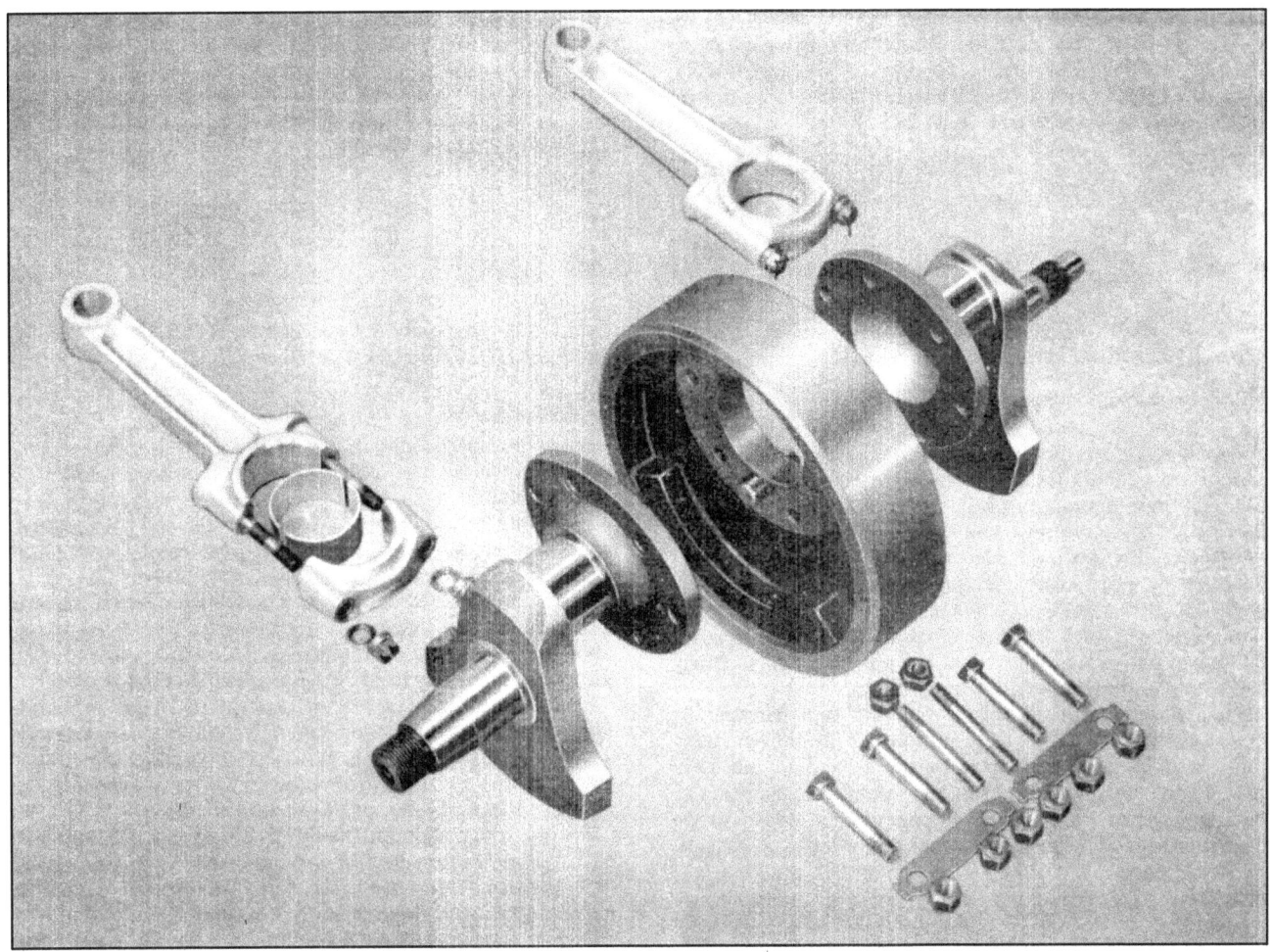

Fig. 22

Crankshaft Dismantled

Pass the bolts through the crank cheek shown in fig. 22 —unite the flywheel and the other crank cheek, engage the cheeks with the dowel protruding through the flywheel.

The two long nuts are used in the top position of the crank throw—to permit the use of a spanner. These bolts are made and machined from high tensile steel—they cannot be substituted by bolts made from regular steel. If the crankshaft has been stripped on a previous occasion new bolts should be used.

All nuts must be tightened tight. Turn back the tab washers for the studs—centre pop the thread on the bolts close to the nuts, for security.

Assembling the connecting rods

Treat the journals with a light coating of anti-seize compound, for immediate lubrication, when the engine is first started. Insert the big end shells into the rod and cap—check the marking—to verify they are located correctly.

Assemble the rod to the crankshaft—use new self locking nuts which are tightened with a torque spanner set to 15 foot lbs. Force some clean oil into the crankshaft oil ways with a wesco gun, until it emerges each side of the con rods. Put the crankshaft aside, cover it with clean rag for attention later.

(The figures in parenthesis refer to illustration on page 17).

Checking the oil pump seal (102)

Before installing the timing chains and sprockets—take up the oil pump—attach it to the crankcase with its two nuts for the purpose of this check. Put the timing cover in position, press it home then release it—if the pump oil seal is effective it will push the timing cover away from the crankcase leaving a gap of 0.010″. Either replace the oil seal, or use shims at the back of the seal to make it effective. Take off the cover—examine the oil seal which encircles the plain portion of the crankshaft this must be faultless, if in doubt replace it with a new one—otherwise oil will escape between the seal and the shaft diameter, instead of going through the crankshaft.

To replace the oil seal (114)

Take out the circlip, prise out the seal (it will be useless afterwards). Gently heat the cover—press in the new seal with the **metal backing outwards** thus the knife edge of the seal will be nearest to the cover. Take off the oil pump for final fitting later.

The intermediate shaft (96)

This is a press fit in the crankcase—a circlip prevents the

shaft from moving inwards—during the process of fitting the timing cover. The shaft has a small hole at one end, a larger hole at the other end. There is a oil hole midway in the shaft—which points to 6 o'clock when the shaft is installed. Heat the crankcase to extract and refit.

The driving side crankcase oil seal (79)

After this seal is inserted in the crankcase, the metal each side of the seal is "peened" in two places. To remove the seal scrape away the "peened" places—then push the seal out. Insert the new seal with the widest aperture outwards (like looking down a funnel).

Assembling the Engine

It is preferable to clean engine parts with gasoline, instead of a solvent, as the later tends to collect dust.

Fitting the crankcase bearings

It is a common assumption that these bearings should be an easy push fit on the shafts, certainly they can be removed easily in this condition, but the need to remove the bearings is because they are unserviceable. It has been established that the life of these bearings will be prolonged, if the inner member for the bearing is close "grunting" fit when pressed home on the shaft—also the outer member is a close interference fit in the crankcase. When the crankcase reaches its running temperature the close interference fit is relieved—the bearings are under this condition not subjected to shock load—thus prolonging the bearing life.

When dealing with an engine that has been affected by premature bearing wear—a repetition can be prevented by using selective assembly, by choosing a bearing that is a close fit on the shaft, also knurling the bearing housing in the crankcase to close up the interference fit. Alternatively have an electrical deposit of copper made on the outside diameter of the bearing sleeve to give an interference fit between 0.002″ to 0.003″.

The roller bearing

Press on to the drive side shaft for the crankshaft, the inner member of this bearing—an arbour press is used for this operation.

Heat the drive side crankcase uniformly (do not concentrate the heat in one place) sufficiently to enable the bearing sleeve to fall squarely in its housing.

Heat the other half of the crankcase in a similar manner to insert the ball bearing, with an eye on the intermediate shaft to see it does not come out of position. Apply some clean oil to both bearings when the case has cooled off.

Check both crankcase faces, and get rid of any jointing compound, previously used—use a fine oil stone on the joint faces to remove burrs, or blemish to ensure an oil tight joint. Set the con rods at the bottom of the stroke—then fit the drive side crankcase on to the crankshaft.

Fit the rotary plate for the breather (84) into the camshaft bush, with the two projections outwards—then the spring (85) then the camshaft—make sure the projections on the plate engage with the slots in the camshaft.

Apply some jointing compound to the crankcase face joint—do not use a shellac base compound which becomes "flaky" and can seal off oil holes. Wellseal is best for this application. Fit the timing side crankcase, also the uniting bolts and screws and tighten.

Place the oil seal dished washer (77) on the timing side shaft—then the pinion plate (81). Fit the key for the timing pinion, tap the pinion (80) on to the shaft.

Put on the intermediate shaft washer (95) put back the magneto—lightly tighten the nuts until the chain is adjusted. Fit the key for the camshaft (87).

Rotate engine so that the timing mark on the small pinion is at 12 o'clock.

Take up the camshaft and timing chains with their sprockets undo the wire, assemble both sprockets, with the timing marks lined up (see fig. 17).

Fit and tighten the camshaft nut (88) then the oil pump driving worm (103) this has a LEFT HAND thread.

Fit the oil pump—tighten down the nuts evenly—not one side at a time, check the oil seal (102) is in position.

Assemble the chain tensioner plate (91) with the longest portion from the bolt hole downwards, then the slipper (89) followed by the plate (89) the longest portion of this plate goes upwards. Put back the two nuts—see para chain adjustment. Note if the chain adjustment is limited the plates (90 and 91) have been fitted upside down.

Assemble both pistons to the con rods—as already described in a preceding chapter, then fit the cylinder barrel.

Before fitting the cylinder head, the ignition timing can be set, measuring the piston travel—by placing a straight edge across the cylinder then measure the piston movement down the stroke with a six inch steel rule. The measurement is

FIG. 23
Fitting the Camshaft

given in the technical data. As a rough guide to set up the ignition timing—turn the crankshaft until the pistons are on the extreme top dead centre of the stroke with the push rods in the tunnels—turn the crankshaft forward again until the inlet push rod for the left hand cylinder goes up and comes down (this will indicate the firing stroke) set the pistons on top dead centre—turn the crankshaft **back** until the third tooth gap (two teeth from the mark) on the small pinion is exactly at 12 o'clock (see fig. 14) this represents approximately 30 degs before T.D.C. with the automatic advance unit in the full advance position. Now set the timing to 32 degs, by moving the armature. Note the cam for the left hand cylinder is at the bottom of the contact breaker compartment (rear brush holder on magneto).

Fit the cut-away timing cover, adjust the timing chains—then finally tighten the magneto fixing bolts. Stick a new gasket to the timing cover proper, put it back with six short and six long screws.

Squirt plenty of oil down the push rod tunnels, also on the push rod top cups.

Use a new cylinder head gasket—then follow the instructions previously given for fitting the cylinder head.

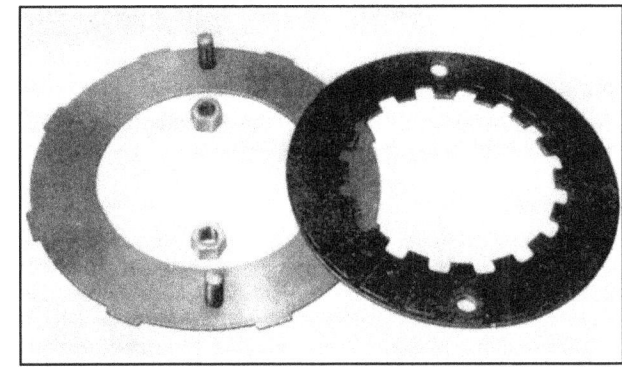

Fig. 24

Tool to Stop Engine Turning

Fig. 25

| Clutch Puller | Timing Pinion Tool | Lightweight | Lightweight | Heavyweight |
| All Models | All Models | Cam Wheel Puller | Sprocket Puller | Sprocket Puller |

Lightweight Twin Models

250 Jubilee 350 Navigator 400 Electra models

Basically, the design of the above three models are identical, the ensuing details apply to all three models.

Lubrication

The system employed is similar to that described for the heavyweight twins, to avoid being repetitive, the reader should refer to the chapter on this subject given for the larger capacity models. There are minor differences—such as the sump filter—which will be dealt with subsequently. An exploded view of these engines shown on page 19 will illustrate the similarity of the oiling system used.

Engine service

To remove the cylinder head, have available the following tools:-

One $\frac{1}{4}''$ Whit box key (for head nuts).
One $\frac{1}{4}''$ Whit open end spanner.
One allen key $\frac{3}{16}''$ across the flats.

Start by:

Releasing the two nuts on the top of the rear suspension units, when a sharp jerk backwards will release the riders seat from its front anchorage.

Disconnect the fuel pipe where it joins the fuel tap, take out the rear gas tank fixing bolt see fig. 27 withdraw the fuel

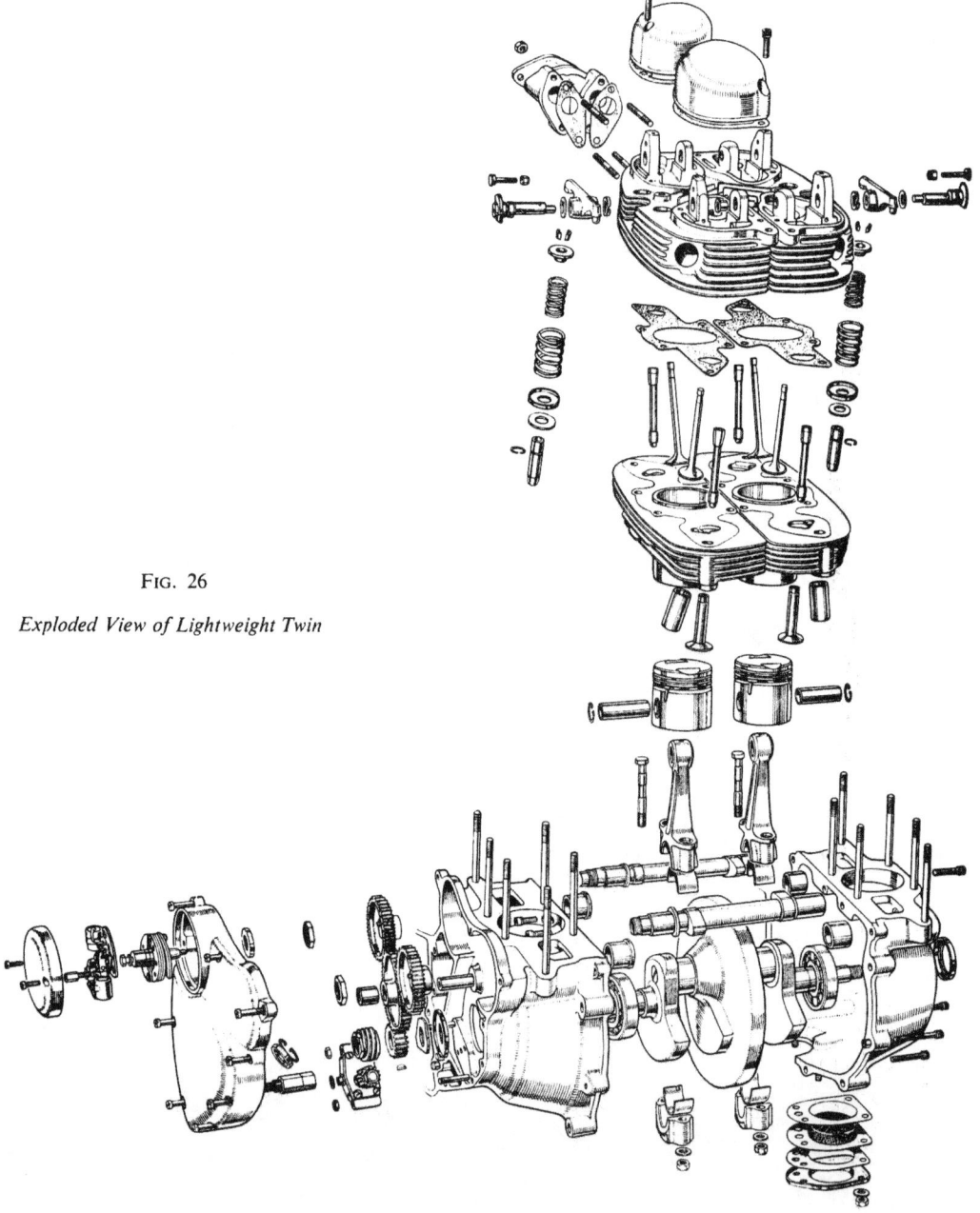

Fig. 26

Exploded View of Lightweight Twin

tank from its front mounting, by pulling backwards.

Take off both exhaust pipes with mufflers—a little solvent squirted around the exhaust ports where the pipes are located

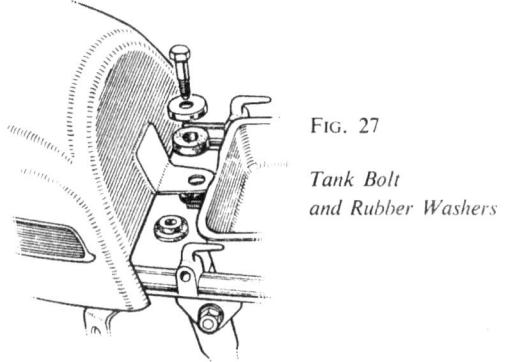

FIG. 27

Tank Bolt and Rubber Washers

will assist removal—avoid racking the pipes to extract—which can make the pipes a loose fit in the ports.

Take off the carburetter, then the manifold. Remove both H.T. wires take out both plugs.

Remove the cylinder head steady stay attached to the frame down member. Either take off—or release both ignition coils for better accessibility.

Remove the rocker box oil feed pipe (watch for the washers each side of the banjo connection).

ELECTRA MODEL ONLY

Take off the frame bracing plates—uniting the front and rear frame, also the flasher unit.

All lightweight twins

Take off in turn the four rocker covers using the allen key mentioned in the list of tools, in service, a portion of this key is cut off, and pressed into a piece of steel tube to extend it so that key can be manipulated clear of the covers, thus avoid the irritation of turning the key a little at a time.

Take off the six nuts securing the cylinder head—their location also tightening sequence is shown in fig. 28.

Raise the cylinder head sufficiently to insert the fingers of one hand to hold the two push rods then the head can be lifted clear of the cylinder. Should the head resist removal—use a short length of wood—with one placed below the inlet port—when a sharp blow with a hammer on the other end of the wood will separate the head from the cylinder. The reader should refer to the details on this subject outlined for the heavyweight engines, which in every way are applicable, when dealing with the valves and seatings, also removing carbon from the piston crowns.

Removing the cylinder

The cylinder should not be disturbed—unless there is good reason to do so. Raise the cylinder sufficient to expose the tappets, and encircle them with a rubber band to prevent them falling into the crankcase, the cylinder can then be lifted clear of the holding down studs.

Removing the valves

A universal valve spring compressor can be used to compress the valve spring to extract the valve spring keepers. The location of each valve and spring should be identified so that they can be replaced in the same order as removed. The inlet and exhaust valves are dissimilar in head diameter—but they can be inadvertently reversed. Check the valve spring free length from technical data renew if $\frac{3}{16}''$ shorter.

Removing the rockers

A study of fig. 29 will indicate the assembly order of the rockers, which can be extracted by removing the self locking nut securing the clamp bolt—early engines used a bolt of this kind with a 2 B.A. diameter—which on current engines has been increased to $\frac{1}{4}''$. The new type bolt can be used on early engines by increasing the bolt hole diameter to take the larger bolt, also grind the radius of the rocker quadrant portion to permit the bolt to be inserted. The four rockers are identical, but the rocker axles are "handed", the quadrant portion is used outwards, in a vertical position. Before refitting check the oil holes for obstruction, and ensure the thrust and spring washer is correctly located as illustrated.

Removing the valve guides

The valve guides are located by a circlip surrounding the guide, which are an interference fit, in consequence the head must be heated to remove the guide, otherwise the interference fit will be impaired, making the guide a loose fit in the head.

Heat the head—use a double diameter drift—of the kind shown for the heavyweight models, drive the guide upwards from inside the port—sufficient to prise out the circlip. Clean the guide with emery tape or to remove burnt oil carbon—reheat the head and drive out downwards through the port.

To refit the guides

Fit the circlip to the guide, ensure it is located in the groove. Heat the head again—put the valve through the guide aperture—then place the guide over the valve and press down. The valve acts as a pilot to start the guide square in the head. Drive the guide home until the circlip abuts against the valve guide boss. Do not spoil the knife edge on guide.

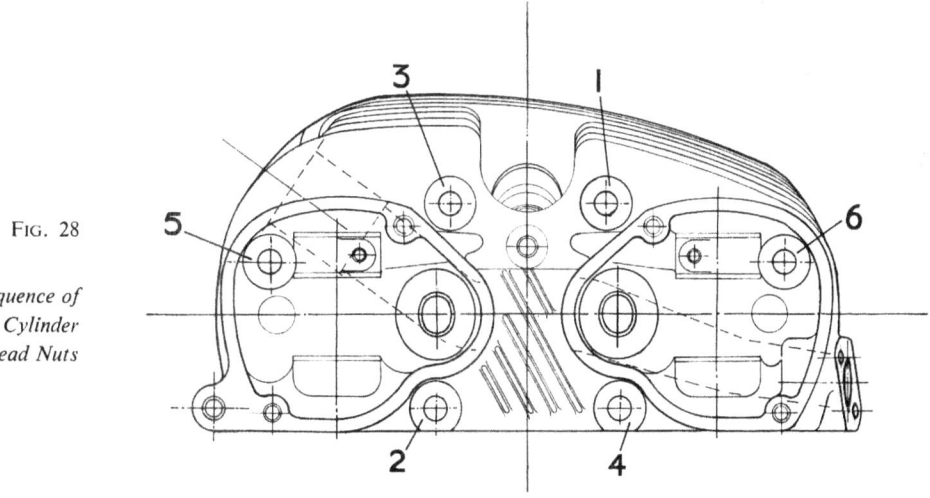

FIG. 28

Sequence of Tightening Cylinder Head Nuts

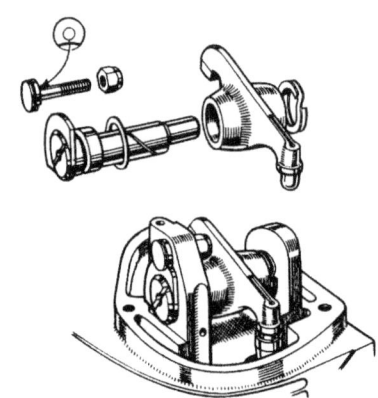

FIG. 29

Rocker Adjustment Details

Valve grinding

Elementary details on this subject are given in the riders handbook, the reader should peruse the paragraph outlined for the heavyweight twins.

Fitting valves

Check the free length of the valve springs first—the inner spring is $1\frac{7}{16}''$ the outer is $1\frac{33}{64}''$. Use new springs if the free length is $\frac{3}{16}''$, or more shorter than the normal free length, the springs are "rated" the two close coils are used against the heat washer.

Removing the pistons

Have available a piece of steel rod about $\frac{1}{4}''$ diameter six inches long. With the cylinder head removed turn the crankshaft until the pistons are on the top of the stroke (Jubilee model) otherwise the wrist pins will score the crankcase during removal. Heat the piston with an electric iron, or its like, take out both outside circlips. Pass the steel rod through the timing side wrist pin—gently tap out the drive side pin supporting the piston at the same time. Do the same with the other piston. Mark the pistons so that they can go back in the same position previously occupied.

Piston rings

Do not disturb unless there is good reason, discolouration on the ring faces indicate gas leakage—use new rings. The ring gap is checked by placing the rings in turn into the unworn part of the cylinder and pushed down by the piston skirt so that the ring is square in the bore. The normal gap is between 0.006" to 0.008"; scrap the rings if the gap exceeds 0.016".

Fitting the pistons

Reverse the procedure described to remove. Fit the circlip with a rotary motion, ensure it is snuggly in its groove.

Refitting the cylinder

To attempt to fit the cylinder without piston ring clamps—particularly on the Jubilee engine—is courting disaster, for ring breakage will inevitably occur. The cost for a tool of this kind will be more than offset by the risk of running with broken rings—not apparent when the cylinder is fitted. This tool in use is illustrated in the heavyweight section. Get rid of all traces of broken base gasket particularly around the cylinder holding down studs, stick a new base gasket onto the cylinder base, do not use jointing compound on both sides of the gasket—it will tear when the cylinder is taken off the next time. Lower the cylinder, discard the rubber band round the tappets.

Refitting the heads

Use a new gasket for the cylinder head to avoid subsequent attention if the original gasket does not work, when the head is put back. Reverse the sequence used for removal. Tighten the head nuts in the order shown in fig. 28 use a torque spanner set to 15 foot lbs for correct tension.

Removing the timing cover

Take off the domed cover for the contact breaker (two screws). Remove the contact breaker assembly, the plate is retained by two screws, passing through the elongated slots also two hexagon pillars, separate the cable connections, the terminals are under the gas tank. The cam operating the contact breakers is a taper fit on the camshaft—use a withdrawal bolt 25016. Take out the bolt fixing the cam, insert the withdrawal bolt and lightly tighten. Give the head of the bolt a sharp blow—the cam will come away. The assembly can be withdrawn. Take out 10 screws fixing the cover, a light tap with a soft faced mallet will separate the cover from the crankcase.

The timing cover oil seals

Two oil seals are used in the timing cover, the most important is the one that surrounds the extension on the timing side of the crankshaft. Should this seal become ineffective, oil can leak past the seal and the shaft instead of going through the crankshaft. The seal is retained by a circlip, which, when removed, will permit the seal to be prised out, and will be of no further use. To fit a new seal warm the cover, press in the seal—with the metal backing outwards, to enable the circlip to be refitted. The other seal is to prevent oil seeping into the contact breaker compartment—the presence of oil here denotes the seal is ineffective, and it must be replaced. The old seal can be taken out after warming the cover, then press in the new one with the metal backing inwards (towards the contact breaker).

Setting the rocker clearance

The clearance between the rocker and the valve end is adjusted by moving the eccentric spindle for the rocker, which is illustrated in fig. 29. To check the clearance—take off the rocker covers. Deal with the inlet rockers first, by turning the engine until the nearside inlet rocker goes down, with the valve fully opened. Use a feeler gauge 0.004" thick—insert it between the valve end and the rocker—the feeler should just pass through—if the clearance is correct. To set, or adjust the clearance—with the engine unmoved—release the self locking nut which clamps the rocker spindle. Use a screwdriver in the slot in the spindle—turn the spindle until the rocker moves away from the valve. Put the feeler on the end of the valve turn the rocker spindle in an opposite direction, until the rocker just "nips" the feeler tighten the spindle lock nut. Pass the feeler again between the valve and rocker to check. Turn the engine until the offside inlet valve is fully opened—repeat the process. Do the same to the exhaust rockers, but use a 0.006" feeler.

Make a mark on the spoke to register with the face for the spark plug on the cylinder head.

Take out the spoke—make a further mark $\frac{1}{8}''$ upwards from the first mark (for the Jubilee and Electra model). Time the Navigator at top dead centre full retarded.

Put the spoke back through the spark plug hole—hold it vertical—turn the engine backwards slowly—until the top mark on the spoke just registers with the face for the plug seating on the head. The points on the contact breaker cam N fig. 33 should be just about to separate. Use a piece of cigarette paper between the points, when a light pull on the paper will indicate when the points are about to separate.

It is best to set up the ignition timing with the auto advance in the full advanced position to offset the possibility if wear on the limit stops, which would then give a fast timing if set with the unit retarded. Details to set up the ignition timing are given in assembling the engine.

Removing the engine from the frame

The machine should be supported by using a stout wood box under the crankcase, do not rely on the central stand. Start by:-

Strip down as far as removing the cylinder head.
Disconnect the negative battery cable.
Disconnect the starter motor cable (Electra only).
Disconnect the three alternator wires at the snap connectors.
Disconnect the contact breaker wire snap terminal.
Disconnect the clutch cable at the gear box end.
Disconnect the spark plug H.T. wires.
Disconnect the two rubber oil pipe connections. The outer one is the feed pipe.
Remove both footrests.
Remove speedo cable at the wheel end.
Remove the rear chain connecting link—try to keep the chain away from the ground.

Remove all the studs passing through the frame and crankcase—that fix the engine.
Remove one of the top front frame member studs—the member can pivot on its remaining bolt.
Get someone to hold the engine during this part of the work.

Warning

There are four allen screws holding the two halves of the crankcase together which are not readily visible. An attempt to separate the crankcase without removing these screws, must cause damage.

There are two of these screws in the spigot bore in the crankcase for the cylinder. The remaining screws are in the crankcase just in front of the gear box casing—they can be obscured by the paper gasket for the cover, which is the object of this warning.

Separating the crankcase

Take off the outer portion of the front chaincase (10) screws.
Remove the outrigger plate (3 nuts) Electra only.
Remove starter drive also chain Electra only.

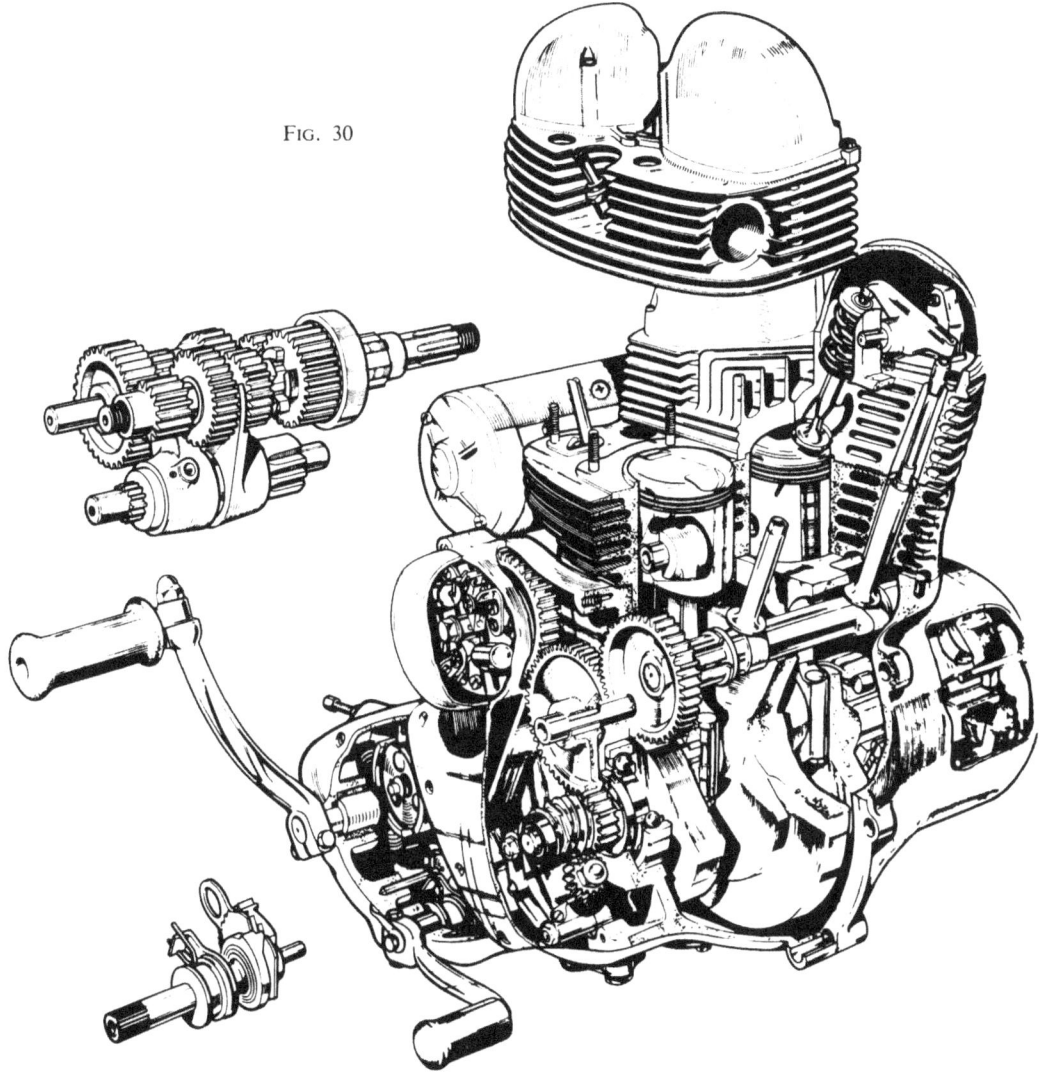

Fig. 30

Fig. 31   *Assembling the Lightweight Engine*

Remove rotor and engine sprocket with chain and clutch assembly. See para chain removal.

Remove the sump filter plate at the base of the sump (4 nuts).

Remove gearbox shafts and internals—see gear box section.

Remove the timing cover (see details on page 28).

Remove the oil pump (2 nuts).

Remove the oil pump worm drive nut **left hand thread.**

Remove the two cam wheels—use a bar extractor bar 24980 then the intermediate pinion.

Remove timing side crankcase, both camshafts, with their springs and plungers.

Remove the crankshaft.

The crankshaft

There are two bronze screwed plugs in the crankshaft, which can be removed to clean the cavity in the crankshaft, before new big end shells are fitted. It is vitally important that these plugs are securely fixed—for if either one or both come out the oil will be cut off from the con rod journals.

The journals for the con rods must have a mirror like finish, that can be restored by using superfine emery tape (do this before the two plugs are put back—to flush out the oilways).

The con rods

These are machined in pairs, so if they are taken off the crankshaft, they must go back in the same position. The con rods and caps are marked with a diagonal line thus / across the cap and rod, so that they can be put back in pairs.

The normal clearance between the big end shells and the crankshaft, with a dry bearing is 0.001″ to 0.0025″.

To take off the con rods remove the self locking nuts—then a sharp jerk upwards on the rod should pull off the cap. If the cap jams half way up the studs, tap the cap square, and try again.

Usually a new set of big end shells will suffice to take up movement in the bearing, caused by wear. Measure the journals which have a diameter of 1.5005″ for the high limit, and 1.5000″ for the low limit. If the wear is 0.001″ to 0.0015″ regrind the journals, fit suitable undersize shells. The journals must have a mirror like finish after regrinding, otherwise the shells will wear rapidly.

Assembling the con rods

Apply a film of anti-scruffing compound to both journals (molybdenum disulphide) use new self locking nuts and tighten with a torque spanner set to 15 foot lbs.

The crankcase bearings

Both the inner member for the roller bearing used on the drive side shaft, also the ball bearing for the timing side shaft, should be a close interference fit on the shafts, the outer portion of the bearings should also be a close interference fit in the crankcase.

Removing the bearings

When the crankshaft is taken out, it will have the inner member of the roller bearing on the shaft, leaving the bearing ring in the crankcase. Heat the crankcase in the region of the bearing sleeve, drop the crankcase—face downwards—the sleeve will drop out.

Heat also the timing side crankcase, then push out the bearing.

Camshaft bushes

It is most unlikely that attention to this part of the engine will be necessary, in view of the robust size of the bushes used. The finished bore diameter reamed in position is 0.9378" to 0.9383".

Intermediate gear

Wear on this bush can cause backlash between the pinion teeth and the gears for the camshafts, to replace the bush it can be pressed out without difficulty. After fitting a new bush it should be reamed to 0.5622" to 0.5627". The shaft for this pinion is an interference fit in the crankcase—located by a circlip—to prevent the shaft moving inwards towards the crankshaft. Heat the crankcase to extract and refit—exercise great care when fitting—to ensure it is square in its housing, as teeth engagement on the pinions will be affected.

Assembling the engine

Prepare to assemble the engine, by washing all parts in gasoline, clean the crankcase joint faces, by removing broken portions of broken gasket, as well as the face for the cylinder. Use a fine oil stone on the crankcase faces, to remove burrs, thrown up by fitting the studs passing through the two halves of the crankcase. Take up the crankshaft, press the inner member for the roller bearing on the drive side shaft with the arbour press—if available.

Heat the drive side crankcase sufficient to allow the bearing sleeve to squarely enter its housing.

Heat the timing side crankcase, insert the ball bearing—ensure it is fully home.

Apply some clean oil to both bearings when the case has cooled down.

All Electra also 1964 Navigator and Jubilee Models

The figures in paranthesis refer to fig. 45.

Hold the drive side crankcase horizontally in a vice, clamp it by the two studs for the primary chain tensioner firmly.

Take up the crankshaft, set both con rods at the bottom of the stroke, then put the crankshaft into the crankcase.

Fit the camshafts with their springs and plungers (the exhaust drives the contact breaker.

Fit the gear box mainshaft (1).

Fit the layshaft (10).

Fit the selector drum (20) with gear cluster as shown in fig. 31.

Fit the selector drum (20) with gear cluster as shown in fig. 31.

Fit the plunger and spring (24/5/6)—with the plunger in the shallowest of the five grooves.

Fit crankcase joint paper washer—use jointing compound on the crankcase only.

Fit the timing side crankcase—check camshafts can move against the springs.

Fit the allen screws and tighten to join the two halves of the crankcase.

Fit selector quadrant (27)—line up the mark on it with mark on selector drum (20).

Fit the actuating plate (29) with letter "O" outwards.

Fit gear box inner cover—six nuts and washers (45).

Fit mainshaft (1) with nut (9) and tab washer.

Fit clutch operating body—split pin outwards then the circlip (40).

Fit footchange ratchet (30) the spring (31).

Fit footchange pedal shaft (32) and spring (33).

Fit the spacer (34) **this has been inadvertently reversed in the drawing.**

Fit the gear box end cover (41).

Fit both camshaft pinions.

Fit dished washer—star shaped backing washer to timing side crankshaft, then the pinion line up the valve timing marks—fit the intermediate pinion.

Fit the oil pump worm drive nut—**left hand thread.**

Fit the oil pump (see notes on heavyweight twins)—check the oil seal on the pump is OK.

Fit the timing cover with new gasket (10) screws.

Fit the sump filter with four nuts, and washers.

Hold the engine upright in a stand—or in a vice—use a razor blade trim off surplus gasket around the crankcase joint.

Fit the pistons—right side first.

Fit the cylinder—with tappets secured by a rubber band.

Fit twelve cylinder holding down studs to crankcase—coarse threads go in the crankcase.

Fit the auto ignition advance unit with contact breakers—set the ignition timing before the head is fitted—the piston travel can be measured—see para on ignition timing.

Fit a new gasket then put back the cylinder head.

Fit the four push rods—tighten the nuts as per fig. 28.

Fit the inlet manifold see the gaskets are sound.

Set the rocker clearance 0.004" for inlet 0.006" for exhaust.

Fit the four rocker covers.

Fit the back portion chain case (four countersunk allen screws).

Fit the engine sprocket key.

Fit together the engine sprocket—chain and clutch assembly.

Now follow the details given for the strip down.

All Lightweight Twins

Ignition timing

To ensure satisfactory engine performance and avoid possible damage to the engine, it is vitally important to make this setting accurately also identical on both cylinders. For this purpose, two contact breakers are fitted (see fig. 33) which can be adjusted independently of each other. As the ignition lead (advance) is limited to 30° before top dead centre with the automatic ignition advance unit in the fully advanced position, it is extremely difficult to measure the piston travel with any degree of accuracy other than by the use of a timing disc, or degree plate attached to the driving side main-shaft. The two contact breakers, with one detached, are shown in fig. 33. Unscrew the two hexagon pillar nuts and two screws to remove contact breaker plates.

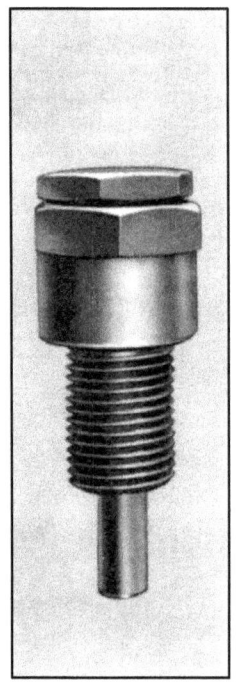
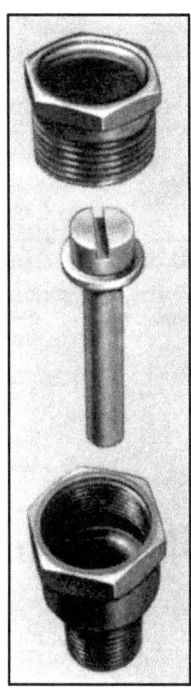
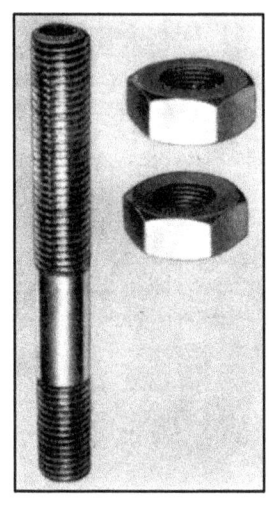

FIG. 32

Timing Plug and Stud

To check the ignition timing

Have available:-
A timing disc 022011.
A stud ¼ BSF 4″ long and two nuts for the stud.
A feeler gauge .012″.
A short length of stiff wire as a pointer for timing disc.
Commence by removing both sparking plugs, the contact breaker cover and the outer portion of front chain case.

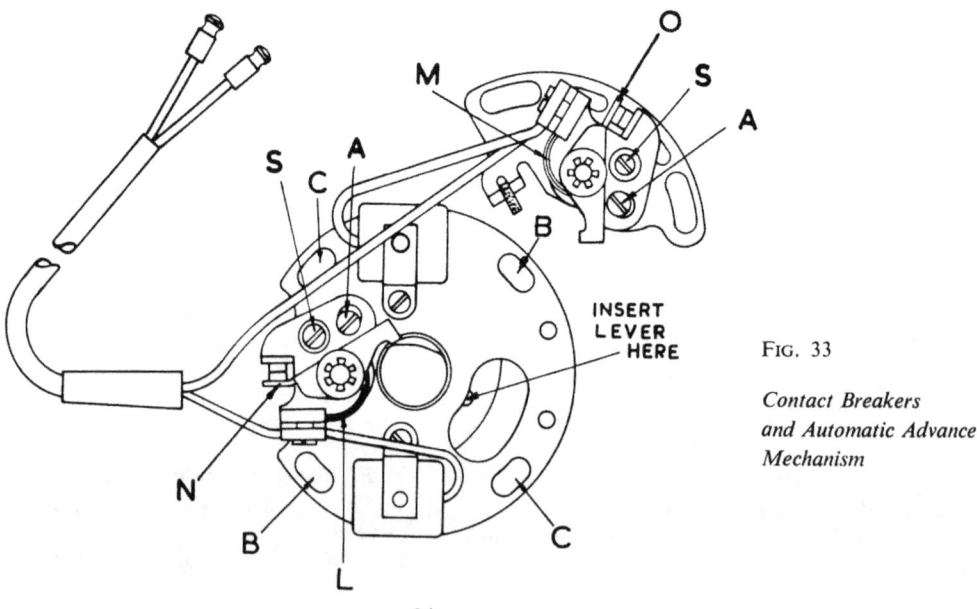

FIG. 33

Contact Breakers and Automatic Advance Mechanism

34

It will be seen that the timing disc will have to be used away from the rotor to clear the stator coils and chain case to do this:-

Take out the bolt securing the starter dog to the mainshaft and screw firmly home into the crankshaft, the **6″** stud mentioned above and run down one of the two nuts.

Fit the timing disc and lightly tighten the second nut.

Make a loop to one end of the wire and attach it in a convenient place on the chain case and secure it with one of the chain cover screws. Bend the free end of the wire at right angle to the timing disc to act as a pointer, just clear of the disc. Check the contact breaker gap (N fig. 33) for the near side cylinder by rotating the engine until the points are at maximum separation, viz when the fibre pad is on the peak of the cam lobe. Use the feeler gauge, which must be free from oil or grease, which should just pass through the contact points.

Reset the gap if necessary by releasing the clamp screw S (fig. 33) and moving the eccentric screw A (fig. 33) until the correct gap is obtained then re-tighten the clamp screw. Repeat this process and check the other contact gap.

For contact breaker service see Electrical section.

Remove the rocker covers, and take off the small contact plate as shown in fig. 33.

Rotate the engine until the left side piston is on the extreme top of its stroke with both valves closed, (rockers free) which is the firing stroke.

Position the timing disc so that the zero mark is approximately midway between the cylinder and firmly tighten the nut securing the timing disc, without moving the engine.

Set the end of the wire pointer to register with the zero mark on timing disc. As the ignition timing must be accurate within two degrees of the specified setting it is vital to accurately position the piston on top dead centre.

Owing to the steep angle of the sparking plug hole in the cylinder head, a rod or wire cannot be used sufficiently vertical to record the piston position. Other than removing the cylinder head, the alternative is to use a timing plug as shown in fig. 32 which can be easily fabricated and consists of a scrap sparking plug with the negative point removed and the insulated portion discarded.

Insert through the plug body a ¼″ diameter cheese-headed screw 1⅜″ long. Use a suitable washer against the screw head and secure the rod by tightening the plug gland nut. The rod should protrude ¾″.

To locate the top dead centre:—

Turn the engine **backwards** about 30° with a spanner on disc nut.

Insert timing plug.

Turn the engine slowly in a **forward** direction until the piston touches the timing rod.

Record from the timing disc the number of degrees that register with the pointer.

Again slowly rotate the engine **backwards** past the 180° mark until the piston comes in contact with the timing plug on its upward stroke and, again record the number of degrees that register with the pointer.

Add together the two figures recorded and divide by two, for example, if the first reading is 35 degrees and the second 25 degrees, giving a total of 60 degrees, half this figure is 30 degrees, thus if the pointer is adjusted to register with 30° on the timing disc and the engine is turned until the zero mark registers with the pointer, this is the true top dead centre piston position.

Take out the timing plug.

To adjust the timing

If the timing is incorrect, adjust by releasing slightly the two hexagon pillars B fig. 33 also the two screws C fig. 33 and move the contact base plate in the required direction. Moving the plate anti-clockwise will advance the ignition timing.

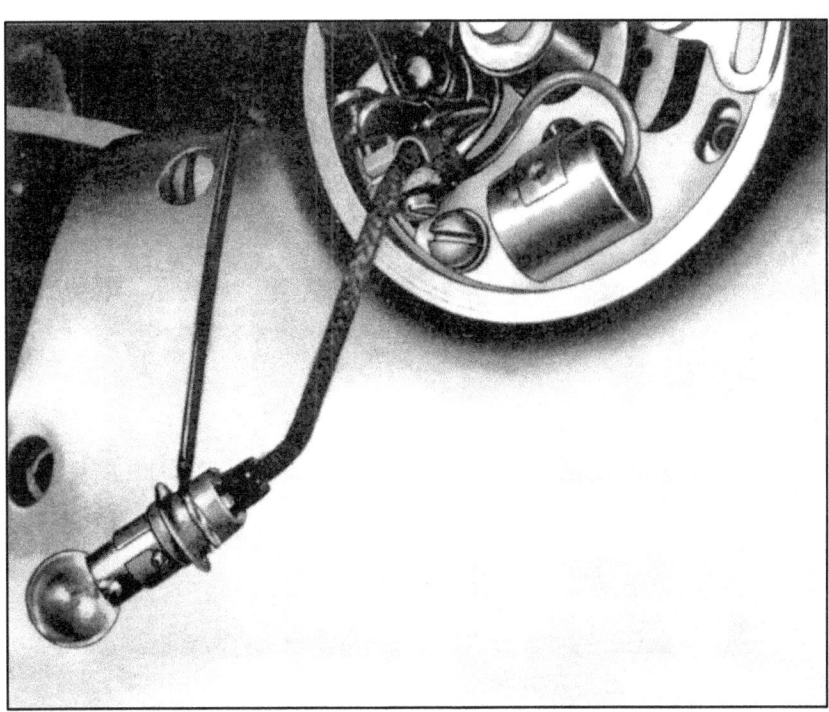

Fig. 34

Bulb Connection

Timing the left side cylinder

To determine the exact firing point (contact gap separation) use a 12 or 6 volt bulb with a short length of wire attached to the bulb body and a similar wire attached to the bulb filament connection.

Connect one wire to a convenient point on the engine, the other to the contact breaker spring L fig. 33 for the left side cylinder.

For technical reasons the timing must be checked with the auto advance unit in the full advanced position, for the left side cylinder.

Turn the engine backwards, switch on the ignition, the bulb will light then insert a lever or the point of a pen knife into the hole as shown in fig. 35 and lever towards the rear of the engine to move the flyweights into the full advance position, maintaining this position turn the engine forward very slowly and stop immediately the bulb light goes out.

Look at the timing disc and the pointer should register 30° if the timing is correct.

To reset the timing

If the timing has been deranged and there is insufficient latitude in the elongated slots in the contact breaker base plates to adjust, the operating cam must be released from its taper fit. Remove the cam central fixing bolt and use in its place a withdrawal bolt 06508 and lightly screw home. A light blow on the extractor bolt will dislodge the cam.

When resetting the timing, the cam rotates clockwise when in use.

Timing the right side cylinder

Having established the correct full advance timing for the left side cylinder, record from the timing disc the number of degrees shown with the auto advance in the RETARDED position which may be 8°.

Fit the small contact breaker plate. Recheck contact gap fig. 33, turn engine one complete turn in direction of rotation until the pointer registers zero on the timing disc. Turn engine slightly backwards until the pointer registers 8° before top dead centre the same amount as for the left side cylinder. Adjust the small contact breaker plate (using the lamp bulb connected to spring M fig. 33) so that the contact points are just about to separate. The timing correctly set will then be identical on both cylinders.

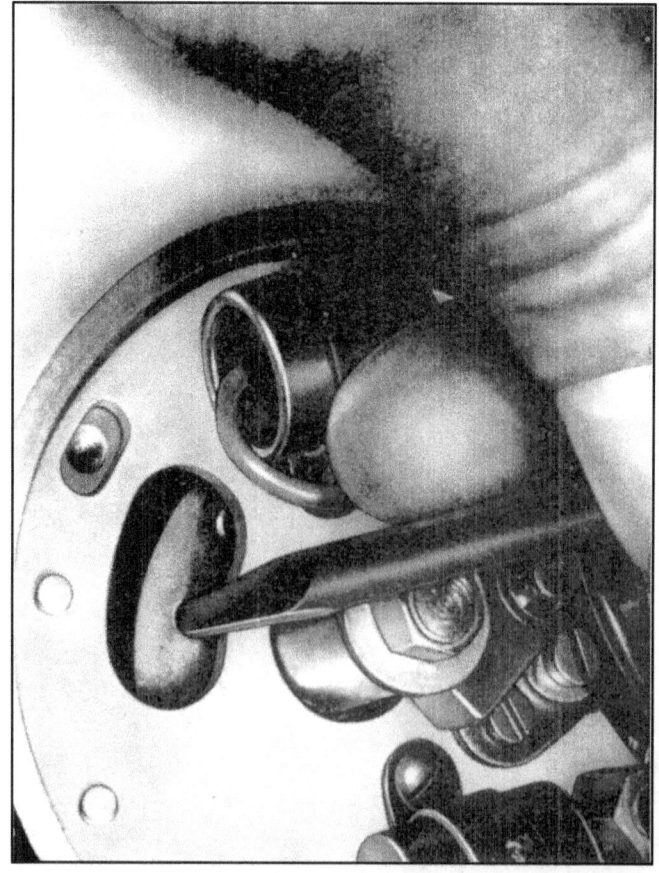

FIG. 35
Ignition Timing

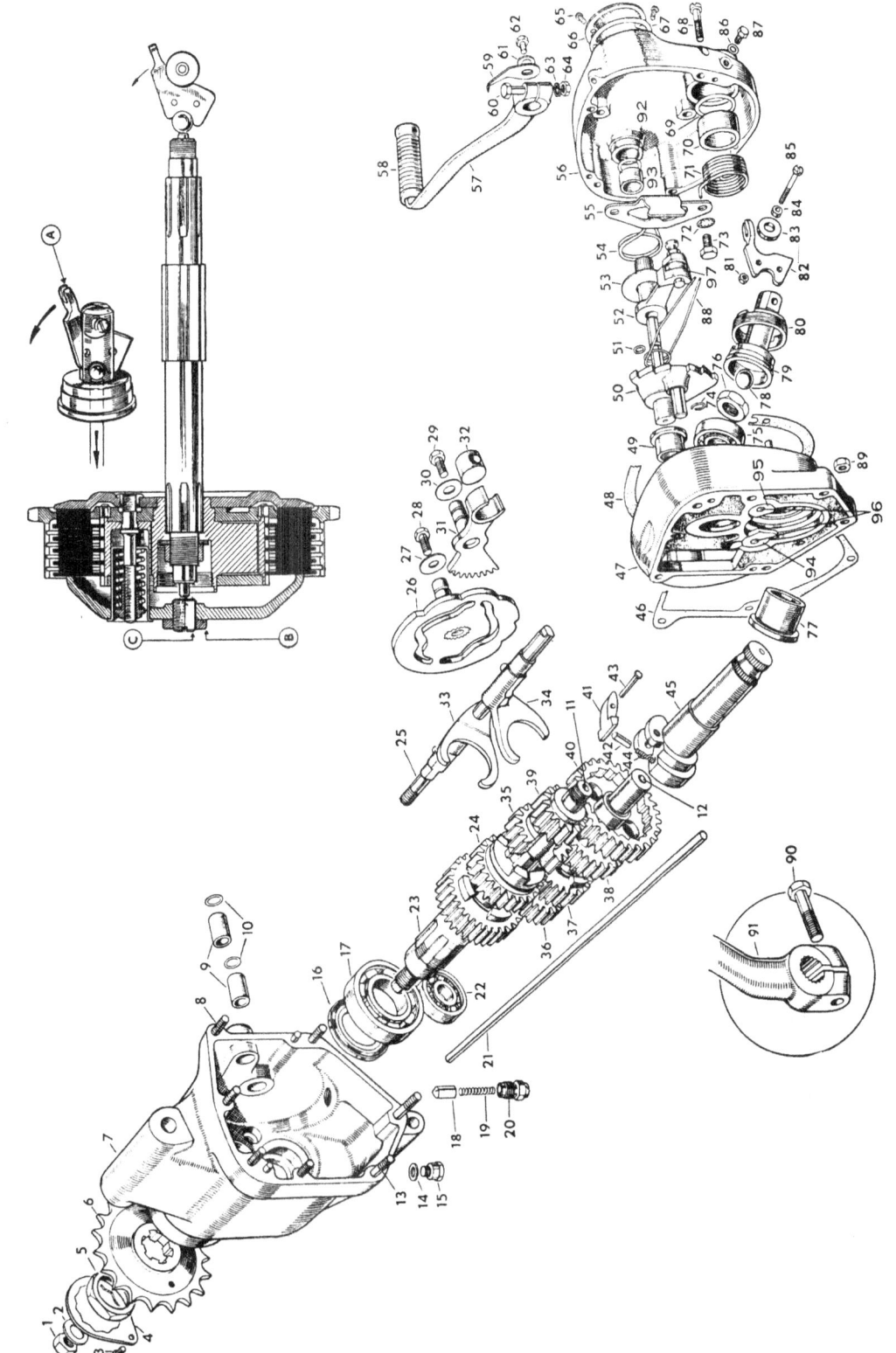

Fig. 36
The Heavyweight Twin Gearbox

TRANSMISSION

The gear box (heavyweight twins)

A stripdown condition of the gear box is shown in fig.36—the figures in parenthesis apply. There is only one left hand thread, viz. the sprocket nut for the rear chain.

Removing the outer cover

Remove the drain plug (15) to drain oil.
Remove the inspection cap (66) take off the clutch cable.
Remove the bolt for gear shift indicator—leave the pedal on.
Remove the kickstarter crank bolt (90) take off the crank.
Remove the five cheese head screws fixing cover (68).
Remove the cover by pulling off—using the gear shift pedal.

Removing the inner cover (47)

Remove the ratchet plate and spindle (5).
Remove the clutch operating arm and roller (82).
Remove the lock ring (80) take away the body and ball.
Remove the mainshaft nut (74).
Remove the seven nuts fixing the cover (89).
Remove the cover—tap the edge and pull off (47).

Removing the internals

Remove the low gear pinion on mainshaft (39).
Remove the striker fork spindle (25) by unscrewing.
Remove the two striker forks (33 and 34).
Remove the clutch push rod (21).
Remove the mainshaft with the gears on it (11).
Remove the layshaft with gears (12) waggle it and pull

Removing the sleeve gear (23).

Remove the screw fixing the lock plate (4).
Remove the sleeve gear sprocket nut (5) left hand thread.
Remove the sprocket (6) from the splines.
Remove the distance piece—behind sprocket.
Remove the gear from the bearing (17).

Removing the cam plate (26).

Remove the dome nut (20) take out the plunger and spring.
Remove the two bolts (28 and 29).
Remove the cam plate and quadrant (26).

Removing the gear bushes

Remove the bushes by pressing out—note location first the bushes are brittle (oilite) use care in fitting. Size in situ 0.81325"—0.81200".

Removing the main bearing (17)

Remove the oil seal (16) by prising out.
Remove the bearing by warming the case and press out.

Removing the bushes

Remove the kickstarter bush (77) by warming the cover by pressing out from the **outside**—ream new bush to 0.6875" to 0.6865".
Remove the footchange spindle bush—it has a blind hole, heat the cover—screw into the bush a coarse threaded tap and pull out.

Assembling the gear box

Fit the main gear bearing (17)—heat the case.
Fit the sleeve gear (23) the distance piece and seal (16).
Fit the sleeve gear sprocket and nut—this must be very firmly tightened.
Fit the lock plate and its screw.

Fitting the cam plate

This plate must be correctly positioned to index the four gears.
Fit the quadrant (31) with bolt and washer. Lift the lever portion of quadrant, with radius on lever to be in line with the top stud for the cover (top gear).
Fit the cam plate with the first two teeth in the quadrant is visible through the slot in the cam plate—then fit the bolt and washer (27 and 28).

Fitting the internals

Fit the mainshaft with the third gear (24) on shaft.
Fit the second gear (35) with striker fork (33) in the slot in the pinion.
Fit the projection on striker fork in cam plate.
Fit the first gear (39).
Fit the layshaft assembled with gear (36) gear (37) gear (38) with the other striker fork in (38) engage projection in cam plate insert the layshaft in its bush.
Line up the two holes in both striker forks, insert the spindle (25) and screw home.
Fit the first gear (40).

To complete the assembly

Put back the roller (32) line up to take foot shift spindle use new gasket—fit the inner cover. Before tightening the body lock ring (80) position the lever (82) so that it is in line with the clutch cable entry to give a straight pull. Refill one pint of S.A.E. 50 oil.

Replacing the gear shift spring

Take off the outer cover (56) then the quadrant (50) with the pawl spring behind it. Tap out the gearshift sleeve (52) washer (53). Take out two bolts (73) remove plate. The spring assembled is shown in fig. 37.

The clutch

To dismantle the clutch, take off the outer portion of the front chain case as described elsewhere.
Unscrew the three clutch adjusting nuts—if difficulty exists—use a penknife blade between the back of the adjuster screw and the spring. There are two protrusions on each screw, which abuts against the start of the spring—to prevent the adjuster involuntarily unscrewing—the penknife will keep the spring clear of the abutment on the adjusters.

To remove the clutch body

With the pressure plate removed, take out the clutch plates, fit the tool shown in fig. 24, remove the gear box mainshaft nut (the tool will stop the assembly turning) take out the chain connecting link, the clutch will come away from the mainshaft, if it resists removal use extractor 040449.

The clutch plates

Should clutch slip or clutch drag develop check the steel plates to see if they are buckled. Friction plates that are impregnated with oil should be washed in a highly volatile solvent—not gasoline, a dusting with Fullers Earth will absorb the oil, and make the clutch effective.

The shock absorber

See Lightweight Models

The clutch bearing

Three nuts, which are centre "popped" will probably become unserviceable after removal, which fix the back plate. The bearing will be exposed when the plate is taken off. Use anti-centrifuge grease to lubricate this bearing before the plate is put back, and centre pop the nuts when finally tightened.

Assembling the clutch

Reserve the order described for dismantling. The clutch adjusting nuts should be just flush with the end of the clutch spring studs.

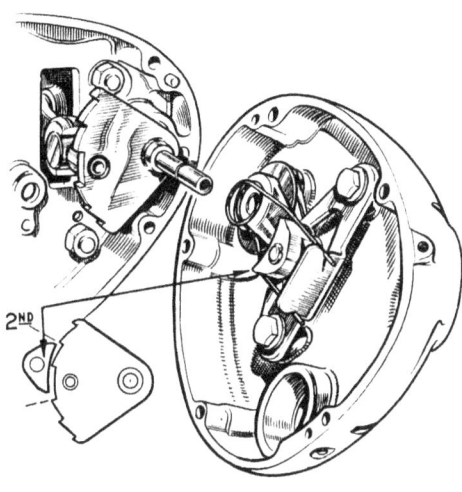

FIG. 37

Adjusting the clutch cable

The clutch cannot possibly function correctly, unless there is free movement between the clutch push rod and the operating mechanism. It is common belief that providing there is play, or lost motion in the clutch operating cable, the clutch push rod has free movement. A study of the clutch operating mechanism, will readily indicate that this assumption is incorrect. The only way to ensure free movement is to: Run down the clutch cable adjuster as far as possible—the lever will be very slack. Take off the outer portion of the front chain case—release the nut for the slotted stud. With a screwdriver screw in the slotted screw in gently—until it just touches the push rod, then unscrew, exactly one half turn—then lock the screw with its nut—with care that the screw does not move, whilst the nut is being tightened.

Now unscrew the clutch cable adjuster—until there is about $\frac{3}{16}$" slack between the inner wire and the cable outer casing, free movement is thus assured. Put back the chain case.

Primary chain adjustment

Front chain adjustment is effected by moving the gear box, which pivots on its lower fixing bolt, by altering the position of the nuts on the cross head bolt. As it is possible for the gear box to move, after the fixing bolts have been tightened, this adjustment must be made in the following sequence. To tighten the front chain: Take off the chaincase inspection cap. Release slightly the nut for the top gear box fixing bolt—leave the lower one. Release and run back several turns, the nut on the cross head bolt—nearest to the engine. Screw down the other nut on the cross head bolt slowly—checking the chain tension through the inspection hole—until the chain is just tight. The importance of this adjustment, is the last movement made, must be one of moving the gear box forward—then the gear box cannot move. With the chain just tight, run down the nut on the adjuster bolt nearest to the rear wheel several turns. Now screw on the adjuster nut—nearest to the engine a trifle at a time checking the chain tension, until there is a minimum of $\frac{1}{2}$" slack in the centre run of the chain. If the chain gets too slack—start all over again. Check the chain tension in several positions—there may be a tight place. Run down the loose nut against the adjuster, tighten the pivot bolt nut.

Rear chain adjustment

Check the front chain adjustment first—as the position of the gear box affects also the rear chain adjustment. Release slightly the rear wheel spindle nuts to enable the wheel and brake drum to move. Unscrew the chain adjuster locknuts, press down hard on the bottom run of the rear chain—to bring the spindle into contact with the adjuster bolts. Move each adjuster bolt an equal amount (to maintain wheel alignment) get someone to sit on the riders seat, adjust the chain until there is a total up and down movement—in the centre run of the chain to the extent of $\frac{3}{4}$" to 1 inch. Tighten the spindle nuts, then the adjuster locknuts (watch the adjusters do not move) check the rear brake, which is also affected when the rear wheel is moved.

Front chain adjustment G15 CS Models

The arrangement used to adjust the front chain on this model is shown in fig. 38. Remove the inspection cap on the front chaincase. Slacken the nut (5) on the right side engine plate. Slacken the nut (3). Screw in the bolt (1) into the crosshead to take up slack in the chain—press hard on the bottom run of the rear chain to tighten the front one, the correct chain whip is $\frac{1}{8}$". Check in several positions—adjust for tightest point. When the correct adjustment is made tighten nuts (3 and 5). Should the front chain be tight—screw the bolt (1) out of the crosshead. Check rear chain adjustment after dealing with the front one.

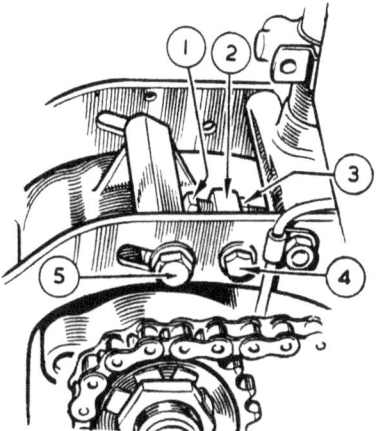

FIG. 38

Front Chain Adjustment

1. Adjusting bolt.
3. Adjusting bolt lock nut.
5. Engine plate bolt.

Rear chain adjustment

Slacken the rear wheel spindle nut also the nut fixing the brake drum dummy spindle. Unscrew the lock nuts for the chain adjusters, unscrew the adjuster an equal amount each side—to keep the chain line correct—until there is $1\frac{1}{8}$" whip in the centre run of the chain—or $\frac{1}{2}$" when someone is sitting on the riders seat.

Tighten the dummy spindle nut first then the wheel spindle nut, finally the adjuster lock nuts. Put back the inspection cover.

Check the rear brake after altering the rear chain adjustment.

Removing the rear chain

The rear chain is closely shrouded by the chain guard, which leaves little room to operate, other than releasing the chain guard from its fixings. If a new chain is to be fitted, disconnect the connecting link in the fitted chain and connect to the new chain at the top run. Select a neutral position in the gear box then with the left hand holding the bottom chain run and the top with the right hand, the new chain can be pulled into position until the chain joint is accessible, when the connecting link can be fitted.

Note: The closed end of the spring link should face direction of rotation.

The Care of Chains

The primary chain

This chain operates under ideal conditions as it is totally enclosed and runs in a bath of oil. Nevertheless, periodical attention is necessary to verify the oil level is maintained, also that the adjustment is correct. As this chain is not readily visible, this maintenance can unintentionally be overlooked.

The rear chain

Each chain joint is in fact a plain bearing of steel to steel on a hardened surface. To prevent metal to metal contact, it is essential to maintain a film of lubricant between the bearing surfaces, which will minimise friction and prolong the life of the chain.

If lubricant is applied with the chain in situ, oil should be diverted firstly to the joint formed by the roller and link edges (a Wesco gun is best suited for this purpose). Apply oil whenever the chain has a dry appearance.

When the machine has been used frequently during inclement weather it is preferable to remove the rear chain for attention. All traces of road grit should be removed with a wire brush and the chain thoroughly washed in paraffin. Wipe the chain dry.

Use a shallow tray sufficiently large enough to accommodate the chain, fill it with a quantity of anti-centrifuge grease, heat the grease until it reaches a state of fluidity and immerse the chain. Agitate the chain sideways to assist penetration of the fluid and leave for about ten minutes. When cool, remove the chain and take off surplus grease. After refitting and adjusting, and with short use, the chain will slacken off slightly, when the surplus grease has been squeezed out of the joints and will need further adjustment.

Checking the chain for wear

The chain should be washed in paraffin so all joints are free. Use a flat board and anchor one end of the chain with a nail, using a foot rule, measure the elongation from the following table.

Chain pitch	Pitches measured	Rejection limit or over
$\frac{5}{8}''$	16	$10\frac{7}{32}''$
$\frac{1}{2}''$	23	$11\frac{3}{4}''$
$\frac{3}{8}''$	24	$9\frac{3}{16}''$

Removing the front chaincase—heavyweight twins

Catch the oil drained in a suitable receptacle.

Release the left side exhaust pipe.

Take off the left side foot peg, then the large foot peg tube nut in the centre of the case.

Depress the brake pedal, only sufficient to take off the case, to avoid stretching the pedal return spring.

The rubber sealing strip is fitted with the small lip—or protrusion facing outwards and nearest to the outer portion of the case. Do not overtighten the foot peg tube nut two threads exposed is enough. If oil leaks because the rubber strip moves, stick it to the case with adhesive, leave over night to set. Paint the strip with soapy water to prevent "sticksion" when the outer portion is put back.

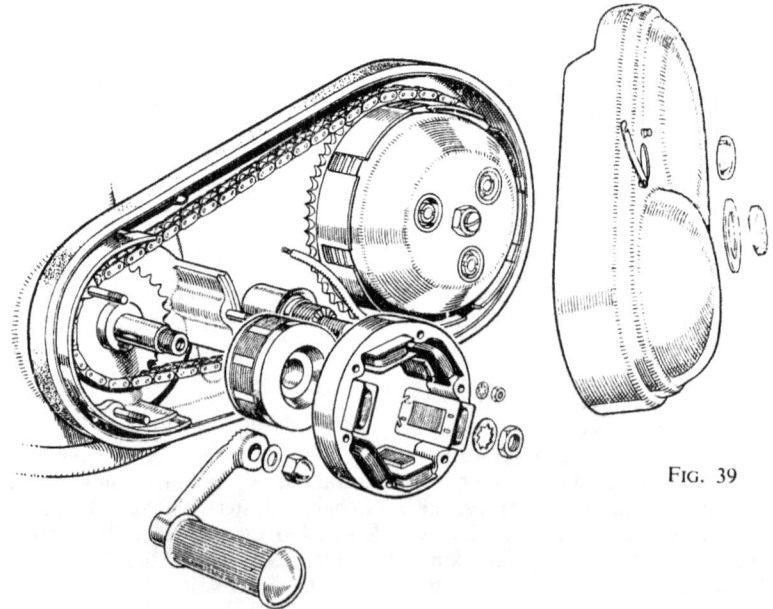

Fig. 39

Removing the front chaincase G15 CS twin

On early models it is necessary to release the foot peg arm from its rod and move the arm forward before the chaincase can be taken off. Later models have a chamfer machined on the arm to permit the case to be taken off.

Catch the oil drained, take off the brake rod adjusting nut.
Disconnect the three alternator wires (between engine plates).
Take out 14 screws, pull off the case gently, feeding the alternator wires through the grummet in the rear portion of the case.

Jubilee and Navigator Models

The gear box—engines before 106838

The oil content is 1¾ pints of S.A.E. 50 grade oil.

Outer cover removal

Take out the drain plug to empty gear box.
Remove the kickstarter pinch bolt take off the crank.
Remove the gear indicator plate and gear change pedal.
Remove the five screws fixing the cover, take away the cover.
Remove the clutch cable gear box end.
Remove the lockring for clutch operating body.
Remove the mainshaft nut inside the body.
Remove the six nuts fixing the cover and take it off.
Remove the footchange quadrant, with its spindle.

Remove the shaft for selector fork (use a spanner on the flats).

The internals can now be taken out. To take out the mainshaft take off the clutch assembly, see para on clutch.

The sleeve gear sprocket

The nut fixing the sprocket has a LEFT HAND thread. It should come off the splines easily—if not use two levers behind it. The sleeve gear can be pressed out, and into the gear box.

The oil seal

With the gear removed the seal can be prised out—it is

FIG. 40 *Gear Box Internals—Before 106838*

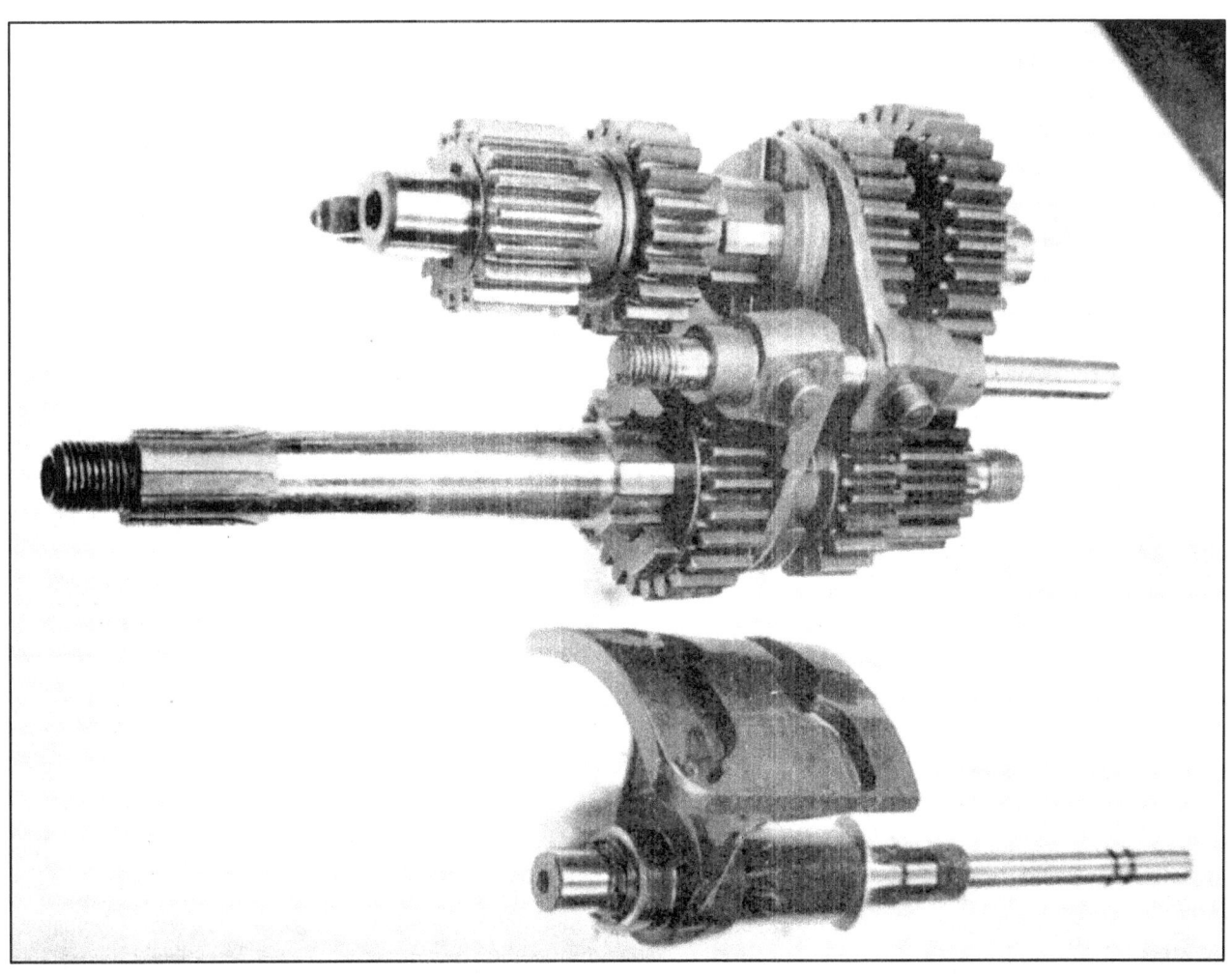

also possible to do this without taking out the gear. Note the metal backing for the seal faces outwards.

Gear box bushes

Two bushes are used in the sleeve gear, where the mainshaft operates. They are a press fit. New bushes fitted should be reamed to 0.689″ to 0.688″. The bushes are thin and brittle, be careful when fitting. The oilite bushes in the cover are made to size and do not require reaming.

To assemble the internals

The assembly sequence is shown in fig. 41 start by:
Put the plunger and spring in position.
Fit the footchange quadrant and spindle.
Fit the mainshaft, then the first—second—and third gear pinions.
Fit the mainshaft selector fork with the protrusion in the quadrant.
Fit the second and third gear to the layshaft and put it in the gear box.
Fit the layshaft selector fork and locate it in the quadrant.
Fit the selector fork spindle and screw home.
Fit the low gear pinion.

The clutch (all models)

As the primary chain is endless, the clutch body together with the engine sprocket are taken off together.
Remove the chain cover (10) screws.
Remove the outrigger plate (3) nuts—Electra only.
Remove the starter chain connecting link (Electra only).
Remove the stator (3 nuts) disconnect the alternator wire connections.
Remove the crankshaft bolt—straighten the tab washer—pull out starter ratchet (Electra).
Remove the rotor.
Remove the clutch pressure plate, with springs.
Remove the gear box mainshaft nut fixing clutch.
Remove the clutch assembly a little from the mainshaft.
Remove the engine sprocket by a puller.
The engine sprocket with clutch are taken off simultaneously.

Assembling the clutch

Put the clutch together in the following sequence:
Fit the thick steel back plate—with the step inwards.
Fit the double sided friction plate.
Fit the plain steel plate.
Fit the double sided friction plate.
Fit the plain steel plate.
Fit the double sided friction plate.
Fit the plain steel plate.
Fit the single sided friction plate—steel side outwards.
Fit the pressure plate, with the cups, springs and adjusters.
The adjusting nuts should be flush with the spring cups, with even tension.

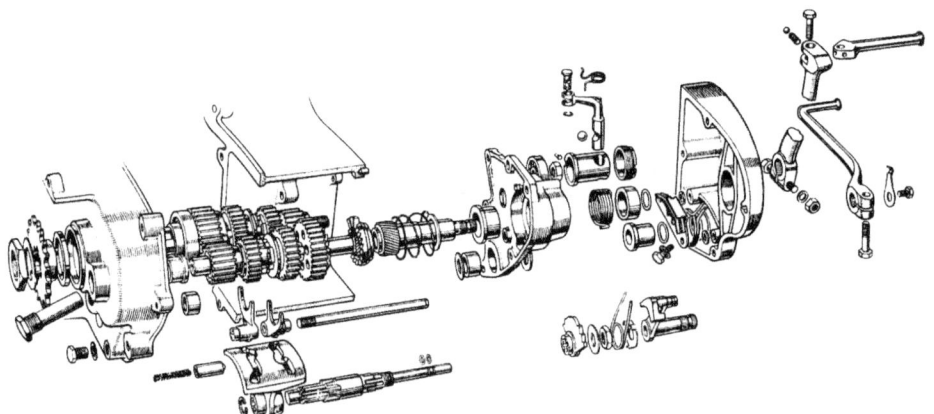

Fig. 41 *Exploded view of Gearbox, Engines before* 106838

The Transmission

Clutch adjustment

In order to obtain clean gear changing and freedom from clutch drag or clutch slip, correct adjustment is essential.

Screw in cable adjustor on rear of engine/gearbox casting to ensure excessive slack in cable. Remove the ten screws securing the primary chain cover and withdraw the cover, taking care not to tear the paper washer. Release the nut locking the adjuster stud in the centre of the clutch pressure plate and screw in the stud until contact with the push rod can be felt. Screw back exactly half a turn and relock the nut. Re-adjust the cable until there is $\frac{1}{8}$″ to $\frac{3}{16}$″ idle movement before tension occurs when the handlebar lever is operated.

Correct spring adjustment has been made when the adjusting screws are flush with the ends of the spring boxes and when individual adjustment has been made to ensure that the pressure plate withdraws squarely when clutch lever is operated.

Primary chain adjustment

It is best to adjust the primary chain when the gearbox/crankcase unit is warm as this is the normal running condition.

Inside the chaincase and held against the bottom run of the chain by two nuts is a nylon or steel slipper. Slackening the nuts enables the slipper to be raised or lowered to adjust the chain. There should be $\frac{3}{16}$″ to $\frac{1}{4}$″ up and down movement in the slack side of the chain when the engine is warm. Check the amount of slack in three or four places and adjust with chain in tightest position.

Rear chain adjustment

With the weight of the machine on the wheels there should be $\frac{3}{8}$″ × $\frac{1}{2}$″ up and down movement in the centre of the slack run of the chain. Check in three or four places and adjust at the position least slack. The rear wheel may be moved backwards by slackening the spindle nuts and rotating

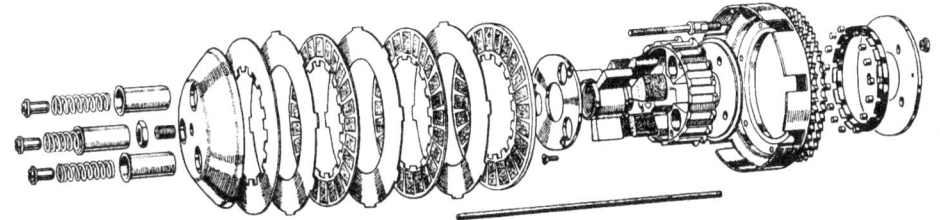

FIG. 42
Exploded view of Clutch

the adjusting screw which presses against the plain part of the nut in an anti-clockwise direction. It is important that both screws are rotated an equal amount in order to maintain wheel alignment.

To move the wheel in a forward direction slacken the spindle nuts as before and rotate the adjusters in a clockwise direction maintaining the plain portion of the spindle nut against the end of the adjuster. Adjust rear brake after moving the rear wheel.

Primary chain removal

The chain is "endless" and can only be removed by withdrawing simultaneously the engine sprocket and clutch assembly.

Remove chain cover 10 screws (see clutch adjustment).

Remove outrigger plate (three nuts).*

Remove starter motor chain (connecting link).*

Remove stator assembly (three nuts). Disconnect snap connectors.

Remove bolt in crankshaft (straighten tab washer) and put out starter ratchet.

Remove the rotor from parallel portion of shaft.

Remove clutch pressure plate with springs and cups.

Remove gear box mainshaft nut securing clutch.

Release only clutch assembly, use extractor 030449 if difficulty exists.

Release engine sprocket by using extractor JEST/12.

The engine sprocket, clutch assembly together with the primary chain, can be withdrawn.

*Electra only.

Primary chain re-fitting

Refit parts removed in the reverse order described for removal, with the following precautions:

Ensure key for rotor is correctly located before fitting the rotor. Run down the stator nuts evenly before finally tightening. The connecting link for starter chain is fitted with the CLOSED end facing the direction of rotation.

The bolt for mainshaft is finally tightened (use hammer tight spanner) and turn back tab washer.

Check chain adjustment.

When the clutch is assembled, operate the clutch lever on handlebar and observe if the clutch pressure is parallel to the plate behind it. If not adjust the clutch spring adjusting nuts until the gap between both plates are equal. Use a little jointing compound on the chain case to secure gasket and tighten cover screws diagonally.

Fill $\frac{1}{2}$ pint (.28 litres) of engine oil.

Clutch dismantling and assembly

To dismantle the clutch see details given for primary chain removal. To dismantle the clutch bearing, take off three nuts securing the clutch spring studs and back plate and take off the sprocket and clutch case. The bearing uses $15\frac{1}{4}'' \times \frac{1}{4}''$ rollers in a steel spacing cage, use a little anti-centrifugal grease on rollers when assembling. Finally tighten the stud nuts and "centre pop" the threaded portion of the stud and nut.

To renew the shock absorber rubbers take off the steel plate see fig. 43.

If the rubbers are badly worn they will come out easily, if not compress the thick rubbers by using a tool as shown in fig. 44. Alternatively use an old steel clutch plate with a handle welded to it, the thin rubbers can then be picked out. Take care to very firmly tighten the three countersunk screws and "centre pop" them for security. Assemble the clutch in the following sequence:

Thick steel back plate (step facing inwards).
Friction plate (double sided).
Steel plate (plain).
Friction plate (double sided).
Steel plate (plain).
Friction plate (double sided).
Steel plate (plain).
Friction plate (single sided) plain side outwards.
Pressure plate with spring cups, spring adjusting nuts.

Note. The adjusting nuts should be flush with the spring cups when finally adjusted.

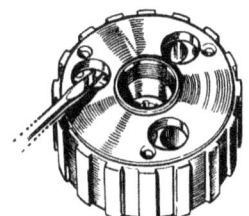

FIG. 43
Removal of Clutch Shock-Absorber Cover Plate

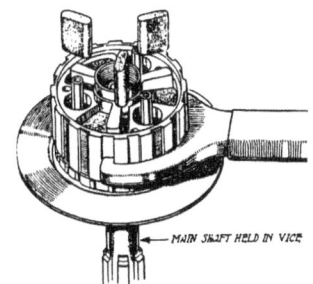

FIG. 44
Removal of Shock-Absorber Rubbers

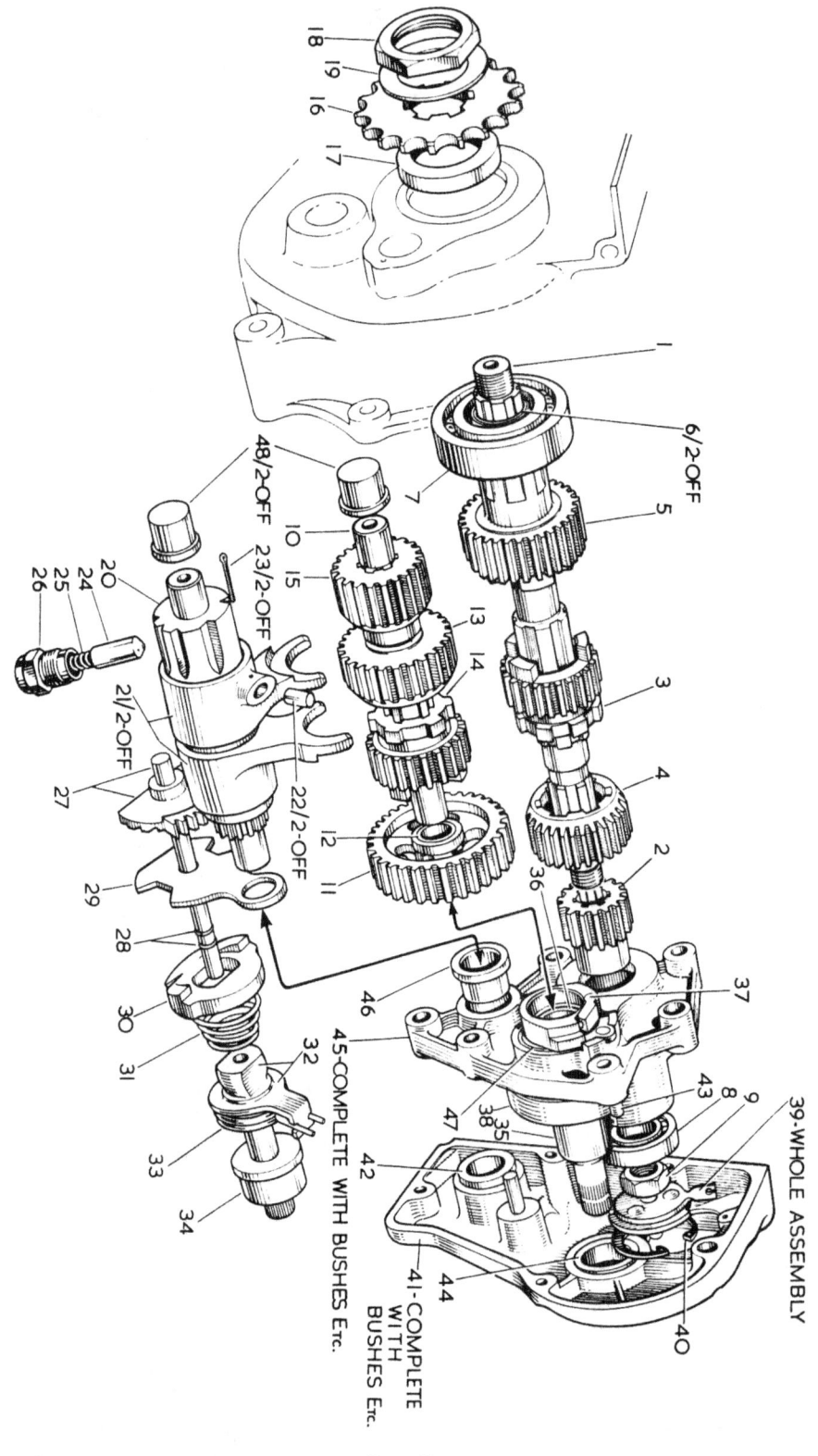

FIG. 45

Exploded view of Gear Box—Gear Box Internals—After 106838

To remove the clutch cable

Remove the clutch cable inspection cap (two screws), the styling panel (two nuts) alongside the clutch cable entry. Use a screwdriver through the inspection cover aperture to prise the clutch operation lever in a forward direction, and disconnect the inner cable. Unscrew the clutch cable adjuster then disconnect the cable from the handlebar end.

Gear Box after 106838

Lubrication

The oil content, after draining, is 2¼ pints (1.25 litre).

Use one of the recommended engine oils SAE 50, drain and refill with fresh oil at first 500 miles and again at intervals of 5,000 miles. Check oil level at frequent intervals and top up as required. Oil is filled via the inspection plate the oil level plug is below this plate. Remove level plug, fill oil until excess drains from oil level aperture. Allow a little time for the oil to settle.

Special Note. There are two plugs in the bottom of the gear box casing.

The drain plug is the SMALLEST of the two.

The gear box

A strip down condition of the gear box is shown on fig.45. There is only one left hand thread used viz the nut retaining the rear chain sprocket on the main gear. The gear box internals can be removed in a cluster if the clutch is taken off the gear box mainshaft. The figures in parenthesis refer to fig. 45.

Dismantling the gear box

Remove the clutch (see para 'primary chain removal' for method.

Remove the drain plug, the selector plunger and spring (24) from underneath the gear box shell.

Remove the kickstart crank bolt, loosen the footchange pedal bolt and take off both levers.

Remove five outer cover screws, then the cover.

Remove clutch inner wire from operating lever 39.

Remove circlip retaining clutch actuating assembly and take out the assembly.

Remove clutch push rod.

Remove gear change shaft assembly 20.

Remove mainshaft fixing nut (9)

Remove five nuts and washers for gear box end plate 45.

Remove gear box end plate complete with kickstarter mechanism (45).

Remove gear change ratchet and plate.

Take out together the mainshaft, the layshaft and selector shaft, which will bring with it the gear cluster.

Dismantling the main gear

Turn back the tab washer (19), remove sprocket nut (18) LEFT HAND THREAD. The sprocket can be held by a short length of rear chain attached to a steel bar.

The sprocket should come off the splines without difficulty. Take away the distance piece and tap the main gear into the gear box shell.

The oil seal removal

To remove prise it out of the bearing housing.

Removing the bearing (7)

The gear box shell must be gently heated, when the main bearing also the two bronze bushes can be drifted out. Pre-heat the gear box shell when re-fitting these bearings to avoid "scruffing" the housings.

To assemble the main gear (5)

If the oil seal is replaced it should be fitted with the metal backing outwards.

Remove circlip retaining clutch actuating assembly and take out the assembly.

Remove clutch push rod.

Remove gear change shaft assembly 20.

Remove mainshaft fixing nut (9).

Remove five nuts and washers for gear box end plate 45.

Remove gear box end plate complete with kickstarter mechanism (45).

Remove gear change ratchet and plate.

Take out together the mainshaft, the layshaft and selector shaft, which will bring with it the gear cluster.

The oil seal removal

To remove prise it out of the bearing housing.

Removing the bearing (7)

The gear box shell must be gently heated, when the main bearing also the two bronze bushes can be drifted out, pre-heat the gear box shell when re-fitting these bearings to avoid "scruffing" the housings.

To assemble the main gear (5)

If the oil seal is replaced it should be fitted with the metal backing outwards.

The sprocket for the rear chain is refitted with the flat face outwards. Do not omit the distance piece ¼" wide between the bearing and sprocket (17). The left hand sprocket nut must be firmly tightened as it is subjected to reversal loads.

Turn back the tab washer.

Gear box end plate bearings (48)

The two bronze bearings (48) also the small mainshaft bearing are a force fit in the plate. To remove apply gentle heat, support the plate and press out the bearings.

Assembling gear box internals

The assembly sequence is shown on fig. 45.

To refit:

Take up layshaft (10) fit gear (14) (13) (15).

Take up mainshaft and fit second gear (3).

Take up selector assembly (20) engage striker forks (21), with gears (3) and (14) then introduce the parts assembled into the gear box. Fit mainshaft third gear (4) and first gear (2). Complete assembly by fitting layshaft first gear (11).

The footchange assembly

The footchange ratchet (27) also the small pinion on the selector shaft are marked so that the gears can be correctly indexed.

Insert the footchange ratchet with line mark on it to register with the line mark on the small pinion.

Fit the footchange actuating plate (29) with letter "O" outwards.

Fit the gear box end cover with kick-starter assembled (five nuts and washers) (45).

Fit the mainshaft nut (9) and tab washer.

Fit the clutch operating assembly (split pin outwards) (39).

Fit the circlip securely in its groove.

Fit the footchange ratchet (30), over the spindle (flat side of ratchet facing the left, or rear of the gear box).

Fit the ratchet spring (31)

Fit the footchange pedal shaft (32), with pedal spring and plate over the footchange spindle and engage the two flats with the ratchet.

Fit the spacing collar (34).

A new or undamaged gasket for the end cover must be used which can be held in position with jointing compound on one side. Alternatively use some grease. Connect the clutch cable to the lever, refit the cover and tighten five screws. Put back the drain plug and spring loaded plunger and refill 2¼ pints (1.25 litres SAE 50 engine oil).

Dismantling the kickstarter (35)

Dismantle the gear box as far as removing the gear box end plate described elsewhere. Temporarily fit the kickstarter crank to the kickstarter shaft, then press the kickstarter axle inwards to clear the stop to allow the spring to unwind. Take off the kickstarter crank, press the axle right through the cover, the spring can then be taken away. To refit the kickstarter spring, put back the kickstarter axle, do not engage it with the stop. Fit the spring on to the anchor stud and engage the turned in end with the slot. Fit the kickstarter crank to axle and wind up the spring 1½ turns then press home axle to engage with its stop.

Wheels and Brakes — Heavyweight Twins

To remove the front wheel

With the machine on the central stand: Detach the brake cable from the expander lever. Detach the brake cable adjuster from the brake plate. Detach the right hand spindle nut. Release the pinch stud in left fork slider end. Take the weight of the wheel by the left hand, pull out the wheel spindle. The wheel can be taken out of the forks.

To refit the wheel

Reverse the procedure described for removal, with the following precautions. Remove traces of rust from the spindle and grease. Exercise care to correctly locate brake plate in the fork slider. Do not tighten unduly the slider pinch bolt, overtightening can cause a fracture.

Note—If the fork motion is stiff after refitting the wheel, slack off the spindle nut and work the forks up and down (the fork tubes will take up alignment), then retighten the spindle nut.

To remove the rear wheel

The rear wheel is detachable from the brake drum. With the rear wheel clear of the ground: Take out the three rubber grommets (4). Remove the sleeve nuts (8) which retain the wheel to the brake drum. Unscrew the wheel spindle (20) and remove it. Take away the distance piece, between the speedometer drive, which will come away also, there is no need to separate the cable from the drive. Pull the wheel away from the driving studs in the brake drum. Incline the machine to the right side, then pass the wheel under the left side silencer, clear of the machine.

To remove the brake drum

With the rear wheel removed: Take off the brake rod hand adjuster, then remove the rear chain connecting link. Release the nut securing the dummy spindle, pull back the brake drum clear of the fork ends.

To dismantle the front hub

The wheel hubs are packed with grease during initial assembly, and should not need further lubrication for at least 10,000 miles, when the hubs should be dismantled for cleaning and fresh grease used. To dismantle the front hub, with the wheel removed take away the brake plate with brake shoes.

Unscrew bearing lock plate on left side of hub, holes are provided for a peg spanner or use a punch. If the plate resists removal use a little heat which will facilitate removal, take out felt sealing washer and distance piece.

To eject the bearing use a drift through the brake side (the front wheel spindle can be used for this purpose) when a few light blows from a mallet will drive out the bearing until it is clear of the hub, and no more, as the other bearing goes into the hub during this process.

Take out the spindle, or drift, invert the wheel and repeat the process to eject the double bearing which will bring with it the large steel washer, the felt washer, also the thin steel washer.

Assembling the hub

Clean and repack both bearings with fresh grease (see table of lubricants). Press into the left side of the hub the single bearing, fit the distance washer (flat side against the bearing), then the felt washer and secure with the lock plate.

Invert the hub, insert the distance tube (small end first) against the bearing.

Enter the double bearing square with the hub, use the drift through both bearings and drive home until the bearing abuts against the distance tube.

Fit the smallest of the two washers, the felt washer, then the large steel washer.

With a suitable punch peen the hub material, where it joins the washer in three equidistant positions to retain the washer.

Rear hub dismantling

With the wheel removed, remove the speedometer drive lock ring (this has a *left hand thread*), take out felt washer and distance piece. To eject the bearing use the wheel spindle with its washer also the distance piece that goes between the speedometer drive and the frame placed on the spindle. Partially drive out the bearing until it abuts against the reduced diameter inside the hub. Take out the spindle, use a short length of steel tubing with the outside diameter slightly smaller than the inside diameter of the bearing and drive out the bearing.

Invert the wheel, then drift out the other bearing, which will take with it the steel cup, felt washer and the thin steel washer.

Assembling the hub

Deal with the bearings as already described and assemble by first fitting the single row bearing, in the reverse order described for dismantling, with the following precaution: when tightening the *left hand* lock ring avoid damage to the slots for the speedometer drive. Finally "peen" the hub dished washer to the hub. The hub assembly sequence is shown in fig. 46.

Dismantling the brake drum

A bearing is not used in the brake drum; when the spindle

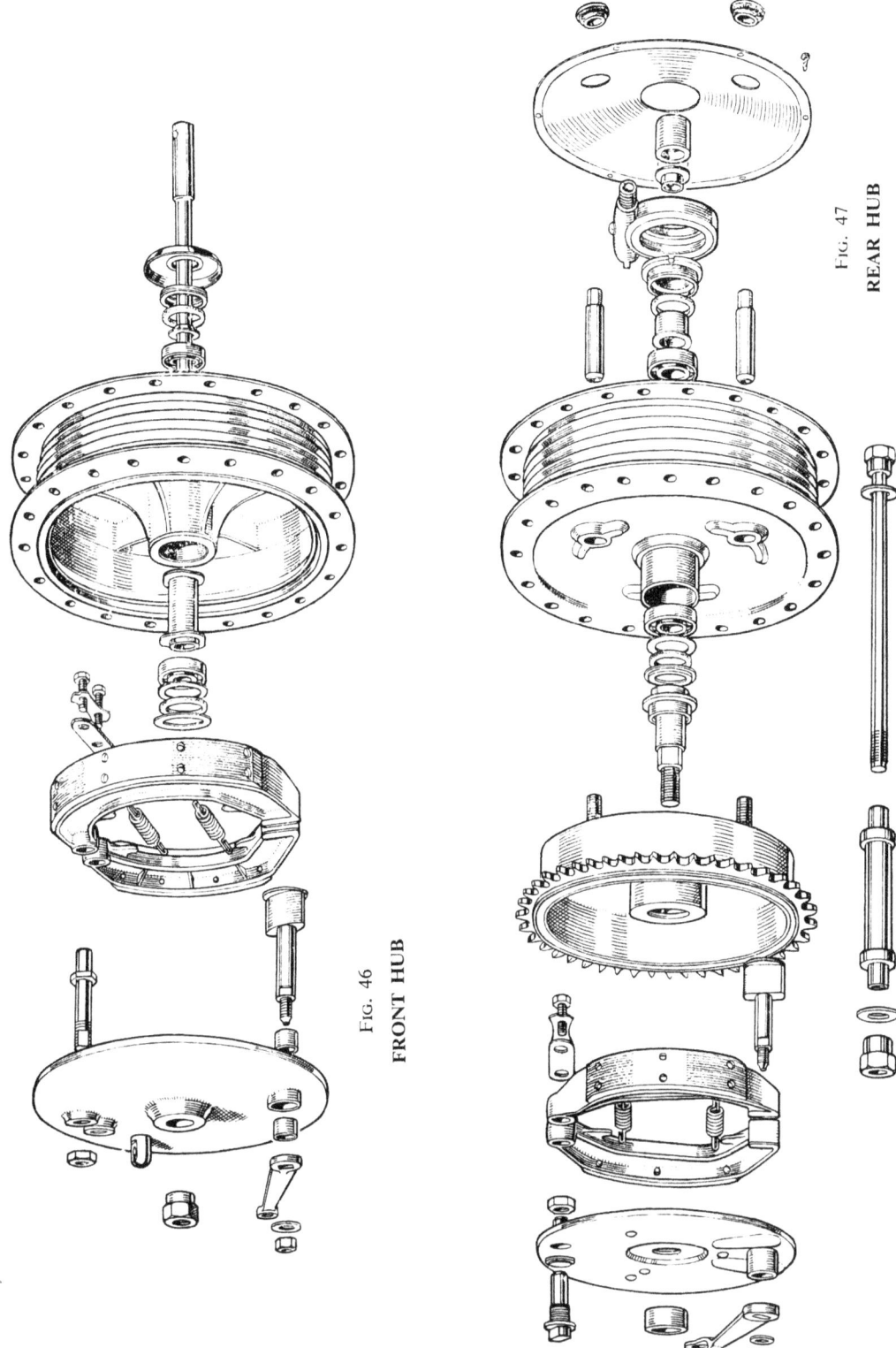

Fig. 46
FRONT HUB

Fig. 47
REAR HUB

nut is removed together with the spacer and washer, the spindle can be taken out.

Brakes, adjustment, front

Clearance between the brake shoes and drum can be reduced by unscrewing the adjuster on the cable. Continual adjustment causes the expander lever to occupy a position with lost leverage. To restore leverage, take off the cable and reverse the expander lever.

To improve brake efficiency, release the spindle nut a few turns, hold the brake hard on, retighten the spindle nut at the same time. The brake shoes will then centralize. On models before 1964 enlarge spindle hole in brake plate by $\frac{1}{32}"$ to centralize.

Rear

If the rear brake pedal is depressed in excess of its normal travel, the return spring (in the pedal) will stretch and become ineffective. The pedal position can be adjusted, within limits, by releasing the pedal spindle and setting the stop to the desired position. If the brake has been disturbed, centralize the brake shoes, by releasing the left hand spindle nut and press hard on the pedal and tighten the spindle nut at the same time. On machines made before 1964 enlarge spindle hole in brake plate by $\frac{1}{32}"$.

Brakes, dismantling and assembly

Remove brake plate from drum. Remove nut and washer from cam spindle. Remove cam lever.

Remove springs from shoes. This is best done with a screwdriver placed against one of the spring hooks and held in position with one hand, now knock the screwdriver with the palm of the other hand to push the spring off the lug on the shoe. The spring may fly off so care should be taken that it is not lost.

Turn back the tabwasher and unscrew the two hexagon headed set screws which secure the shoes to the pivot pins. Lift off the pivot pin tie plate and remove the brake shoes.

The cam can now be withdrawn. It may be tight in its bush if the cam lever nut has been overtight as this causes the end of the spindle to become swelled. When this happens the end immediately behind the flats should be eased down with emery tape.

If the cam will pass through the bush but is tight, it can be eased down more easily after removal.

On the rear brake plate only, the cam spindle bush can be removed after unscrewing its locknut from the inside.

To re-assemble

Remove all traces of rust and dirt from the expander cam and pivot pins, apply a slight smear of grease. For ease in working the brake plate can be held in a smooth jaw vice, clamping it by the torque stop. Fit the brake shoes, tie plate and tab washer and set screws. If the tab washer has been used on more than one occasion discard it and use a new one. Fit the shoe springs, by anchoring the end farthest away from the operator, use a length of stout string in the free end of the spring, stretch the spring with one hand and guide the spring onto its anchorage with the other hand. Alternatively use a narrow blade screwdriver. Finally fit the expander lever with its nut and washer. The washer on the rear brake expander, together with the rim on the brake plate, prevents the rear brake shoes being removed from the pivot pins, unless the linings are badly worn. Removing the expander cam will allow the shoes to be detached from the plate.

Balancing the wheels. At high speeds, if the tyres are out of balance, the steering can be affected and in extreme cases the front forks can 'flap' at maximum speed. As oil seals are used on both wheel spindles, the wheel cannot be accurately balanced until the friction caused by the seals is removed. The courses open are:
(1) Remove the oil seals.
(2) Obtain two ball races with an internal diameter sufficiently large enough to take the wheel spindle, mount the wheel on two boxes as shown in fig. 46A.

If the wheel is correctly balanced, it should remain stationary in any position in which the wheel is placed. The most likely out of balance position will be where the valve is situated or where a security bolt is fitted. The heaviest part will of course come to rest at 180° or 6 o'clock. To counterbalance, use thin strips of lead twisted round the spoke. Special weights for this purpose are supplied by the tyre makers. When the wheel is in perfect balance, secure the strips of lead with insulating tape which should be painted with jointing compound. The effect of a balanced wheel has to be tried to be appreciated if continued high speeds are permissible.

All models—except G15-CS and Jubilee
Front Forks

Lubrication

Use one of the grades of oil, S.A.E. 20 as shown in the table of lubricants. The normal oil content is five fluid ozs. (142 c.c.). Attention is only necessary at the first 1,000 miles and again at 10,000 miles when the oil should be changed by draining. An exploded drawing of the front forks is shown in fig. 48 from which it will readily be seen that the fork springs abut against the filler plugs (34), before removing these plugs weight must be taken off the front wheel, by placing the machine on its central stand to avoid the forks collapsing.

To drain the forks

With the machine on the central stand: Unscrew the two filler plugs (34). Have available a container to catch oil drained, then remove the drain plug screw (7) with its washer, with the container under the fork leg. If the wheel is inclined to one side, draining will be more complete. Deal with the other fork leg in a similar manner.

Filling oil

It will be seen the air space between the fork spring, and the inside of the tube is very close; therefore fresh oil must be filled with extreme care, to avoid losses by spilling. Use a measured container for the correct content of 5 ozs. Replace the drain plugs before filling, also firmly tighten the filler plugs after.

Steering head adjustment

On a new machine the filler plugs (34) should be checked for tightness due to settling down, check as well the steering head bearings at the first 100 miles, and then occasionally, as the mileage increases. Using the machine with movement in these bearings will damage the races. Movement in these bearings can usually be detected when the front brake is applied. To check, raise the front wheel well clear of the ground with a box under the crankcase. Try to raise or lower the front wheel with one hand and use the fingers of the other hand encircling the handle bar lug where it meets the frame, when movement can be felt. To adjust bearings a thin open ended spanner $1\frac{1}{8}"$ across the flats is needed. First release the tube clamping stud nut (28), unscrew the stem nut (37) slightly. Use the thin spanner on the sleeve nut (30) and manipulate as necessary. The bearing should be devoid of play with free movements. Retighten the column nut, also the clamping stud nuts.

The steering head bearings for the 1964 models are of the cup and cone type, with 18 loose ¼″ dia ball bearings in each bearing. The cup portion is a press fit into the head lug. To remove the cups use a piece of steel tubing through the head lug to drive out the cups, shifting the tubing from one side of the cup to the other to eject it square with the lug. Use an old screwdriver, or taper wedge to take off the cone on the fork column.

Dismantling the forks

The forks can be removed as a unit, or the fork legs can be removed individually. To take out one fork leg remove the front wheel as described elsewhere. Take off the front mudguard with stays. Release nut for pinch bolt (28). Remove filler cap plug (34), disconnect it from the damper rod, by using two spanners.

The fork inner tube can now be drawn downwards clear of the handlebar lug and fork crown. If the tube resists removal fit back the filler plug without being connected to the damper rod, screw in a few turns, then give it a few sharp blows with a soft faced mallet to separate the tube from its taper fixing in the handlebar lug.

To remove the forks as a unit

Follow the instructions given for removing a fork leg, as far as disconnecting the filler plugs from the damper rods. Proceed by taking off the headlamp leaving it suspended by the loom. Separate the control cables from the levers, and remove handlebars. Remove the column nut (37) then give the underside of the handlebar lug one or two blows with a mallet until it is clear of the fork tubes. At this stage support the ends of the forks, for after removing the sleeve

1964 Front Fork Assembly

1. Fork main tube.
2. Main tube bush.
3. Main tube bottom bush.
4. Main tube bottom bush circlip.
5. Fork end left hand.
6. Fork end right hand.
7. Fork end drain plug.
8. Washer for plug.
9. Oil damper tube.
10. Oil damper rod.
11. Oil damper tube bolt.
12. Washer for bolt.
13. Washer for tube.
14. Nut for rod top.
15. Nut for rod bottom.
16. Damper tube cap.
17. Piston locating peg.
18. Oil damper valve cup.
19. Oil damper valve cup slotted ring.
20. Main tube lock ring with cup.
21. Main spring.
22. Main spring locating bushes.
23. Spring cover tube.
24. Spring top cover tube securing plate.
25. Screws securing plate.
26. Crown lug complete with column.
27. Pinch stud for crown lug.
28. Nut for stud.
30. Fork head race adjuster nut.
31. Top cover left hand.
32. Top cover right hand.
33. Main tube top cover ring.
34. Fork main tube filler and retaining plug.
35. Washer for plug.
36. Fork head clip.
37. Fork crown and column lock nut.

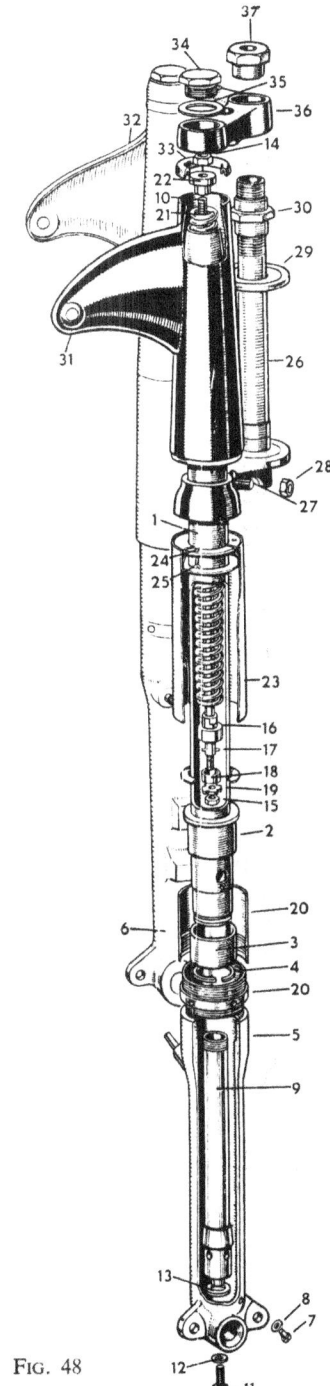

FIG. 48

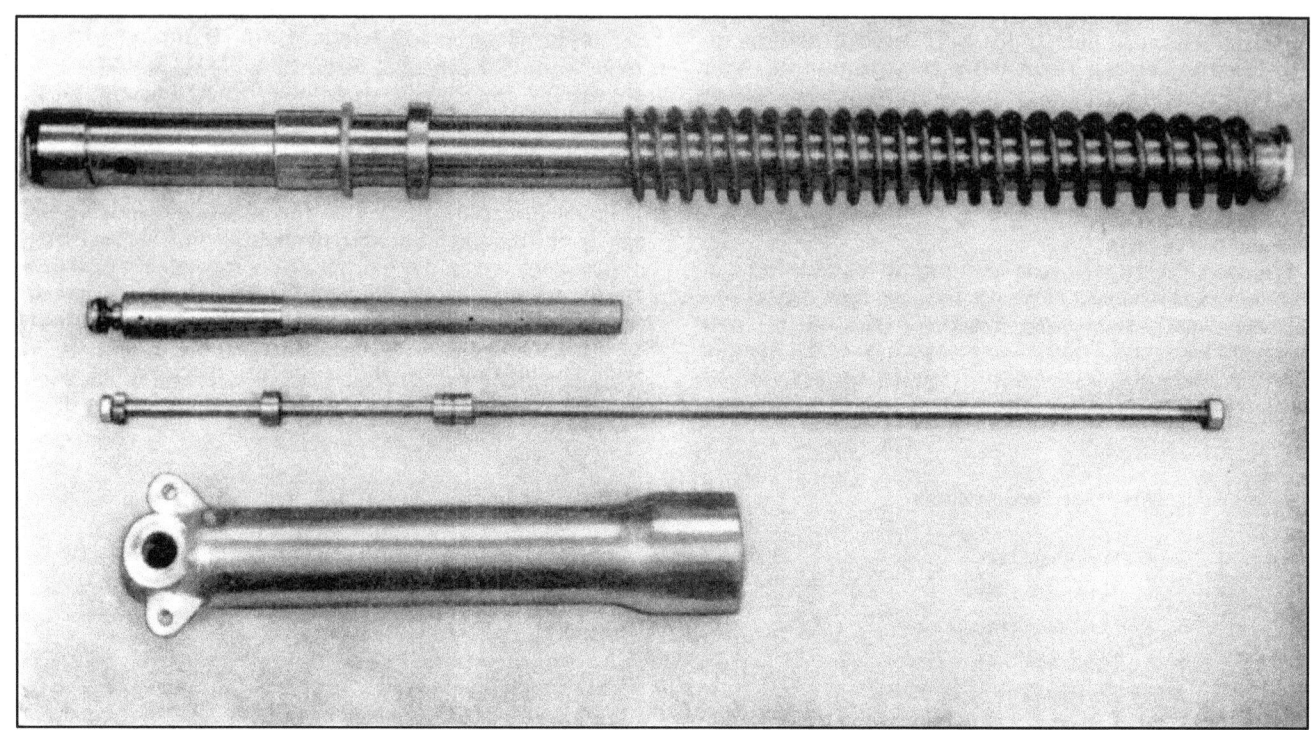

Fig. 49 *G15 CS Fork Damper arrangement*

Fig. 46A *Balancing the road wheels*

nut (30) the forks will drop out. Watch for the steel balls for the races, there are 18 in each race (36 in all), if a steering damper is fitted detach the fixed plate from the frame.

To dismantle a fork slider

Remove from the fork slider the bolt fixing damper tube (11). Unscrew the bottom cover (23), holes are provided for a C spanner. Take away the fork slider (5).

The damper tube with the fork spring can be extracted from the tube. To dismantle further, take off nut securing fork spring, unscrew the damper tubecap (16) with a tommy bar through the holes in the damper tube, for if this is held in a vice it will distort and become useless. The damper assembly sequence is clearly depicted in fig. 48.

Note—When removing the oil seal, sealing washer and flanged bush pass them along the fork tube and take off from the top end past the taper end, if the oil seal is to be used again.

Assembling the forks

It will be apparent from the dismantling instructions given that there is nothing complicated in the fork assembly and if the reverse sequence is used, no difficulty should occur with the following precautions.

The fork tube, where the oil seal operates, must have a smooth finish and free from blemish.

The oil seal is fitted from the top of the tube, with the visible spring facing downwards against the flange for the bush.

The damper tube cap also the damper tube fixing bolt must be properly tightened.

Finally tighten the bottom cover (23) when the front wheel has been put back.

Fill 5 ozs. of S.A.E. 20 oil to each fork leg.

Steering lock

The lock is pressed into the handle bar lug, and can be removed by driving it out from underneath. A number is stamped on the bottom of the lock for key identification.

Front Forks — G15 CS Models

Description

In the main the fork lay out is similar to those used on the street machines with the following exceptions:

The fork inner tubes are 2″ longer.

Large diameter external fork springs.

Special two way damping—designed for rough going.

Fork tube gaiters for dust exclusion.

Note

It has been assumed that metallic contact takes place when the forks are on the rebound—this is purely an assumption—for a hydraulic lock builds up before the forks reach their limit of movement. This can be demonstrated by bringing the forks on to the hydraulic lock—when it will be found that there is additional movement before metallic contact takes place.

To dismantle the forks

Take out the front wheel, front fender, disconnect front brake cable.

Unscrew the two top bolts (34).

Disconnect the damper rod lock nut—take off the top bolt with its washer.

Release the nut for the pinch stud (28).

If available use tool 13685 screwed into the fork inner tube.

A sharp blow on the end of the tool will separate the tube from its taper in the lug.

The handlebar lug also fork crown will remain in the frame.

To dismantle the slider (see fig. 49)

The damper tube together with the damper rod can be removed by taking out the bolt underneath the slider by using a thin walled spanner (pour out the oil first) there is a fibre washer used with this bolt.

Dismantling the fork tube (see fig. 49)

Start from the top end of the tube:

Take off the fork spring, the oil seal paper washer, then the bronze flanged bush.

Take off from the bottom end the fork tube sleeve nut, its washer.

Note—The oil seal is fitted with the exposed wire coil downwards; finally the steel bottom bush.

Dismantling the damper rod

Start at the bottom end:

Take off the bottom rod nut, the brass seat for the damper valve, the valve for damper also the small pin which passes through the rod and checks the valve.

Take off the plunger sleeve, by pulling out the circlip (note the oil groove is nearest to the bottom of the rod when fitted).

To remove the fork crown

Take off the head lamp, also the handlebars.

Take off the fork crown nut (37).

Take off the handlebar lug (36) tap it upwards with a soft faced mallet.

Take off the adjusting nut (30)—support the crown whilst doing this—watch for 18 ball bearings in each race (current models) take out the crown from the frame.

To remove the frame bearings

Refer to details for street machines.

Rear suspension

The damper assembly is, on all models, a sealed unit. The damper fluid filled is sufficient to last the lifetime of the unit.

Should a grating noise develop when the units are moving, press down on the top cover to extract the split collets—then take out the top fixing bolt—the cover can be taken off. Apply some heavy grease on the outside diameter of the springs, and assemble. The spring loading is adjustable, within limits. A cam faced scroll is spot welded to the damper assembly, using a "C" spanner moving the scroll anti-clockwise engages the strongest position—both units must be dealt with at the same time.

Front Forks — Jubilee Models

Dismantling the forks

Remove the front wheel as described in 'Wheels and brakes section'.

Take off the head lamp front and detach bulb holders.

Disconnect the speedometer drive cable.

Detach the black and blue cable plugs.

Detach ammeter wires and dip switch cable.

Detach handlebars.

Detach front mudguard by taking out the two clip bolts, expand the clip a trifle to avoid damage to enamel.

Detach drain plugs (7) and catch the oil.

Detach head stem nut (24), watch for three shim washers.

Detach steering head stem and support the forks (see fig. 51). Watch for head bearings (29), set of 39 and take away forks. Support the forks in a vice (fig. 63), take out screw (2), and pull off the bottom slider extension (13) with fork spring attached.

Detach two screws securing top cover tube, and take tube away.

Detach bolt (15), pull out fork spring and damper. The spring is screwed on to the damper, also the top spring anchor.

Removing the oil seal

The oil seal will come away attached to the slider.

Secure the slider in a suitable clamp fixed in a vice.

Bring the mudguard clip up to the oil seal body, using a series of light blows with a hammer directed on to the ears of the clip. Move the clip round the seal body whilst doing this to remove it squarely.

Re-assembling the front forks

The work involved is straightforward with the following precautions:

(1) After fitting the cover tubes leave the two fixing screws loose. When the forks are assembled and working correctly, retighten the screws.
(2) Assemble the oil seal to the slider squarely.
(3) When refitting the slider bring the seal up to the bush. Use a small radio-type screwdriver or similar tool, insert the tool between the oil seal rubber and the fork bush. Use a rotary motion pressing gently against the slider, the seal will go over the bush without damage.

Refill with 70 cc. of S.A.E. 30 oil.

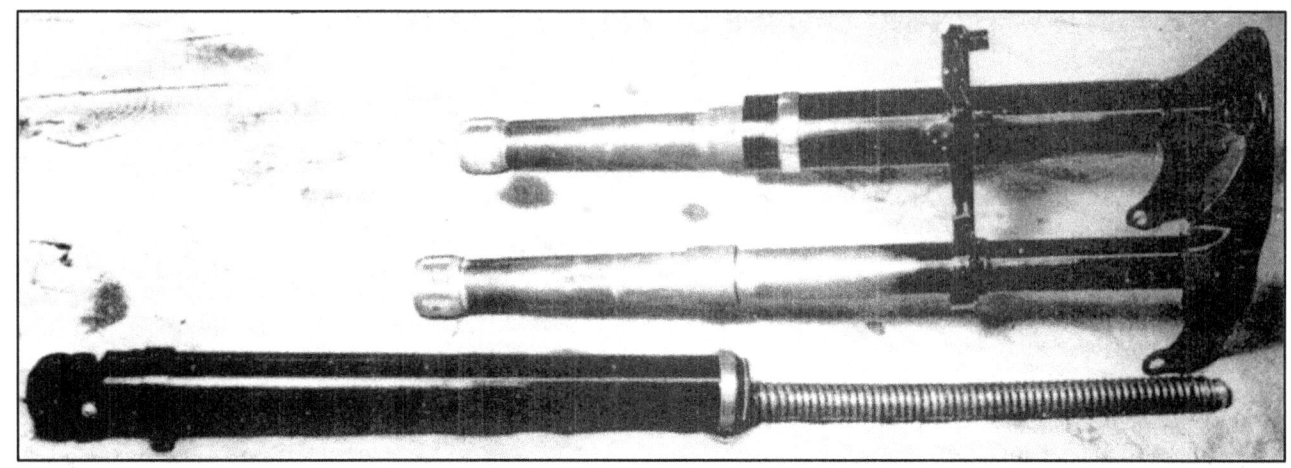

Fig. 50

Note—The fork tube bushes are silver soldered to the tubes 5¾" apart.

Steering head adjustment

With the machine on the stand, need for adjustment of the steering head bearings may be detected by trying to rock the forks with hands holding the fork legs. The bearings should be tested for slackness after the first 200 miles and subsequently every 1,000 miles. Two spanners should be used, one turning the adjusting nut (34), the other to slacken and re-tighten the lock nut when the adjustment has been carried out.

Adjustment should be such that no play be felt, yet the bearings are free to rotate and are not over tight.

Adjusting the bearings too tightly will ruin them and induce heavy steering.

Note—It is important that adjusting and locking nuts are tightly locked together.

JUBILEE FRONT FORKS

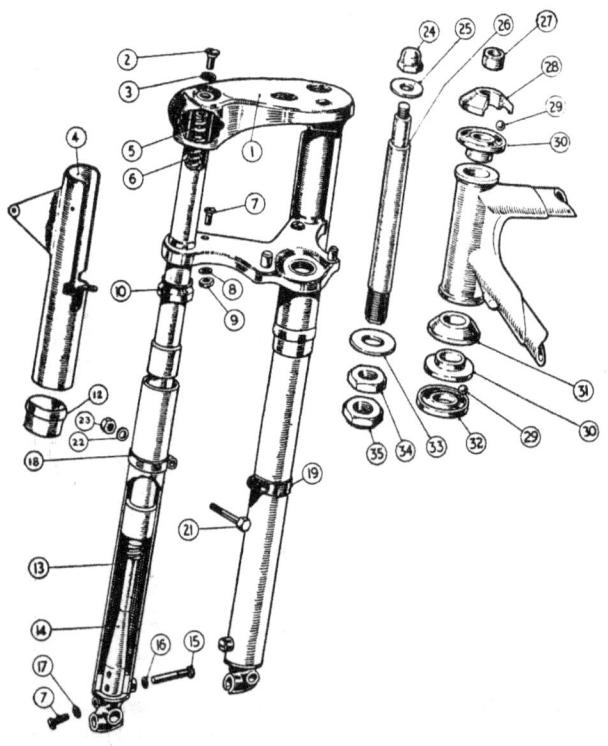

Fig. 51

1	043343	Fork "H" member.
2	043245	Screw, inner tube, top.
3	000201	Washer, fibre, inner tube top screw.
4	043345-6	Tube, cover, top, left and right.
5	043246	Adaptor, inner tube top screw.
6	043259	Spring main.
7	043251	Screw, top cover tube and drain plug.
8	021579	Washer, shakeproof top cover tube screw.
9	000005	Nut, top cover tube screw.
10	043253	Seal, oil, fork tubes.
12	043344	Sleeve, end, top cover tube.
13	043347	Extension, slider.
14	043256	Tube, damper.
15	043257	Screw, retaining damper tube.
16	043258	Washer, fibre, damper tube retaining screw.
17	000203	Washer, fibre, drain plug.
18	043260	Clip, mudguard attachment, left.
19	043261	Clip, mudguard attachment, right.
21	000373	Bolt, mudguard attachment clip.
22	000011	Washer, mudguard attachment clip bolt.
23	000004	Nut, mudguard attachment clip bolt.
24	043262	Nut, domed, head stem, top.
25	043263	Washer, head stem top domed nut.
26	043235	Stem, head.
27	043236	Spacer, head stem.
28	043240	Race, adjusting top.
29	000021	Bearings, ball, head races.
30	043238	Race, frame head lug, top and bottom.
31	043241	Cover, dust, bottom ball race.
32	043239	Race, fork crown, bottom.
33	043244	Washer, head stem bottom nuts.
34	043242	Nut, adjusting, head stem, bottom.
35	043243	Nut, lock, head stem, bottom.

Jubilee Model — Wheels and Hubs

Front and rear hubs, lubrication

Hub bearings are packed with grease during original assembly and should not require attention for many thousands of miles. At around 10,000 miles the hubs should be dismantled, the old grease washed out and the bearings re-packed with grease.

Brake adjustment

Adjustment of the operating rod or cable should be such that a minimum movement of lever or pedal brings the brake into operation. There should be no contact between brake linings and brake drum when the brakes are off.

Brake pedal adjustment

The brake pedal stop is situated at the left hand end of the footrest rod. By slackening off the footrest rod nut the pedal stop may be rotated and locked into another position, thus providing a certain amount of adjustment. Altering the position of the pedal pad will necessitate adjustment of the brake rod.

Front wheel removal and re-fitting

Place machine on stand and disconnect operating cable from lever on hub. Slacken the mudguard stay bolts on the forward side of each fork leg and tap each firmly to release the stay which acts as a cotter on the shank of the nut. Remove the spindle nuts and wheel will drop through the slots in the fork ends.

Before replacing the wheel ensure that the slots in the two fork ends are in line and that the brake plate anchor slot engages with the appropriate peg when the wheel is placed in position.

Fit and tighten the brake side spindle nut first. Tighten the opposite spindle nut and return to the brake side to tighten the mudguard stay bolt. Roll the machine off the stand and bounce the forks a few times to encourage the right-hand leg to assume its normal position sideways on the spindle nut before locking the right-hand mudguard stay bolt. Reconnect brake cable.

Rear wheel, removal and fitting

If the machine is fitted with rear chain enclosure, it will first be necessary to remove this by removing the three bolts visible on the outer side of the case and a fourth bolt underneath the front end of the lower portion and accessible from the opposite side of the machine.

Disconnect rear chain, remove it from rear wheel sprocket and prevent it dragging on the ground. Remove the rear number plate by removing the two screws securing it to the rear fairing. Remove also the brake rod adjuster and the nut securing the speedometer cable to the driving box. Slackening both spindle nuts will enable the wheel to be withdrawn through the slot in the fairing normally covered by the number plate.

When re-fitting ensure that the brake plate stop is engaged with the slot in the swinging arm and that both spindle nuts are hard against the wheel adjusters. Check wheel alignment, chain tension and brake adjustment.

Rear hub, dismantling and assembly

Having removed the wheel, and stripped the spindle of its nuts, distance pieces, locknuts, etc., noting their positions, withdraw the speedometer driving box from the hub. Hold the wheel firmly and drift out the spindle in either direction; it will bring with it one ball race, a plain steel washer, felt washer and dished steel washer. The remaining bearing can be readily drifted out of the hubshell.

Having cleaned the bearings and re-packed them with

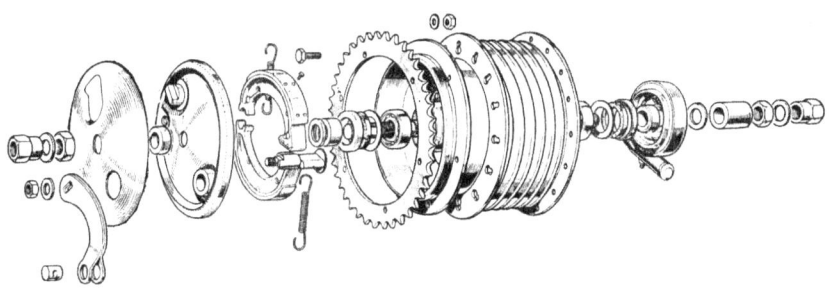

Fig. 52 *Exploded view of Rear Hub*

grease, press or drift one back into position in the hub shell and fit its steel and felt washers. Insert the appropriate spindle end and tap the spindle right home. Thread the other bearing over the opposite end of the spindle and drift it right home, fitting its steel and felt washers. Fit distance piece approximately $\frac{1}{2}''$ long to plain side of hub, fit speedo driving box, taking care to engage driving pegs. Fit $\frac{1}{8}''$ washer and $1\frac{1}{4}''$ distance piece to same side and fit and tighten locknut. Fit $\frac{3}{4}''$ distance piece to brake side followed by brake plate, the remaining distance piece and locknut. This assembly when offered up should slide nicely between the rear fork ends. A plain washer and nut is fitted at each end.

Front hub, dismantling and assembly

With the wheel removed proceed as described for the rear hub, knocking out the bearings in an identical manner. Re-assemble also in similar fashion, fitting the $\frac{5}{16}''$ counterbored distance piece and the thin locknut to the plain side of the hub. Against the bearing on the brake side is fitted the $\frac{1}{2}''$ distance piece followed by the brake plate, the $\frac{3}{8}''$ distance piece, the brake plate cover and the counterbored nut in that order.

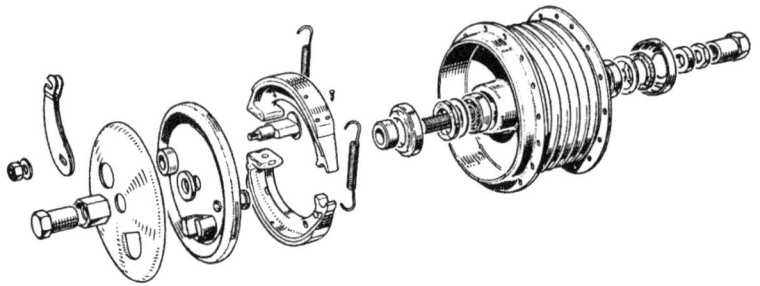

Fig. 53   *Front Hub*

The Frame

The swinging arm (heavyweight twins—except G15 CS

A strip down of the frame is shown in fig. 55. which indicates the parts used, also the assembly order. The figures shown for the various parts are for spares list reference. The arrangement used can be seen in the strip down, the two Clayflex bearings (68) are a press fit in the swinging arm (67) separated by the distance piece (69). An arbour press is used to take out and fit these special bearings—which need no routine attention.

The swinging arm G15 CS only

The bearing for this model uses two oilite type bearings, in a steel sleeve, these two parts are not supplied separately. The bushes operate on a ground steel sleeve, which can be seen in fig. 56. The sleeve is now retained by a cotter pin—early models had two cotter pins. With the rear frame dismantled as depicted, take out the cotter pin, press out the steel sleeve, the arm can be taken away. The two felt washers will come away at the same time.

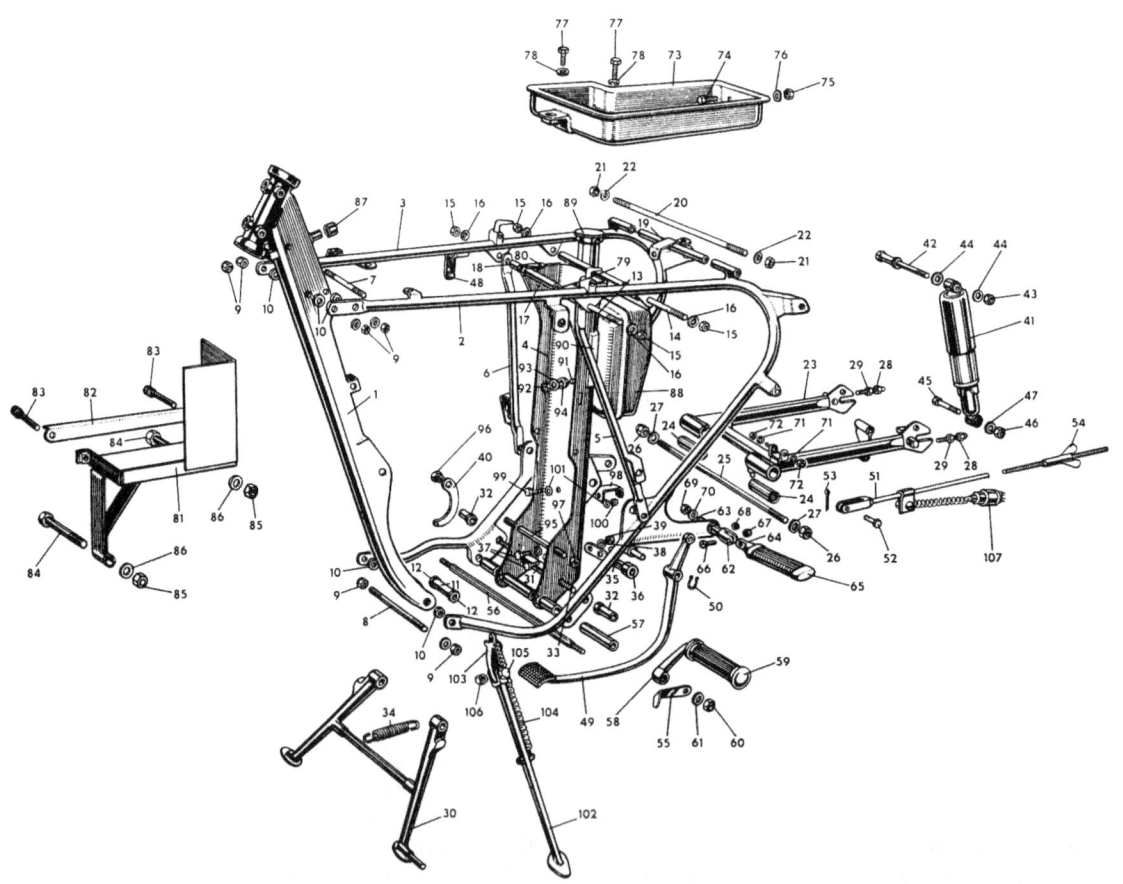

Fig. 54

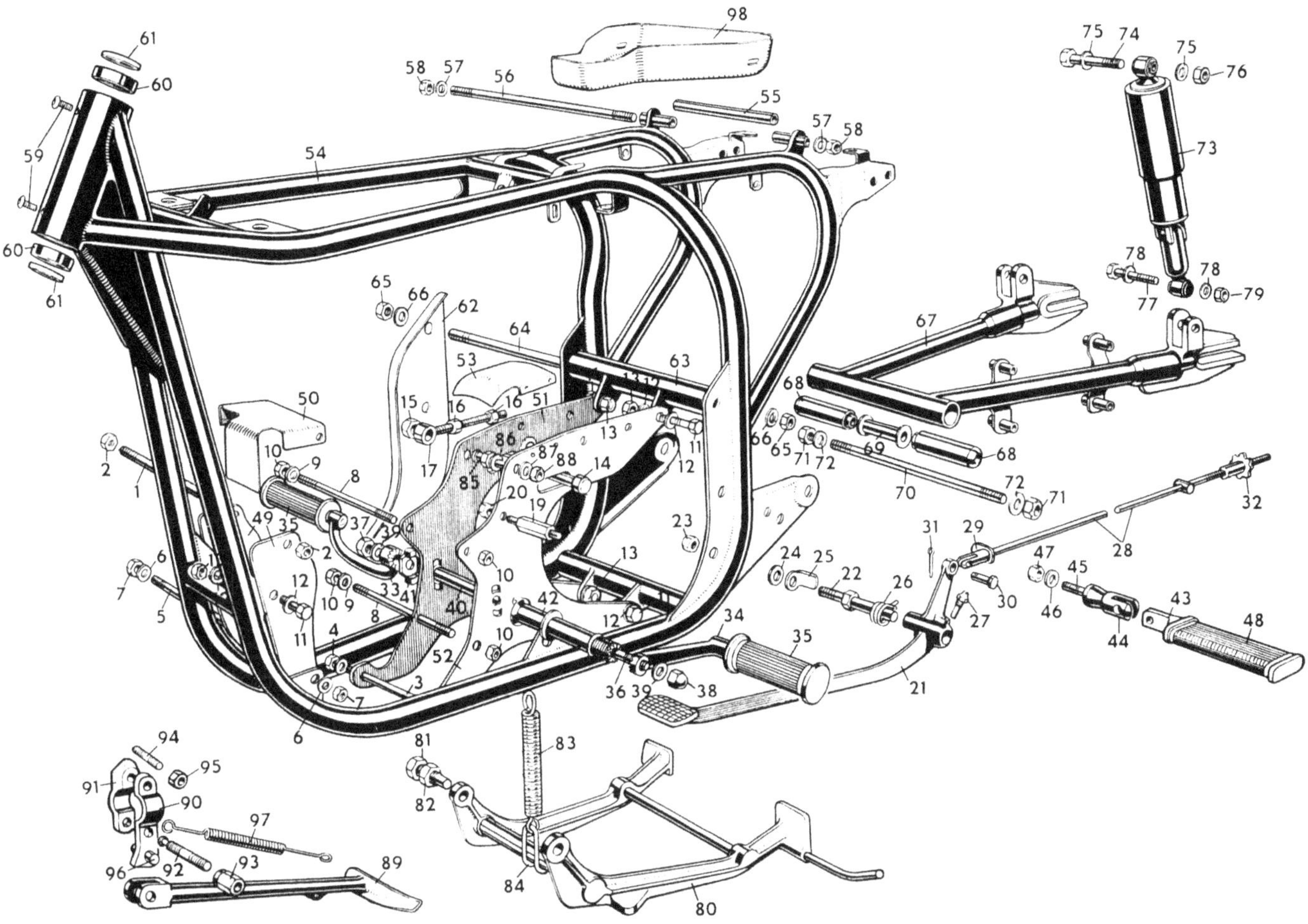

Fig. 55

Lubrication

A filler screw is used in the plate covering the steel sleeve. To lubricate the bushes take out the screw with fibre washer, inject some heavy grade oil, until the cavity is full—some leakage might occur after—which will cease when the normal level is reached.

The bushes

To remove the two bushes—support the arm and press out, in turn each flanged bush.

The spindle diameter is 0.9995″ to 0.990″.

The bushes reamed in situ are 1.001″—a regular one inch reamer will suffice.

The swinging arm—lightweight twins

A frame strip down is shown in fig. 53, to indicate the lay-out, the oil tank shown is used on the early De-luxe models—the figures are for spare parts list.

The arrangement used is similar to the heavyweight counter part, so the details already given apply.

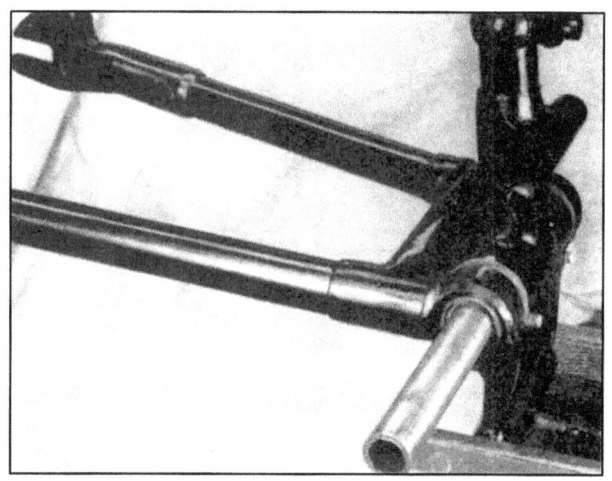

Fig. 56

Carburetter Service

Carburetter function

The petrol level is maintained by a float and needle and in no circumstances should any alteration be made to these parts. In the event of a leaky float or a worn needle valve, the part should be replaced with new. (Do not attempt to grind the needle to its seat.)

The petrol supply to the engine is controlled, firstly, by the main jet and, secondly, by means of a taper needle (see fig. 57), which is attached to the throttle valve and operates in a tubular extension of the main jet.

The main jet controls the mixture from three-quarters to full throttle, the adjustment taper needle from three-quarters down to one-quarter throttle, the cut-away portion of the intake side of the throttle valve from one-quarter to about one-eighth throttle, and a pilot jet, having an independently adjusted air supply, takes care of the idling from one-eighth throttle down to the almost closed position. These various stages of control must be kept in mind when any adjustment is comtemplated (see fig. 57 for location of the pilot jet air adjustment screw). The pilot jet, unlike on earlier models, is now detachable for cleaning.

The size of the main jet should not be altered save for some very good reason. See 'Data' for details of standard sizes of jet, throttle valve and jet taper needle.

With the standard setting it is possible to use nearly full air in all conditions, except perhaps when the engine is pulling hard up hill or is on full throttle, when some benefit may be obtained by slightly closing the air control.

Weak mixture is always indicated by popping or spitting, at the air intake.

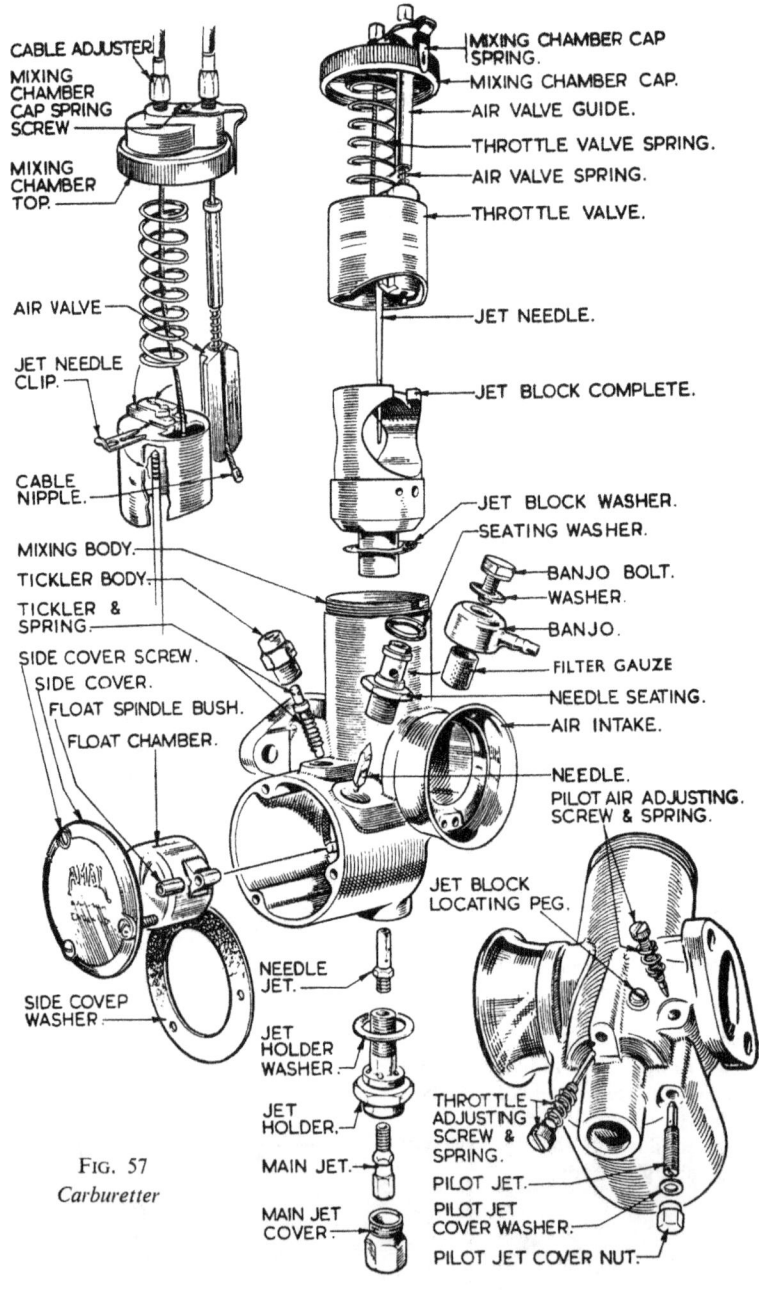

Fig. 57
Carburetter

A rich mixture usually causes bumpy or jerky running and in cases of extreme richness, is accompanied by the emission of black smoke from exhaust.

Carburetter adjustment

With the taper needle projection, main jet size and type of throttle slide specified, correct carburation, except at idling speed is assured.

To check for correct idling mixture, first run engine until it is just warm, but not too hot, when with the throttle nearly closed and air fully open it should fire evenly and slowly. If it fails to do so, first of all make certain that the sparking plug is clean and the point setting correct. Having done this and idling is still uneven try resetting the pilot jet air screw.

Adjustment of this air screw is not unduly sensitive and it should be possible to obtain the correct setting for even firing in a few seconds.

In the event of even firing at idling speed being unobtainable by adjustment of the air screw, look for obstruction in the pilot jet.

Having obtained even firing, all that remains is to adjust if necessary the position of the throttle stop screw until the desired idling speed is obtained.

Setting twin carburetters

It is important that the two carburetters are synchronised—the two throttle slides must open the same amount together. The best way to do this is to use two short lengths of ¼" diameter steel rod (two lead pencils, of the same size would do) insert through both carburetters—so that the throttle slides can rest on them. This may mean taking off the air filter—but the time spent is well worth while. With the slides resting on the rods, run down the cable adjusters to give slack in the wires. Unscrew carefully the cable adjuster to take up the slack (on one carburetter) verify the slide is still sitting on the rod—until the slack in the cable is absorbed. Do the same with the second carburetter, so that when the twist grip is manipulated, both slides sit on the rod simultaneously. Take out the rods.

Check the plug gaps 0.020" to 0.022", for good idling. Start the motor, let it run for a short period, with fast idling. With the motor running take off one H.T. lead—adjust the idling for the cylinder running, by manipulating the pilot air control screw, in conjunction with the throttle stop screw, until an even slow idling is obtained. Do the same with the other cylinder, and when both cylinders are running—the idling will probably be too fast. Unscrew, an equal amount, the throttle stop screws to give the desired idling speed.

If the motor is down on maximum speed, open the twist grip as far as it will go, then check if both slides are both clear of the choke (one, or both wires may be too short).

CARBURETTER SPECIFICATIONS

	Jubilee	Navigator	Electra
Type No.	375/43	375/48	375/54
Main jet	130	170	190
Slide	375/3½	375/3½	375/3
Needle	.1065	.1055	.1055
Needle position	3	4	4
Pilot jet	25	25	25

	Model 88SS	650SS	650 Manx	750	G15
Type No. R/H	376/289	376/289	376/289	389/88	389/88
Type No. L/H	376/288	376/288	376/288	389/87	389/87
Main jet	250	270	250*	350	420
Slide	376/3½	376/3½	376/3½	389/3	389/3
Pilot jet	25	25	25	20	20
Needle	.1065	.1065	.1065	.1065	.1065
Needle position	3	3	3	3	3

*With air cleaner

Electrical Service

WIPAC ALTERNATOR TESTING INSTRUCTIONS

The Series 114 Alternator consists of a six pole Stator ring 5" in diameter with six coils and a six pole permanent magnet rotor. There are three main leads coloured white, light green and orange. Three coils are connected in series to white and light green, the other three coils are connected in in series to white and orange. The output from these coils is a.c. converted to d.c. by means of a bridge-connected metal rectifier. The output of the alternator is controlled through the switch on the headlamp and connects three or six coils according to its position.

Emergency starting

The emergency position is intended for starting when the battery is discharged. This position is marked 'EMG' on the ignition switch.

In this position the two groups of alternator coils are connected in parallel, and if the lights switch is in the 'OFF' position the full output of the alternator goes into the battery. This will raise the voltage of a discharged battery to a level sufficient to start the engine. In the EMG position the charge rate is high—the engine should not be run in EMG too long. The boost charge thus provided may be used to restore a discharged battery. Switch over to IGN after ten minutes.

Rotor demagnetised

Although the WIPAC Rotor is robustly built and holding a very high magnetic charge, it can become demagnetised if the machine is run with battery connections reversed, or if the rectifier breaks down. A demagnetised rotor should be returned to WIPAC for satisfactory remagnetisation.

Testing

Testing of component parts can be carried out if the following instruments are available:

0-12 d.c. Volt Meter.
0-15 a.c. Volt Meter.
1 ohm Resistor (capable of carrying 8 amps.).
10-0-10 d.c. Ammeter.

High grade moving coil instruments must be used and accurate. The 1 ohm. resistor must also be accurate, otherwise correct readings cannot be obtained. *Engine speed* when testing should be in the region of 2,500 r.p.m. Tests should not be attempted at speeds below 2,000 r.p.m. A few revs. above or below 2,500 will not affect the readings of an alternator in good condition.

Charge rate test

(1) First check the battery voltage which, if fully discharged, should be substituted for one that is in good condition.
(2) Disconnect the brown negative lead from the double connector.
(3) Connect the d.c. ammeter in series with the battery wire and the double connector.
(4) Run the engine at 3,000 r.p.m., the minimum permissible readings are shown in the following table:—

Ignition switch	Lights switch	Minimum charge rate
Ignition on	Off	1.0a
Ignition on	Low	1.3a
Ignition on	High	1.0a
Emergency on	Off	6.0a

The rate of engine speed and condition of battery will affect the charge rate recorded. The figures shown in the table in comparison with the recorded figures indicate if the system is functioning correctly.

N.B.: If the charge rate is down with lights on HIGH check the main bulb wattage.

Low or no charge rate test

Check the alternator output by:
(1) Disconnect the white, orange and light green wires from the four-way connector. If a maroon colour lead is also used, leave this in position.
(2) Using the a.c. voltmeter with the one ohm. resistor across the terminals (parallel) join one wire from the voltmeter to the white wire, the other meter wire to the orange wire. Run the engine at a speed equivalent to 30 m.p.h. in top gear, the voltage reading should be between 6.2 and 6.8 volts.

Transfer the meter wire from the orange wire to the light green and repeat the test. A low reading on one of these tests indicates a fault in the coils. A low reading on both tests can be due to a partially demagnetised rotor.

If no reading is shown in both tests, the alternator is defective (see test 3).

(3) A short circuit to earth on one or more coils will affect the a.c. voltage output.

To check, with the front chain case in position, use the d.c. voltmeter in series with a battery in good condition. Connect the wire from the meter to the white wire, the battery wire to a good and convenient earth on the engine. If a reading is shown on the meter, one or both coils are shorting to EARTH.

Note—The white wire is common to all coils.

Remove the outer portion of the chain case, check the alternator wires for damaged insulation, also coil connections before discarding the alternator.

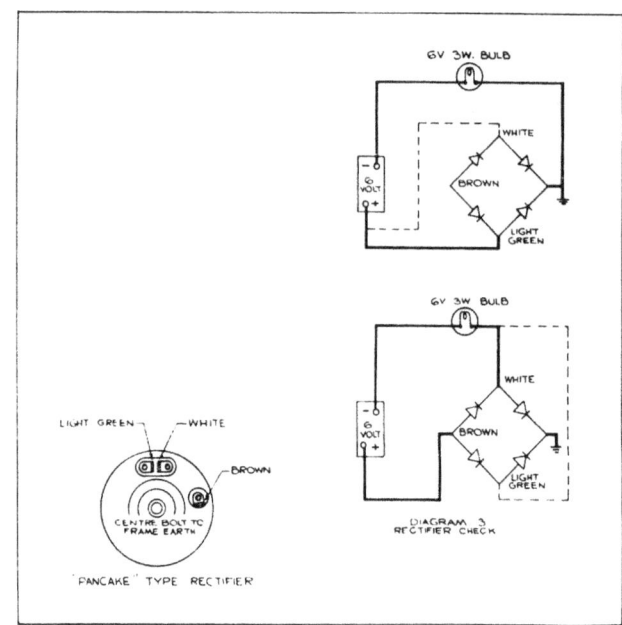

Fig. 58A

When the fault is located, repeat the tests previously described.

Rectifier tests

Before testing, verify the earth connection is clean and secure, check also the wires attached to the rectifier for loose connections. Take out the white, green and brown wires from the rectifier.

For this test use a 6 volt battery connected to a 3 watt bulb and holder. Connect the battery and bulb holder wire across the rectifier as shown in diagram A (fig. 58A).

Test in the following sequence:

Positive wire to Light Green ⎫ Bulb earthed. Bulb lights.
„   „   „ White   ⎬ Rectifier O.K.

„   „   „ Brown   ⎫ Bulb on Green. No light.
„   „   „ Brown   ⎬ Rectifier
                             ⎭ „ , White. No light.
                               Rectifier faulty.

Reverse the battery connections with:

Negative wire to Light Green ⎫ Bulb earthed. No light. Rec-
„   „   „ White   ⎬ tifier O.K.

„   „   „ Brown   ⎫ Bulb on Green. Bulb lights.
„   „   „ Brown   ⎬ „ „ White. Rectifier
                             ⎭   faulty.

Note—The common cause of rectifier trouble is invariably due to reversed battery connections, which can also demagnetise the rotor, if the engine is run with these connections reversed. The battery positive terminal is connected to EARTH (translucent), the negative is the feed line (brown).

Ignition and lighting switches

Both switches in the head lamp are mechanically identical and will interchange, the switch knobs being differently marked. If one switch is suspect take off the lamp rim and glass. Pull off the cable plugs and reverse their location. A further check will indicate if the switch is defective or otherwise. Replace the cable plugs in correct position after changing the switch.

Replacement switches should be of the improved type which can be identified by a NYLON post for the switch knob. Old type switches use a steel post.

Plug location

The blue plug is for the lighting system and the black for ignition.

WIPAC ELECTRICAL SERVICE

Lamp bulb blowing

Premature bulb failure involving all or many of the light bulbs at one time on a full d.c. battery system is caused by a defective connection in the battery 'line'.

This 'line' starts at (1) the frame end of the translucent lead from the positive battery terminal and proceeds:

(2) Positive battery terminal.
(3) Negative battery terminal.
(4) Brown wire from battery negative to 4-hole connector (bullet terminal).
(5) Brown wire from 4-hole connector to ammeter (bullet terminal).
(6) Ammeter terminal with brown wire.
(7) Ammeter terminal with blue wire.
(8) Both ends of short insulated link wire in the ignition switch plug, which joins blue ammeter wire to brown wire going to lights switch.

Should the ammeter develop internal open circuit, bulbs will blow, also should the battery have little or no electrolyte, this is a partial or complete open circuit with the same results. There is finally the remote possibility of one of the actual wires in the battery 'line' being broken—again, bulbs will 'blow'.

For quick checking, test connections in this order:

(1) Both battery terminals.
(2) Both ammeter terminals.
(3) All brown wires into 4-hole connector.

Speedometer bulb

On models made before 1961, the speedometer bulb is in circuit during daylight running and fails from filament fatigue. Transfer the wire attached to the speedometer bulb holder and connect it to the light switch as shown in wiring diagram for 1962 models. to illuminate the speedometer when lights are in use.

Ignition system

Special Note—The star-shaped washer for contact breaker pivot is not detachable. If the engine fails to start and there is no spark at the sparking plug points, examine the contact breaker by:

Check the gap at full separation .012″ and reset if necessary (ensure feeler gauge is free from oil).

Check condition of contact points which should have a grey frosted condition. The presence of oil or grease in the contact breaker compartment will cause a black matt condition.

Clean points with an abrasive strip or alternatively fine grade emery cloth. Pass a strip of clean paper, or rag soaked in petrol, across the points after cleaning.

Check free movement of contact breaker arm on its pivot.

Adjusting contact breaker gap

This adjustment is effected by altering the position of the fixed contact point by:

(1) Releasing slightly the locking screw.
(2) Adjust the gap by turning the eccentric screw (close to the fibre pad) in the required direction, with the fibre pad on the rocker arm on the cam lobe (maximum separation) .012″. Retighten the lock screw when adjustment is correct.

Lubrication

The felt pad should be impregnated with H.M.P. grease. Use sparingly, an excess can affect contact points surface.

Before replacing the contact breaker cover, check the condenser fixing for security.

If attention to the contact breaker fails to produce a spark, check the circuit by:

Swing on the ignition, rotate the engine very slowly until the contact points close. A discharge between three to four amps will be shown on the ammeter if current is passing.

As the ammeter is not closely calibrated, a more accurate check can be made by using the d.c. ammeter in between the brown battery wire and its connector.

If a discharge is not shown on the ammeter with contact points closed, this indicates current is not passing through the primary windings in the h.t. coil.

With ignition switch on check the dark green wire attached to the coil by:

Removing this wire from the coil terminal.

Connect one side of the d.c. voltmeter to the end of the dark green wire, the other side of the meter to earth.

If there is no reading on the meter, check the ignition (black) plug in the headlamp.

If the internal insulated wire bridge across two of the plug terminals (see wiring diagram) is fractured or disconnected, this will allow the engine to start with the switch on either emergency or ignition, but not in both positions, as one switch connection is out of circuit.

Renew the bridge connection.

Ignition coil test

(1) Use a battery with one wire attached to the d.c. voltmeter with a short length of wire attached to the other voltmeter terminal.
(2) Disconnect the two wires attached to the coil, also the h.t. cable.
(3) Use a further wire on the second battery terminal. Connect the free end of this wire, also the meter wire across the coil terminals. If there is continuity, a reading will show on the meter indicating the primary winding is in order.
(4) Transfer one wire from the coil terminal to the centre h.t. connection, if there is continuity a lower voltage reading will show by reason of the higher resistance of the secondary winding.
(5) Place one of the test wires on to one of the two coil terminals, the other to the coil case. No reading should show. Use the test wires on the h.t. connection and the case. No reading should show.

A meter reading on one or both tests means the windings are earthed, the coil should be replaced.

Usually a defective primary winding will produce a weak spark, conversely, an intermittent spark is associated with a faulty secondary winding. Where doubt exists, test by substitution.

The condenser (see 'Ignition system').

If the condenser is suspect, use a sound condenser with two crocodile clips attached to it.

Remove contact breaker cover, attach one clip to the connection on the contact breaker terminal, the other to a convenient earth position.

Running the engine with the external condenser in use will prove if the condenser is faulty or otherwise.

Vivid blue arcing at the contact points is indicative of a faulty condenser.

Where the orthodox electrical testing gear is not available, improvisation can be made by using the following equipment:
(1) A 6 volt 36 watt bulb and holder.
(2) A 6 volt .04 amp bulb and holder (this bulb is used on cycle rear lamps).
(3) A fully charged 6 volt battery.
(4) A short length of wire to join the battery to one side of the bulb holder. Also two test wires about 24″ long connected to the other battery and bulb holder terminals.

Test to ensure the bulb lights then proceed by:

Disconnecting the alternator wires from the connector.

Join one test lead to the white cable, the other test wire to the green cable.

Run the engine at a fast tick over speed when the bulb should show a fairly bright light.

Transfer the test wire from the green cable only to the orange cable and repeat the test.

Conclusions from test
(1) If the lamp bulb is not uniformly lighted on both tests, there is a fault in the alternator (see 'Earth test').
(2) Should the bulb fail to light, the alternator is defective.
(3) A dull light on both tests indicates a partially demagnetised rotor, due to battery connections being reversed at some time or other. Use a.c. voltmeter to check voltage output.

Alternator coils earthed

Use the test set with the 6 volt .04 bulb.

Connect one test wire to a convenient earth position on the engine.

Connect in turn, the other test wire to the white, green and orange wires.

Should the bulb light on any of these tests, the coils are shorted to earth.

Rectifier (forward flow test)

With the ignition and lights switches 'OFF', use the 36 watt bulb for this test, then:

Disconnect the wire from the brown connector on the rectifier (keep the wire end clear of the frame and engine).

Connect one test lead to rectifier brown terminal, the other test lead to earth.

Switch on to EMG and run the engine at tickover when, if the rectifier is O.K. the bulb will light brightly (six coils in circuit).

Repeat the test with the switch at IGN (three coils in circuit), the bulb will light, but not so brightly if rectifier is O.K.

Warning: Do not attempt to run the engine with an open circuit for the rectifier. The brown wire or the test set must be connected to prevent high voltage which will cause damage.

Rectifier (reverse flow test)

With the light and ignition switches 'OFF' test by:

Taking off one of the battery wires from the battery.

Connect the test set with the .04 amp bulb between the battery terminal and the battery wire.

If the reverse flow is normal, the bulb will light dimly, a bright light indicates a defective rectifier.

Alternative rectifier tests

An alternative method of testing can be effected by using the following equipment:

(1) A moving coil ammeter, scale 10-0-10.
(2) A fully charged 6 volt battery.
(3) A 6 volt 30 watt lamp bulb and holder.
(4) A 6 volt 0.040 amp bulb and holder.
(5) Three short test wires.

Forward flow test

Make a series circuit as shown in diagram B (Fig. 59B). The bulb will light with a reading of approximately 4.5 amps on the meter.

Take off the wire from the positive battery terminal, connect the third test lead to the positive battery terminal, also to the brown terminal on rectifier (d.c. negative).

Take up the wire taken from the battery and connect in turn to the green, then white, terminals (a.c. side).

In each test the bulb should light with a reading of 4.5 amps on the meter.

For clarity, remove test wires from rectifier, remake the series circuit B.

Next remove the battery negative wire, connect the third test wire to the negative battery terminal, also to the rectifier earth bolt or case.

Connect in turn the wire removed from the battery to the green and white terminals. Again, in each test the bulb should light with a reading of 4.5 amps.

If the meter readings on these tests are above 3 amps, the rectifier is satisfactory. Discard the rectifier if the readings are below 3 amps.

Note: Whilst a new rectifier will show 4.5 amps, this value will decrease after considerable service.

Reverse flow test

Make the circuit shown in diagram C (Fig. 60C) for this test.

A rectifier that is normal will have a reverse flow which should not exceed 0.040 milliamps, by using the 0.040 bulb with a current consumption of 40 milliamps it can be established if the reverse flow is abnormal by:

Removing the positive lead from the battery.

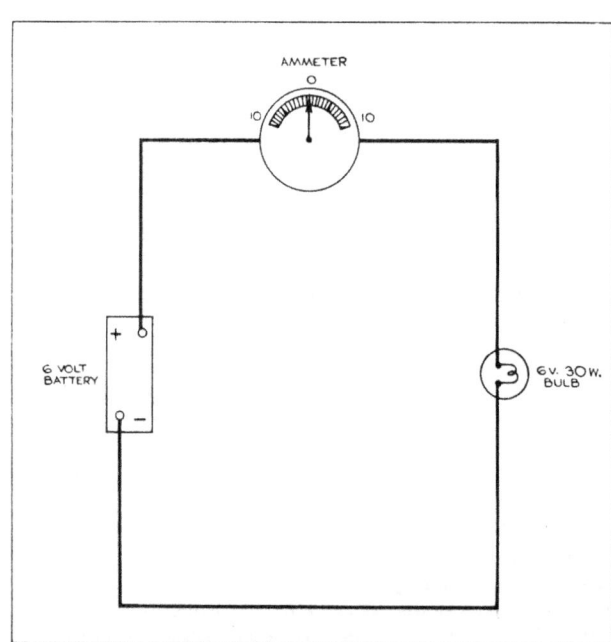

Fig. 59B

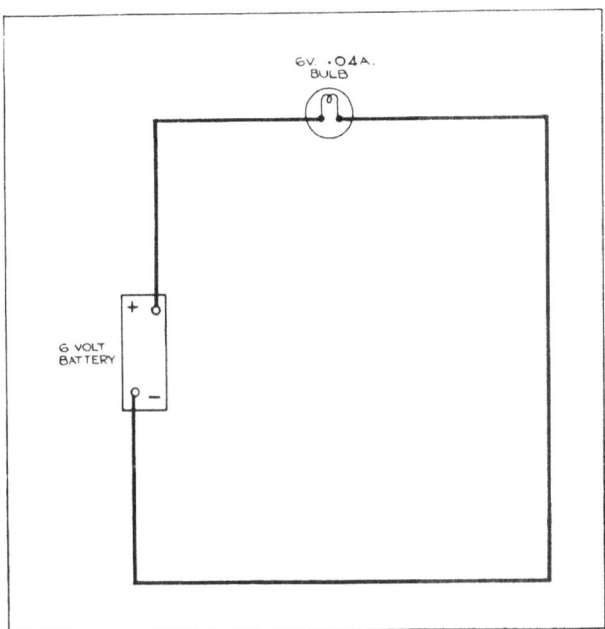

Join the third test wire to the battery positive, also to the rectifier earth bolt or case.

Connect the wire removed from the battery, in turn, to the white and green terminals.

If the bulb lights in these two tests the rectifier is defective.

Take off the test wires from rectifier and remake the circuit C.

Remove the negative wire from the battery.

Join the third test wire to the battery negative terminal, also to the brown rectifier terminal.

Connect the wire removed from the battery in turn, to the green and white terminals.

Should the bulb light in either of these tests the rectifier is defective.

Fig. 60C

Lucas Electrical Service

SINGLE CYLINDER AND ALTERNATOR TWINS — LUCAS A.C. LIGHTING-IGNITION UNIT

ALTERNATOR MODEL RM 15

The alternator consists of a spigot-mounted 6-coil laminated stator bolted to the outer portion of chaincase with a rotor carried on and driven by an extension of the crankshaft. The rotor has an hexagonal steel core, each face of which carries a high energy permanent magnet keyed to a laminated pole tip. The pole tips are riveted circumferentially to brass side plates, the assembly being cast in aluminium and machined to give a smooth external finish.

Thus there are no rotating windings, commutator, brush-gear, bearings or oil seals and consequently the alternator requires no maintenance apart from occasionally checking the snap connectors in the three output cables are clean and tight, which are located behind the frame cover which is located by two knurled screws.

If it is necessary, for any purpose, to remove the rotor, there is no necessity to fit keepers to the rotor poles. When the rotor is removed wipe off any metal swarf which may have collected on the pole tips. Place the rotor in a clean place.

Normal running

Under normal running conditions (i.e., ignition switch in IGN position) electrical energy in the form of rectified alternating current passes through the battery from the alternator—the rate of output depends on the position of the lighting switch. When no lights are in use, the alternator

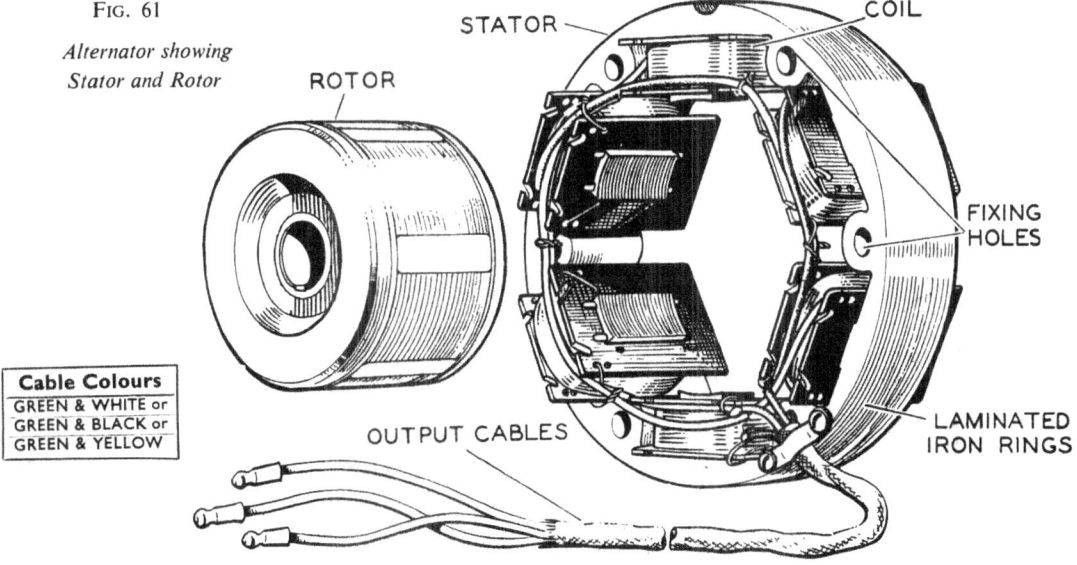

Fig. 61

Alternator showing Stator and Rotor

Cable Colours
GREEN & WHITE or
GREEN & BLACK or
GREEN & YELLOW

output supplies the ignition coil and trickle-charges the battery. When the lighting switch is turned, the output is automatically increased to meet the additional load of the parking lights and again when the main bulb is in use.

Emergency starting

An EMERGENCY starting position is provided in the ignition switch for use if the battery has become discharged. Under these conditions, the alternator is connected direct to the ignition coil, allowing the engine to be started independently of the battery.

Once the engine is running, turn the ignition switch back to the normal running position, otherwise misfiring will occur.

Emergency charging

Should the battery become discharged a temporary boost charge can be effected during daylight running, by an alteration to the alternator connections.

The snap connectors are located behind the frame plate, which is secured by two knurled screws.
(1) Disconnect the green and yellow and green and black connectors.
(2) Reconnect the green and black to the green and yellow.
(3) Do not interfere with the green and white cable.

It is stressed that this is a temporary measure, prolonged use will adversely affect the battery.

Rectifier

The rectifier is a device to allow current to flow in one direction only. It is connected to provide full-wave rectification of the alternator output. The rectifier is mounted on the tool box under the twin seat.

The rectifier requires no maintenance beyond checking that the connections are clean and tight. **The nut clamping the rectifier plates together must not under any circumstances be slackened, as it has been carefully set during manufacture to give correct rectifier performance.** A separate nut is used to secure the rectifier to the frame of the motor cycle.

Note—It is important to check periodically that the rectifier is firmly attached to its mounting bracket.

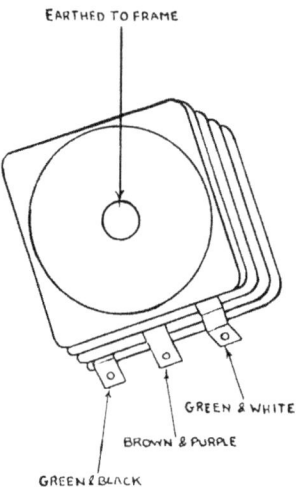

FIG. 62 *Rectifier*

Lucas Coil Ignition (Alternator Twins)

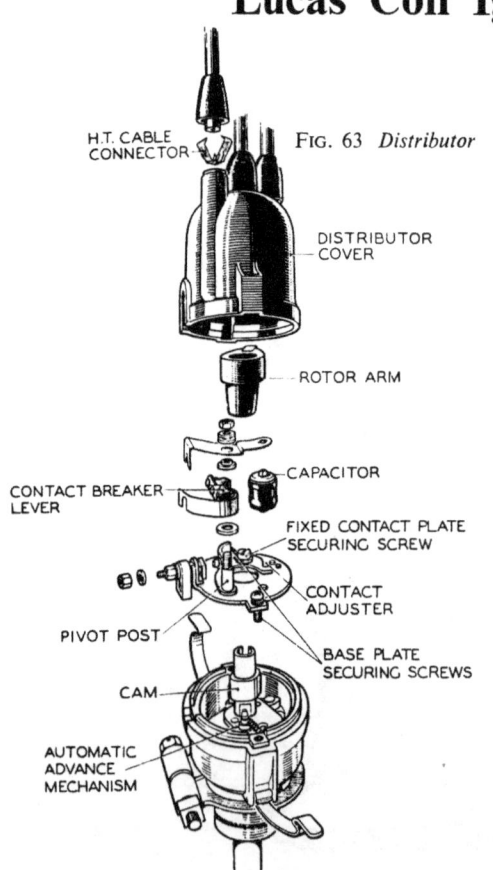

FIG. 63 *Distributor*

The ignition equipment comprises a Model MA6 coil with a Model 18D2 distributor assembly. The contact breaker with automatic advance mechanism is mounted in the distributor body.

The distributor has a flange fitting retained to the crankcase by one bolt and two nuts.

The drive is by gear pinion on the distributor shaft which is located by a parallel pin passing through the distributor shaft and the pinion. The parallel pin is retained by a circlip encircling the boss on the pinion.

An efficient oil seal encircles the distributor shaft to prevent oil entering the contact breaker compartment with an 'O' ring on the body for oil retention. A bronze thrust washer is fitted between the pinion and the distributor body. A clamp incorporated in the flange mounting, when released, will allow the distributor to be moved for ignition timing. The rotation is anti-clockwise.

Cleaning

To be carried out every 6,000 miles. Remove and clean the distributor cover, which must be handled with care. Pay particular attention to the spaces between the metal electrodes in the cover, and check that the small carbon brush moves freely in its holder.

Lubrication

Lift off the rotor arm, and unscrew the two screws securing the contact breaker base plate. Remove the base plate and lubricate the automatic advance mechanism with clean engine oil, paying particular attention to the pivots.

Re-fit the base plate and rotor arm.

Examine the contact breaker. The contacts must be free from grease or oil. If they are burned or blackened, clean with fine carborundum stone or very fine emery cloth, afterwards wiping away any trace of dirt or metal dust with a clean petrol-moistened cloth.

Contact cleaning is made easier if the contact breaker lever carrying the moving contact is removed. Before re-fitting the contact breaker lever, lightly smear the cam and pivot post with clean engine oil.

No grease or oil must be allowed to get on or near the contacts.

After cleaning, check the contact breaker setting.

Contact breaker setting

The contact breaker gap should be checked at the first 500 miles and subsequently at every 6,000 miles. To enable the engine to be rotated freely and slowly, remove both sparking plugs and distributor cover. Turn the engine slowly until the heel for the moving contact is on the peak of the cam (maximum separation). Check the gap by introducing a feeler gauge (which must be clean) between the points which should be a sliding fit with the correct gap, the correct setting is .014″—.016″.

To adjust the gap, ensure maximum separation, slacken slightly the screw securing the fixed contact plate.

Insert the screwdriver between the two projections on the base plate and the notch in the fixed contact plate and adjust to obtain the correct gap.

Re-tighten the fixed contact screw and re-check the gap.

Ignition Coil (Alternator Twins)

The coil, Type MA6, requires no attention whatsoever beyond keeping its exterior clean, particularly the terminals and occasionally checking that the connections are tight.

When the high tension cable shows signs of perishing or cracking it must be renewed, using 7 mm. p.v.c.-covered or neoprene-covered rubber ignition cable.

To remove the old cable from the ignition coil, pull the cable together with its connector from the moulded terminal socket. It is advisable to fit new connectors when renewing ignition cables.

The coil is clipped to the front-frame top tube underneath the petrol tank.

Capacitator (Alternator Models)

The capacitor is now attached to the base plate by a screwed extension. Take away the base plate to remove capacitor. fig. 64 shows the early type.

Magneto Models

Electrical equipment

Lucas electrical equipment is fitted and this comprises three independent electrical circuits, as follows:
(1) IGNITION—Magneto, High-tension wires, Sparking plugs and Cut-out switch.
(2) CHARGING—Dynamo compensated voltage control unit and Battery.
(3) LIGHTING AND ACCESSORIES—Lamps, Horn, Switches and Wiring.

Ignition

A Lucas type K2F magneto is fitted. The replacement part number is 42230-A and the part number of the complete contact breaker is 492854.

Lubrication and adjustment is required every 3,000 miles, cleaning is required every 5,000 miles and every 10,000 miles the complete unit should be handed to a Lucas Service Station for dismantling, replacement of worn parts, cleaning and lubrication.

Lubrication every 3,000 miles

Smear the cam ring inside and out with Mobilgrease No. 2. Apply a spot of clean engine oil to the tip of the pivot post. **No oil must be allowed on or near the contacts.**

To remove contact breaker

Take out the hexagon-headed screw from the centre of the contact breaker, then pull the assembly off the tapered shaft. When refitting, ensure the projecting key on the assembly engages with the keyway cut in the armature shaft. Incorrect assembly will affect ignition timing.

Adjustment every 3,000 miles

Remove the contact breaker cover and turn the engine until the contact points are fully opened. Check the gap with a gauge having a thickness of .012″ (spanner 015023 has a gauge of this thickness as an integral part of it). If the setting is correct the gauge should be a sliding fit, but if the gap varies appreciably from the gauge it should be adjusted by releasing the fixed contact plate securing screw and using a screwdriver as shown in fig. 64.

Cleaning every 5,000 to 6,000 miles.

Take off the contact breaker cover and remove the contact breaker. If the contact points are burned or blackened, clean them with a fine carborundum stone or with very fine emery cloth, and afterwards wipe away any dust or dirt with a petrol-moistened cloth. After replacing the contact breaker check the point gap and, if necessary, re-set it.

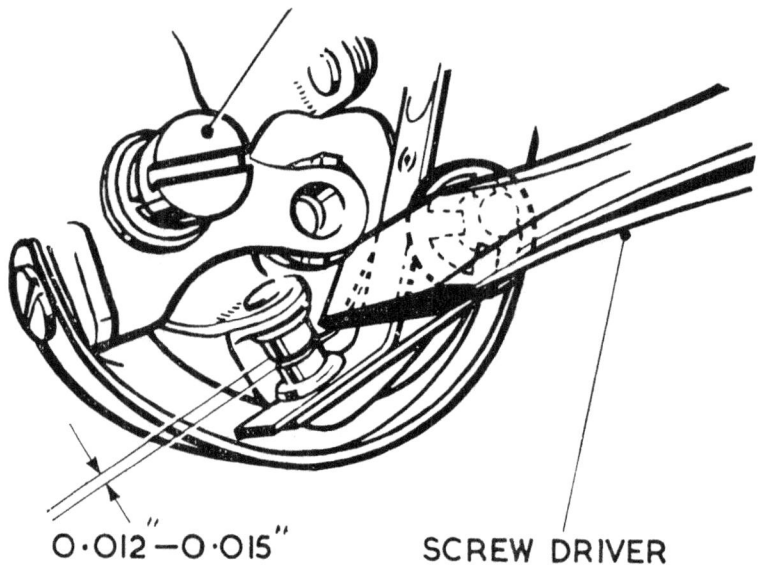

Fig. 64

Remove the high tension pick-ups (held by swinging spring clips), wipe clean and polish with a fine dry cloth. The high tension pick-up brush must move freely in its holder.

If it is dirty, clean with a cloth moistened with petrol. If the brush is worn to within ⅛" of the shoulder it must be renewed. Treat both pick-ups and their brushes.

While the pick-ups are removed, clean the slip ring track and flanges by holding a soft cloth on the ring by means of a suitably shaped piece of wood, while the engine is slowly turned.

If, on inspection, the high tension cable shows signs of perishing or cracking, it must be replaced by a suitable length of 7 mm. p.v.c.-covered, or neoprene ignition wire.

Battery—All Models (MLZ9E)

A lead-acid battery Lucas type is used on all models.

The voltage is 6, the the capacity is 12 ampere hours, at the 10 hour rate.

Machines are issued with dry charged batteries, the acid is filled by the dealer.

All models have the POSITIVE battery terminal connected to 'EARTH'.

Topping up the battery

Fortnightly or more often in warm climates, check if the electrolyte in each cell is level with the top of the separators. Top-up, if necessary, with distilled water. Do not allow distilled water to come into contact with metals—always only use a glass or earthenware container and funnel.

If a battery is found to need an excessive amount of topping-up, steps should be taken to find out the reason. If one cell in particular needs topping-up more than another, it is likely the case or container is cracked, in which event the battery must be replaced and arrangements made to clean up the battery carrier. Metal parts should be well cleaned and, if possible, washed with a solution of ammonia or bicarbonate of soda, in water.

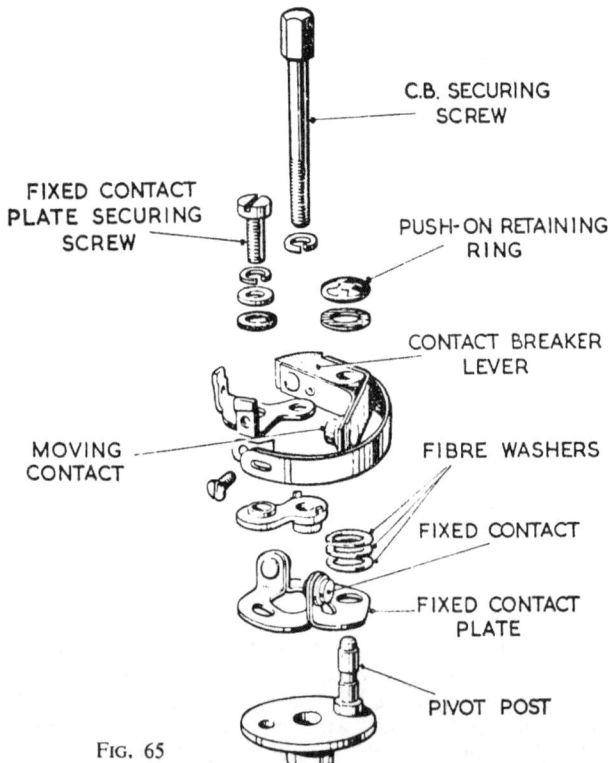

Fig. 65

Lighting and Accessories

Headlamp
A pre-focus main bulb, also a pilot bulb are mounted in the lamp reflector. The reflector and lamp glass are made up as one assembly and are not sold separately.

To remove the head lamp rim, release the screw retaining the lamp rim with one hand and support the light unit with the other.

The light unit can then be taken off the lamp.

To refit
Engage bottom tag on lamp rim with the small slit in the shell and gently force the top of the rim back into the shell, after which re-tighten the retaining screw on the top of the lamp body.

The main bulb is secured by a bayonet fixing holder, which is removed by turning anti-clockwise.

The pilot bulb is a plug-in or push fit.

The headlamp rim is detachable from the light unit by removing six spring clips.

Main bulb
Home and general export Lucas No. 446-12 volt vertical dip.

Export Europe Lucas No. 370
Pilot bulb Lucas No. 12 volt 989
Stop tail lamp Lucas No. 12 volt 380.

Main bulb

Home Models	Lucas No. 373 6-volt 30/24 watt prefocus (left hand dip).
General Export Models	Lucas No. 312 6-volt 30/24 watt prefocus (vertical dip).
Continental Models	Lucas No. 403 6-volt 35/35 watt prefocus duplo (vertical dip).
French Export Models	Lucas No. 379 6-volt 36/36 watt 3-pin duplo (vertical dip).

Parking Bulb .... Lucas No. 988 3-watt M.C.C.

Setting
The headlamp should be set so that when the machine is carrying its normal load the driving beam is projected straight ahead and is parallel with the road surface.

Dipper switch
Every 5,000 miles the moving parts of the dipper switch should be lubricated with thin machine oil.

Headlamp (Alternator Models)
A separate ignition switch is incorporated in the right side of the headlamp body.

Lucas stop tail lamp (Model 564)
The correct size of bulb to be used in rear lamps is based on the cubic capacity of the engine. The replacement bulb for this lamp is Lucas No. 384, 6-volt, 6/18 watt. Small bayonet cap.

Lucas horn (Model HF1441)
Horns are pre-set to give their best performance and, in general, no further adjustment is necessary.

If the horn becomes uncertain in its action, giving only a choking sound, or does not vibrate, it does not follow that the horn has broken down—the trouble may be due to a discharged battery, a loose connection, or short-circuit in the wiring of the horn.

In particular ascertain that the push-horn bracket is in good electrical contact with the handlebars.

It is also possible that the performance of a horn may be upset by its mounting becoming loose.

Terminals
All models have the POSITIVE battery terminal connected to 'EARTH'.

The earth connection, for the electrical system, is connected to the frame, on top of the seat lug tube.

Remove the twin seat for access.

Alternator Model RM15

The following data applies to three versions of Model RM15, namely, 540, 210, 18, fitted to magneto ignition machines, 047, 534, fitted to coil ignition machines, and 540, 210, 05, fitted to two-way radio equipped machines.

Test equipment required
(1) First-grade moving coil a.c. voltmeter. 0.20 volts.
(2) First-grade moving coil d.c. ammeter. 0.25 amps.
(3) One ohm load resistor (capable of carrying 20 amperes without overheating.)

Test No. 1
For this test, the battery must be in good condition and more than half charged.
(1) Connect the d.c. ammeter between the battery negative terminal and the battery main cable.
(2) Start the engine and set it to run at approximately 3,000 r.p.m.
(3) Observe the ammeter readings in each of the positions of the lighting switch.

The figures given in the following table are the minimum acceptable battery input currents. If the readings obtained are lower than the figures quoted, proceed to Test No. 2.

Minimum acceptable battery charging currents			
Switch	Despatch number of unit		
	540, 210, 18	047, 534	540, 210, 05
			Boost switch Open / Boost switch Closed
Off	2.75	2.5	4.0 / 9.0
Parking	2.0	1.5	2.5 / 7.0
Head	2.0	2.5	3.5 / 3.5

Minimum acceptable voltage readings			
Voltmeter and Resistor connected between	*Despatch Number of unit* 540, 210, 18	047, 534	540, 210, 05
White-with-Green and Green-with-Black cables	4.0	4.0	9.5
White-with-Green and Green-with-Yellow cables	6.5	6.5	13.0
White-with-Green and Green-with-Black (with Green-with-Yellow connected to Green-with-Black)	8.5	9.0	15.5
Each cable in turn and earth	Zero	Zero	Zero

Unsatisfactory readings can be due to defective wiring or connections.

Ensure that all snap-connector joints and earth connections are in good condition before proceeding to Test No. 2.

If considered necessary, check the rectifier by substitution.
(1) Disconnect the three alternator output cables.
(2) Start the engine and set to run at approximately 3,000 r.p.m.
(3) Connect the one ohm load resistance in parallel with the a.c. voltmeter and check the voltage between the alternator output cables.
(4) Conclusions to be drawn from results of above tests:
Demagnetised rotor magnets indicated by all readings being low.

Short-circuited coil indicated by individual reading being low.

Open-circuited coil or coils indicated by aero reading(s).

Earthed coil or coils indicated by voltage reading between any output cable and earth.

Alternator, Model RM15, with rotor, withdrawn (REC 728).

Batteries

Model:	PU7E	SC7E
No. of plates per cell	7	7
Ampere-hour capacity:		
At the 10-hour rate	12	22.5
At the 20-hour rate	13.5	26
Electrolyte to fill one cell (approx.):		
Pint measure	1/5	½
Cubic centimetre measure	115	280
Initial-charge current in amperes (not applicable to 'dry-charged' batteries)	0.8	1.5
Re-charge current in amperes	1.5	2.5
Examination of electrolyte level	Fortnightly	Weekly

Notes for putting the battery into service

It is necessary to use different filling-in specific gravities, according to shade temperature, when preparing electrolyte solutions. When filling batteries for the home trade and in climates having shade temperatures ordinarily below 80° F. (26.6 C.) add one part (by volume) of acid (1.835 S.G.) to 2.8 parts of distilled water, to obtain a filling-in solution having a specific gravity of 1.270 at 60° F. (15.5 C.).

For use in climates where shade temperatures are frequently over 80° F., the acid-to-water ratio must be 1:4 to give a specific gravity of 1.210 at 60° F. Specific gravity readings taken at electrolyte temperatures other than 60° F. can be corrected to this reference temperature by deducting 0.002 from the observed reading for every 5° F. (2.7° C.) that the temperature is below 60° F. Conversely, 0.002 must be added to the observed reading for every 5° F. that the temperature exceeds 60° F. The temperature of the filling-in solution should be 60° F. to 80° F. When applicable, allow battery to attain room temperature before filling. Fill to the top edge of separators or separator guards in one operation with acid of appropriate strength. Then initial-charge uncharged batteries and if time permits, give 'dry-charged' batteries a four-hour charge at the appropriate re-charge rate.

Maintenance

At the intervals given in the above table, remove the battery lid, unscrew the filler plugs and if necessary, add distilled water carefully to each cell to bring the electrolyte just level with the separator guard or, if visible, with the top edges of the separators. *Do not use tap water.* Wipe away all dirt and moisture from the top of the battery.

If the motor-cycle is to be laid up for a while, give the battery a fortnightly freshening charge at the appropriate re-charge rate until the electrolyte in the cells is gassing freely, in order to replace the energy lost during standing.

Contact Breaker Units and Distributor

Model:	18D2	CA1A	CA1A	CA1A
Part No.	40589	47578	47579	47595
Contact Gap Settings:				
Inch measure	0.014-0.016	0.014-0.016	0.014-0.016	0.014-0.016
Centimetre measure	0.356-0.406	0.356-0.406	0.356-0.406	0.356-0.406
Centrifugal Advance Curve	ECM 667	ECM 674	ECM 675	ECM 748

Model:	18D2	CA1A	CA1A	CA1A
Part No.	40589	47578	47579	47595
Contact Breaker Spring Force (Measured at contacts)—				
In ounces	18-24	18-24	18-24	18-24
In grammes:	511-680	511-680	511-680	511-680
Capacity of Capacitor in microfarads:	0.14-0.20	0.18-0.23	0.18-0.23	0.18-0.23

Condenser Check

When investigating a misfire, and where the condenser is suspect, the use of an external condenser will prove if this component is defective.

Use a sound condenser with two crocodile clips attached. Attach one clip to the low tension terminal on the distributor, the other to a convenient earth position.

A short test, by running the engine, will indicate if the condenser is defective.

In the case of Single Cylinder Models, remove contact breaker cover, fit one clip to terminal for contact breaker pivot post, the other to earth.

Maintenance

Check the contact breaker gap setting after the first 500 miles (800 km.) running and subsequently every 6,000 miles (9,660 km.).

Every 6,000 miles examine and clean the contacts and also the moulded cover of Model 18D2.

At this period carry out the following lubrication procedure:

(1) **Cam.** Smear the surface of the cam very lightly with Mobilgrease No. 2 or clean engine oil.
(2) **Cam bearing.** Model 18D2. Inject a few drops of thin machine oil into the arm spindle.
Model CA1A (every 3,000 miles, 4,830 km.). Remove the central securing bolt and inject a few drops of thin machine oil (this will also lubricate the timing control mechanism).
(3) **Contact breaker pivot post.** Apply a spot of clean engine oil to the exposed tip of the contact breaker pivot post.
(4) **Centrifugal timing control mechanism.** Model 18D2. Lift off the rotor arm and unscrew the two screws securing the contact breaker base plate to the body. Lubricate with clean engine oil the centrifugal timing control mechanism thus exposed, paying particular attention to the pivots.
Model CA1A. See (2).

High tension cable.

Renew as required, using 7 mm. p.v.c.-covered or neoprene covered rubber insulated ignition cable.

Oil seal replacement (Model 18D2 only)

The oil sealing ring which is fitted in a groove round the shank is simply replaced, but the oil seal fitted inside the shank requires the use of a suitable extractor to remove it from its housing.

Bearing replacement

Use a hand press to remove the old bush from the shank of the unit.

Before fitting the replacement bush (Part No. 425498), allow it to soak in medium viscosity engine oil for at least 24 hours. In cases of extreme urgency, this period of soaking may be shortened by heating the oil to 212° F. (100° C.) for two hours and then allowing the oil to cool before removing the bush.

A shouldered mandrel must be used to press the new bearing into the shank. This mandrel must be hardened and polished and be 0.0005" (0.013 mm.) greater in pin diameter than the distributor shaft. To prevent subsequent withdrawal of the bush with the mandrel, a stripping washer should be fitted between the mandrel shoulder and the bush.

Magnetos — Models K2F and NC1

Endurance test

With the contact breaker cover in place, run the magneto for one hour at 3,000 r.p.m. with the high tension cable (or cables) connected to an 8-kilovolt annular spark gap.

Inspection

After the above run, disconnect the magneto and examine it as follows:

Remove the pick-up brush (or brushes) and check for signs of sticking movement, of flashover or of fouling against the slip ring moulding. Examine the slip ring for signs of flashover, burnt or rough track, presence of swarf or of eccentricity. Examine the contact breaker. The contacts must be in line and have a maximum opening setting of 0.012"—0.015" (0.305-0.381 mm.).

The contact breaker arm must be free to turn on its pivot. Remove the earthing brush and check that it is free to move in its holder. Check the armature for excessive end float or binding. Up to 0.005" (0.127 mm.) end float is permissible. Shims of 0.005" and 0.003" (0.075 mm.) thickness are available for correcting excessive end float.

High speed test

Connect the high tension cable (or cables) to a rotary gap set to spark at 8 kilovolts. A loading resistor must be connected in parallel with the spark gap to simulate 'leaky' sparking plugs.

With model K2F magnetos use a 1.5-micromho load. With model NC1 use a 2.5-micromho load. Remove the contact breaker cover and run the magneto over the speed range 1,000—3,000 r.p.m. No missing must occur. Observe the contact braker for excessive sparking.

While running at 3,000 r.p.m., the primary winding should be short circuited at least six times, by touching the contact breaker spring with an earthed cable.

Low speed test

Connect the high tension cable to a 3-point spark gap set to 5.5 mm., using independent spark gaps for the two cables of twin-cylinder magneto model K2F. Not more than 5 per cent missing must occur under the following conditions of speed and ignition timing:

Magneto model	NC1	K2F
Part No.	423, 47	422, 30 and 422, 64
Maximum speed (r.p.m.):		
Ignition advanced	130	150
Ignition retarded	170	180

Maintenance

Every 3,000 miles check and (if necessary) reset the contact breaker gap to 0.012″—0.015″.

Apply a spot of clean engine oil to the exposed tip of the contact breaker pivot post.

Every 6,000 miles clean exterior and interior of magneto. Renew earthing and pick-up brushes if worn to within $\frac{1}{8}$″ of shoulder. Clean contacts with carborundum stone, silicon carbide paper or very fine emery cloth.

Checking the Rectifier

If a spare rectifier known to be in good condition is available, the simplest check is that of substitution. (In this connection, Lucas rectifier 47132 is used with alternators 540, 210, 18 and 047, 534, while rectifier 47142 is used in conjunction with alternator 540, 210, 05.)

When a satisfactory substitute is not available, the rectifier is best checked by removing it from the machine and bench testing it as detailed.

Test equipment required

(1) Two first-grade moving coil 0-20 direct current voltmeters.
(2) One-ohm load resistor (capable of carrying 12 amperes without overheating).
(3) Fully charged 12-volt battery of about 50 ampere-hours capacity at the 10-hour rate, e.g., any typical nine-plates-per-cell car battery, as fitted to medium-sized cars.

N.B.: When testing, it is essential that the battery terminal voltage (as indicated by voltmeter V2) is at least 12.

When testing, it is essential to make the individual tests as quickly as possible to avoid overheating of the rectifier plates.

Forward resistance test

With the test equipment connected as shown in the illustration, proceed as follows to check in turn each of the four cells which form the rectifier:

In sequence, connect the
 +ve test prod to terminal '2' and the —ve to terminal '1'
 +ve test prod to terminal '2' and the —ve to terminal '3'
 —ve test prod to centre bolt and the +ve to terminal '1'
 —ve test prod to centre bolt and the +ve to terminal '3'

In each check, not more than 2.5 volts should be shown by voltmeter V1.

Back leakage test

With the test equipment connected as before, proceed as follows:

In sequence, connect the
 —ve test prod to terminal '2' and the +ve to terminal '1'
 —ve test prod to terminal '2' and the +ve to terminal '3'
 +ve test prod to centre bolt and the —ve to terminal '1'
 +ve test prod to centre bolt and the —ve to terminal '3'

In each check, the voltage shown by voltmeter V1 should be within 2 volts of that shown by voltmeter V2.

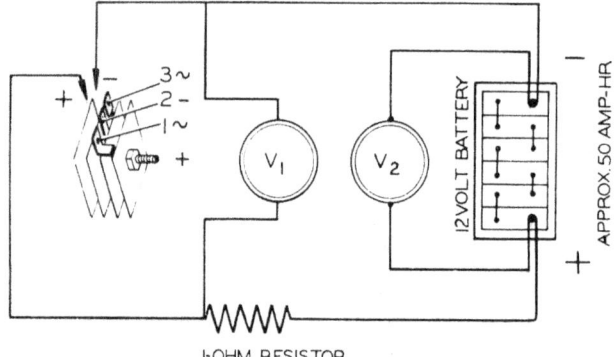

V_1 — WILL MEASURE THE VOLT DROP ACROSS THE RECTIFIER PLATE
V_2 — MUST BE CHECKED WHEN TESTING THE RECTIFIER PLATE TO MAKE CERTAIN THE SUPPLY VOLTAGE IS THE RECOMMENDED 12 VOLTS ON LOAD

FIG. 66

Lucas 88SA Switch

General

Model 88SA switches have superseded the equivalent versions of model 63SA as initial equipment on motor-cycles, and will eventually replace the model 63SA in service.

Unlike the model 63SA, which has terminals crimped directly to the cable harness, the model 88SA consists of a switch fitted with contact pins that engage with a specially designed socket. In this latter case it is the socket that is permanently connected (resistance brazed) to the cable harness. This plug-in feature of the 88SA switch simplifies disconnection for replacement, or test purposes.

There are three versions of the 88SA switch which are as follows: Lighting switch, ignition switch knob operated and ignition switch key operated. Alternative positions of the ignition switch are ignition off, ignition on and emergency. The emergency position on the key operated model is obtained by *pressing the key inwards* and then turning it in an anti-clockwise direction.

For service purposes sockets pre-wired with 4″ of cable are to be made available.

Rectifier output—circuit simplification

With the improved characteristics of modern rectifiers the possibility of battery discharge due to rectifier leakage can be discounted. The 88SA switch therefore, does not make provision for disconnecting the rectifier from the battery because, first, it is not necessary, and, secondly, its omission permits a degree of switch standardisation.

12 volt system

This improved form of lighting was first introduced for the 1964 models. The heat sink plate, to which the Zener diode is attached, must be kept in the air stream for heat dissipation. Two 6 volt batteries in series are mounted in the battery compartment. It is most important to ensure that the battery cables, as well as the link cable, are securely tightened. The wiring diagrams are shown on pages 78 and 79.

The effects of modern Engines and Fuels on Sparking Plugs

The growing trend these days is for engines to produce more power with improved economy, thus giving more of a sports car performance to the family saloon. As a result of this it is usual for touring engines to employ much higher compression ratios than was the custom a few years ago. Fuels with higher octane ratings have been developed to accommodate the more severe conditions, which have brought in their train many difficult problems for both petroleum chemists and automotive engineers.

The improved high octane fuels are complex blends of petroleum fractions with various additives including tetra ethyl lead in greater or lesser degree. In addition to soot and carbonised oil residues certain products of combustion, including lead and sulphur compounds, settle on the surfaces of combustion chambers, piston crowns, valves and sparking plugs. Unfortunately some of these deposits, although effectively non-conducting when cold, become electrical conductors at high temperatures, and their formation on a plug insulator offers a leakage path to earth for the high tension current. This can cause weak sparking and mis-firing, particularly at wide throttle openings when maximum compression pressures demand a higher voltage to spark the electrode gap. The problem is accentuated by the higher compression ratios now employed which require in any case a greater voltage to produce a spark across the plug gap than was necessary with earlier, low compression engines.

Whilst higher performance engines are now commonplace present day traffic conditions compel many vehicles to spend a large proportion of their running time at low duty, especially in city congestion. Such prolonged slow driving can allow an accumulation of lead fouling to form on plug insulators, although the symptoms may not manifest themselves under low duty operation. A spell of open road driving, however, with wider throttle openings, may well cause the temperature of the plugs to rise sufficiently to render the deposits electrically conductive, thus shorting out the spark and producing misfiring.

This condition is common to, and can occur in, any brand of sparking plug. We have on the one hand better automotive engines with highly developed fuels and oils to suit them, and on the other the increased problem of combustion chamber deposit. Do not blame the sparking plug—it can only work efficiently when clean. Regular cleaning not only prevents heavy deposit formation, it makes it easier to remove, for when plugs start shorting the deposits are virtually baked on, making them difficult to clean satisfactorily.

The higher temperatures reached in modern engines under fast driving conditions cause the sulphur compounds produced when petrol is burnt to have a more corrosive action on plug electrodes. Where corrosion and reduced plug life result from habitual hard driving, the use of a cooler running plug type will be beneficial in minimising the attack.

Careful tuning of carburetter and ignition settings will retard the formation of fuel deposits. Contact breaker points, which make and break four times as often as each plug fires in a four-cylinder engine, are bound to be worn by the time new plugs are needed. When the points become pitted and burned, they cannot supply the correct current to the coil to enable the latter to deliver an adequate output to the plug to produce a good spark. In severe cases this can also have a retarding effect on ignition timing.

No plug is any better than the electrical system backing it up. Examine the contact breaker points and if necessary reface them or renew, making sure their gap is set to the engine maker's specification by using a K.L.G. ignition gauge. Check also that the insulation of the high tension plug leads is sound, and is not frayed or cracked.

Instructions for Cleaning

For maximum efficiency a sparking plug operating under normal conditions should be cleaned and have its gap(s) reset several times during its life. In average motor car conditions this should be at approximately 3-5,000 mile intervals and proportionately less in other engines where running conditions may be more severe. Similarly more frequent attention may be necessary in oily engines. It is sometimes possible to avoid the effects of over-oiling by fitting a softer plug, but if the oiling is due to engine damage or wear, this is only a palliative and should not replace the proper corrective action. Where sustained hard driving is involved it may be necessary to reset gaps more frequently, as the high temperatures cause more rapid erosion of the electrodes, and cleaning at the same time will be amply repaid.

K.L.G. plugs should be cleaned on a reputable sand-blast cleaner. If plugs are oily on removal from the engine, they should be washed out with petrol and blown dry with an air gun prior to sand-blasting to reduce the tendency for sand to stick inside the body.

When sand-blasting, the plug should be slowly rotated and slightly tilted from side to side to allow the sand full access to the inside. It should be done in several short bursts, removing the plug each time for examination and carried on long enough only to effect the desired cleaning. Excessive blasting may damage the electrodes and insulator.

Finally, the plug should be well blown out with air to remove all particles. A final examination should be made for any particles tightly lodged inside and these removed by some pointed object, preferably non-metallic, but if metallic, care should be taken not to abrade metal on to the ceramic, as this could cause shorting.

With overhead earthwire plugs which still have considerable life left in them, it is advantageous before re-setting the gap to file the underside of the earth wire and the end of the centre electrode lightly to restore the sharp edges which existed when the plugs were new. Only the minimum of metal should be removed, but the resultant lower sparking voltage will be of benefit in giving starting, idling and cruising performance approximating more closely to that of new plugs.

Detachable K.L.G. plugs can be cleaned easily and efficiently by hand if preferred or if a sand-blast cleaner is not available. The following instructions are for cleaning a plug by hand:

To dismantle the plug for cleaning, the gland nut must be unscrewed from the body so that the insulated electrode assembly may be withdrawn. This is best accomplished by using two close fitting box spanners, one fitting the gland nut hexagon and the other the body hexagon: the box spanner holding the gland nut should itself be gripped in a vice, whilst the other box spanner is utilised for unscrewing the body. Alternatively, the hexagon of the gland nut may be held gently in a vice, care being taken not to distort by over-tightening. *Never* grip the body hexagon in a vice as this will distort it sufficiently to lock the gland nut in position, making it impossible to take the plug apart.

If the insulator is oily, first *wash it in* an oil solvent such as petrol or paraffin and dry; then, with fairly coarse glass paper, remove the carbon deposit and wash again. Do not scrape with a knife or other object, as metal will be abraded on the ceramic and leave a potential short-circuiting path.

The firing point should be cleaned with a fine emery cloth.

The plug body should be scraped clean internally with a knife or wire brush after removing the old internal gasket, paying particular attention to the earth electrodes. With overhead earth plugs which have a considerable life still left in them, the electrodes should be lightly filed as already described, but this can be done if preferred before re-assembly.

Finally rinse in petrol or a cleaning spirit.

A new internal washer should be lightly smeared with thin oil. Make sure that it is properly seated in the plug body before re-inserting the central electrode assembly.

Screw up the gland nut and tighten sufficiently to give a gas-tight joint.

Before refitting the plugs to the engine adjust the gaps to .020" to .022". Coat the threaded portion with oil Dag or graphite paste.

Always remember the golden rule—never try to move the central electrode. It is surrounded by insulation which cannot bend. Move the earth electrodes only.

Sparking plug tightening torque: 22 ft. lbs. (3.05 M/KG).

Electra Electrical Service

Voltage regulator

The voltage regulator is of the relay type and depending on the state of charge of the battery will switch in or out additional generator coils to increase or decrease the charge rate as necessary. The unit has been carefully adjusted at the factory for optimum performance and any attempt to alter the settings can only impair its efficiency and invalidate the guarantee.

Charge rates

Load Condition	Battery Condition	Charge Rates at 3,000 r.p.m.
No Lights	Regulator in (Battery Low)	7 amps minimum
No Lights	Regulator out (Battery chgd.)	2 amps minimum
Pilot Lights	Regulator in (Battery Low)	6 amps minimum
Pilot Lights	Regulator out (Battery chgd.)	Balance minimum
Head Light	Regulator in (Battery Low)	2 amps minimum
Head Light	Regulator out (Battery chgd.)	4 amps maximum

Bulbs

Headlamp	12v. 40/50w. Pre-focus
Rearlamp	12v. 21/6w.
Stop Lamp	12v. 21/w.
Pilot Lamp	12v. 2.2w.
Speedometer Bulb	14v. 0.8w.
Flashing Indicators	12v. 18w. Festoon type

DO NOT run with the battery disconnected otherwise the voltage regulator will constantly chatter and accelerate wear on the contacts and pivots, the rectifier will also over-heat. If you switch the lights on all the bulbs will blow.

DO NOT reverse the battery connections, which will burn out the rectifier. Running the machine in this condition will also de-magnetize the rotor.

Batteries (positive earth)

Two Exide type 3-EV11 batteries of 12 amp hour capacity are housed in the tool compartment also in a carrier underneath the riders seat, both are secured by a rubber band.

"Dry charged" batteries are supplied without electrolyte, but with their plates in a charged condition. No initial charging is required and to bring the battery into service it is only necessary to fill the cells with electrolyte, prepared by mixing concentrated sulphuric acid and distilled water.

Preparation of electrolyte

In the U.K. and countries where the temperatures are normally below 90°F (32°C) electrolyte of 1.270 S.G. is required, viz. 1 part acid (1.835 S.G.) to 2.8 parts distilled water. In tropical climates where temperatures frequently rise above 90°F, electrolyte of 1.210 S.G. is recommended, viz., 1 part acid (1.835 S.G.) to 4 parts distilled water.

Warning. ALWAYS ADD ACID TO WATER—NOT WATER TO ACID.

ON DRY CHARGED BATTERIES THE FILLING OF EACH CELL MUST BE COMPLETED IN ONE OPERATION AND LEVELS RESTORED AFTER STANDING FOR AN HOUR OR MORE BY SYPHONING OFF EXCESS ELECTROLYTE.

Electrolyte should be mixed in a glass or earthenware vessel, or lead lined tank.

Temperature of filling room, battery and electrolyte should be maintained between 60°F and 80°F.

Batteries filled in this way are 90 per cent charged. After filling, a dry charged battery needs only the attention normally given to lead-acid type batteries.

Battery maintenance

Deterioration soon sets in if left standing without attention for any length of time. To keep the battery in good condition, maintenance must be carried out whether the machine is in use or not.

Every month (every fortnight in summer) remove battery, clean terminals and top up the three cells with distilled water—NOT tap water, as this contains impurities detrimental to the battery. Pour the distilled water through a glass funnel or syringe to the level shown on battery.

Many lighting troubles can be traced to unseen corrosion between the surfaces of the battery terminals; keep the terminals clean. A little grease smeared on them will help to prevent corrosion.

Do not keep distilled water in receptacles made of any kind of metal as this will quickly render it impure—make use of a clean glass bottle or jar. Rain water collected in a jar makes a satisfactory substitute for distilled water.

Never bring a naked light near a battery with vent plugs removed or when the battery is being charged; the gas given off by the electrolyte is dangerously explosive.

Battery acid is highly corrosive; therefore, throw away any cleaning rags used to clean the battery lest their use on other parts of the machine causes rust.

Never let a battery completely run down; if this does occur get it charged as soon as possible or its length of life may be seriously shortened.

Warning. When refitting the battery to the tool box compartment the POSITIVE terminal must be on the left side (facing front of machine) this terminal is earthed on the crankcase.

Electric self-starter mechanism

This equipment is comprised of the following components:
Lucas starter motor 12 volt type M3.
Epicyclic gear in housing attached to starter motor body.
Starter drive sprocket.
Starter drive chain with detachable link.
Starter drive ratchet on engine shaft.
Outrigger plate bolted to chaincase housing the overriding clutch.
Solenoid starter switch 12 volt mounted between the frame channel and rear mudguard.
Starter switch incorporated in "Triconsul" switch mounted on left handlebar.

Electric starter operation

The electric starter operates when the ignition is switched ON and the red button in the "Triconsul" switch mounted on the left side of the handlebar is depressed. The drive, from

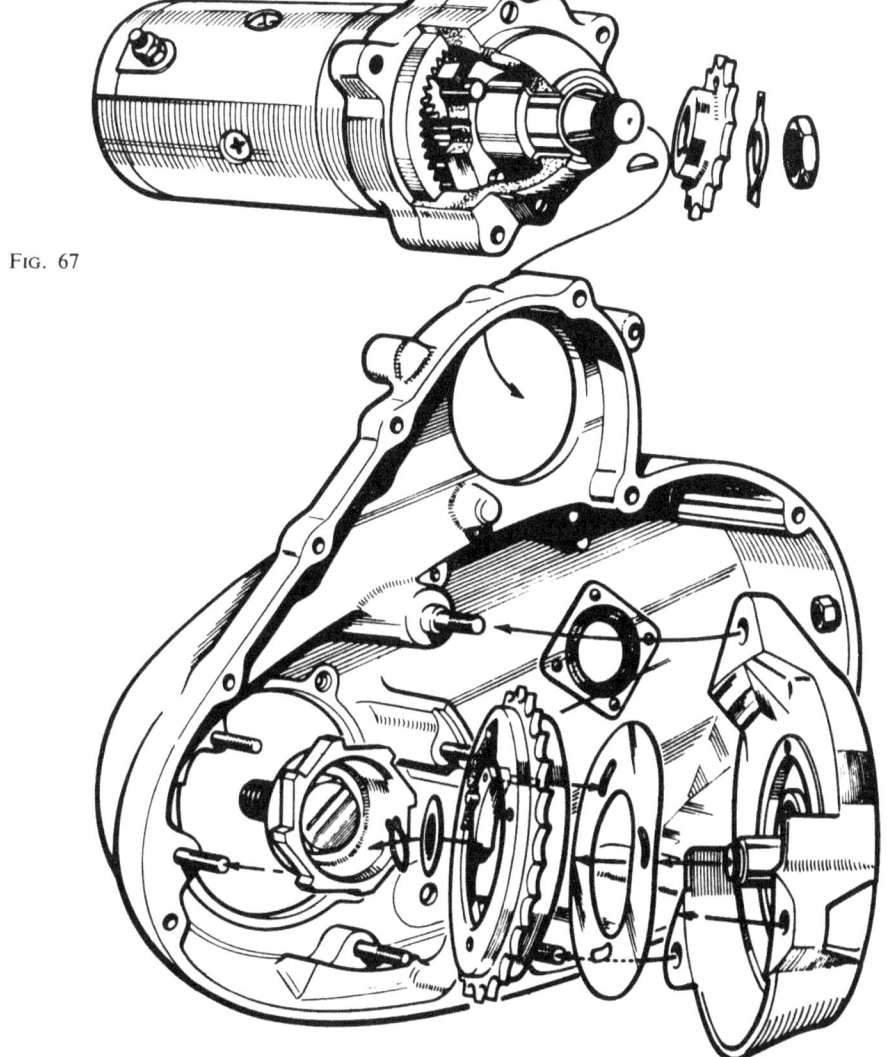

Fig. 67

the starter motor, is taken through the Epicyclic gear, rotating the overriding clutch via the drive chain.

Three pawls, which are lightly spring loaded by a wave plate, engage with the dogs on the starter ratchet thus rotating the engine. Immediately the engine commences to run, the pawls disengage with the drive on the engine mainshaft.

The electric starter is simple in design yet robust in construction and does not need frequent attention.

The following precautions are however necessary:—

If the machine is used when the temperature is in the region of 32° Fahrenheit (zero Centigrade) the engine should be rotated several times by means of the kickstarter to relieve 'gumminess' between the pistons and cylinder caused by oil adhesion.

Periodically check the electrolyte level in both batteries and top up to the visible level indicated on the battery case.

If the machine is left standing for any length of time, the batteries should have a freshening charge, until all cells are gassing freely, to replace energy lost during standing.

To remove starter motor

Take off the heavy duty cable attached to the starter motor.
Remove the outer chain case cover.
Remove the chain connecting link.
Remove three self locking nuts fixing the motor to the chain case. The starter motor together with the Epicyclic gear in its housing can be withdrawn.

Direction lights (12 volt 18 watts)

The operating switch is mounted on the right side handlebar in front of the air control lever. To exchange a bulb, remove four screws retaining the amber plastic covers. Take out the large screw in light body, the bulb can be removed with the fingers.

To remove the light body

With the bulb removed, pull out slightly the connector and wire, use a screwdriver and release two or three turns (no more) the expander screw inside the handlebar. A sharp tap on the end of the screwdriver will separate the taper plug retaining the light body.

When refitting, it is preferable to take off the switch and pull back the cable, after tightening the taper plug. A circuit diagram is printed on the flasher unit.

Warning. Do not overtighten amber cover fixing screws.

Lucas Constant-Mesh Starting Motor

Model M3 Part No. 26509

General

Model M3 constant-mesh starting motor is a four-pole, four-brush, earth return machine with series-connected field coils. The armature shaft is extended to carry a ten-toothed pinion, which acts as the 'sun' gear of an epicyclic reduction gear assembly, through which the starting torque is transmitted, via a chain drive and free-wheeling device, to the engine crankshaft. The free-wheeling device—incorporated between the driving chain sprocket and crankshaft—ensures that the starting gears and motor remain stationary unless actually engaged in turning over the engine.

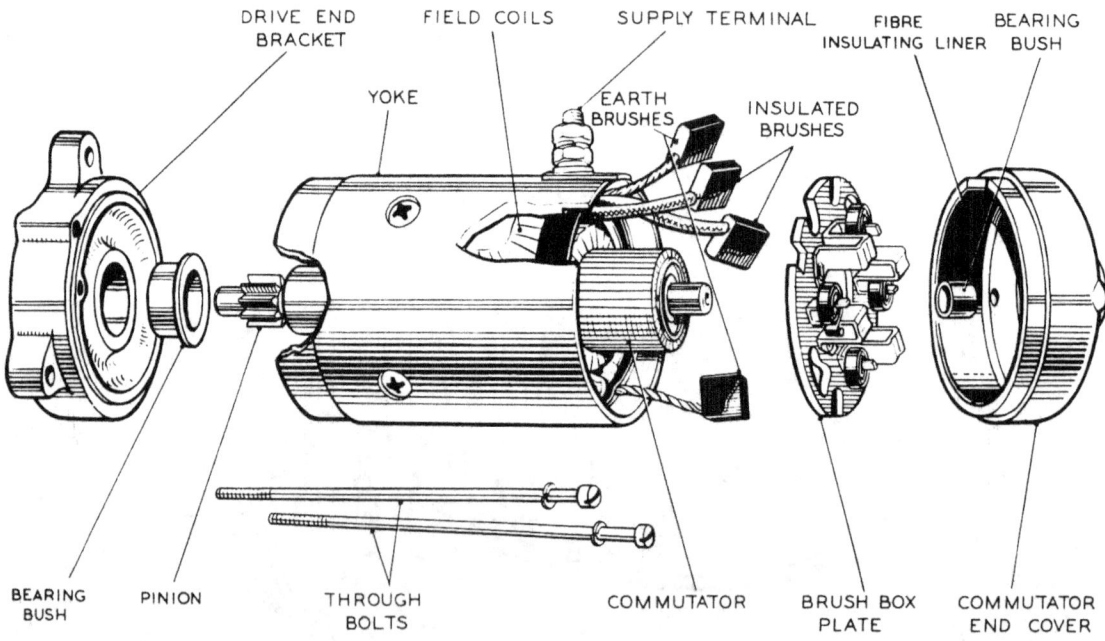

Fig. 68

Maintenance

Keep the supply terminal on the starter yoke clean and tight. If the connection has become dirty, clean the contacting surfaces and lightly smear with petroleum jelly, No periodic lubrication is necessary, but when the engine is stripped down for a general overhaul the starting motor should be removed and given a thorough examination on the bench.

Performance data

(a) Light running on 12 volts: 50 amp (max) at 6,500-7,500 r.p.m.

(b) Lock torque: 4.5 lb.-ft. with 260 amp (max) at 7 terminal volts.

Servicing (a) Testing in position

Switch on the lamp(s) (or connect a moving coil 0-20 voltmeter between the battery terminals), operate the starter and watch for the following symptoms.

Electra starter motor

Cases are known where the sprocket for the starter motor has become detached from the starter motor shaft. It is imperative that the shaft fixing nut is securely tightened—this is best effected by using a short length of suitable chain attached to a bar (see fig. 68A) to secure the sprocket whilst the sprocket nut is tightened.

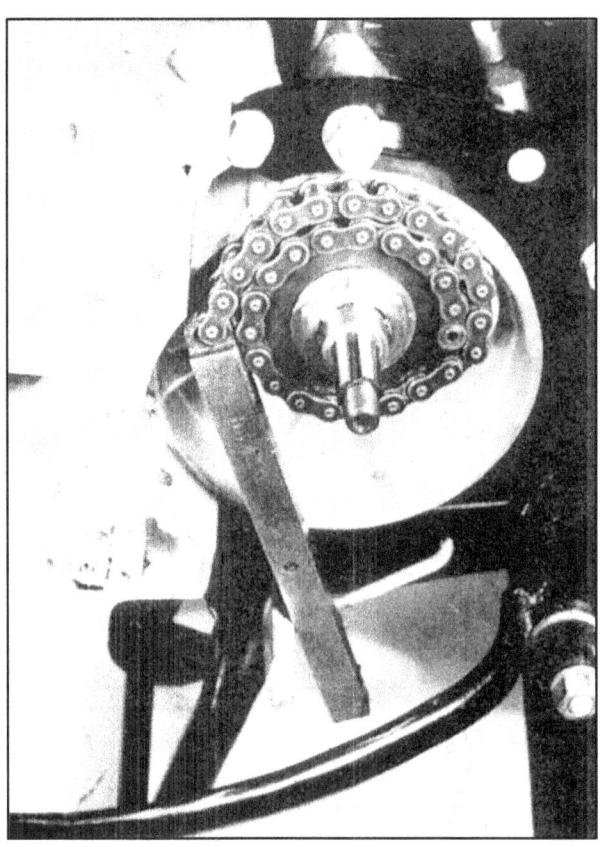

FIG. 68A

Chain Bar Tool

ELECTRA
DIAGRAM OF ELECTRICAL WIRING

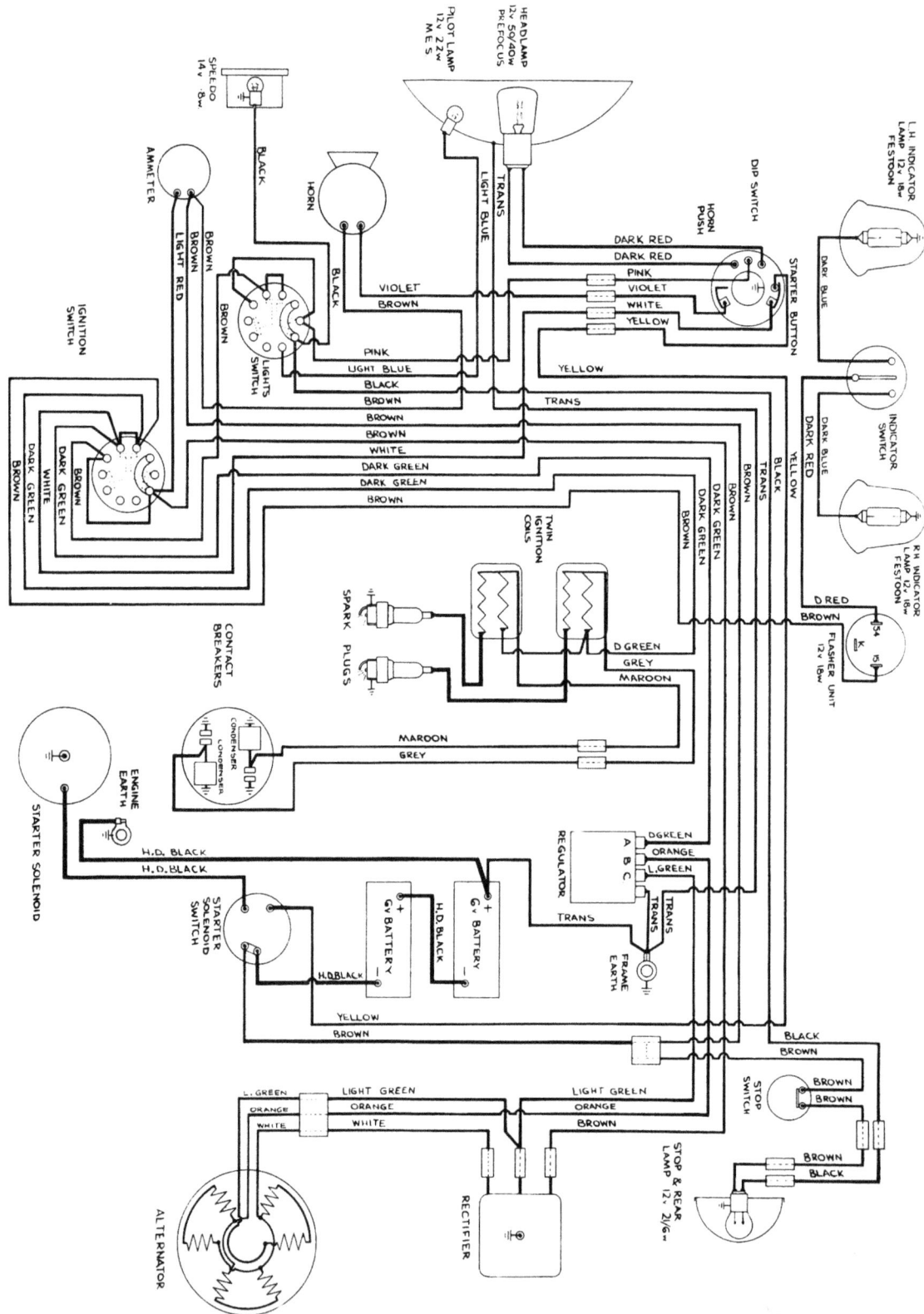

Fig. 69

JUBILEE AND NAVIGATOR

DIAGRAM OF ELECTRICAL WIRING

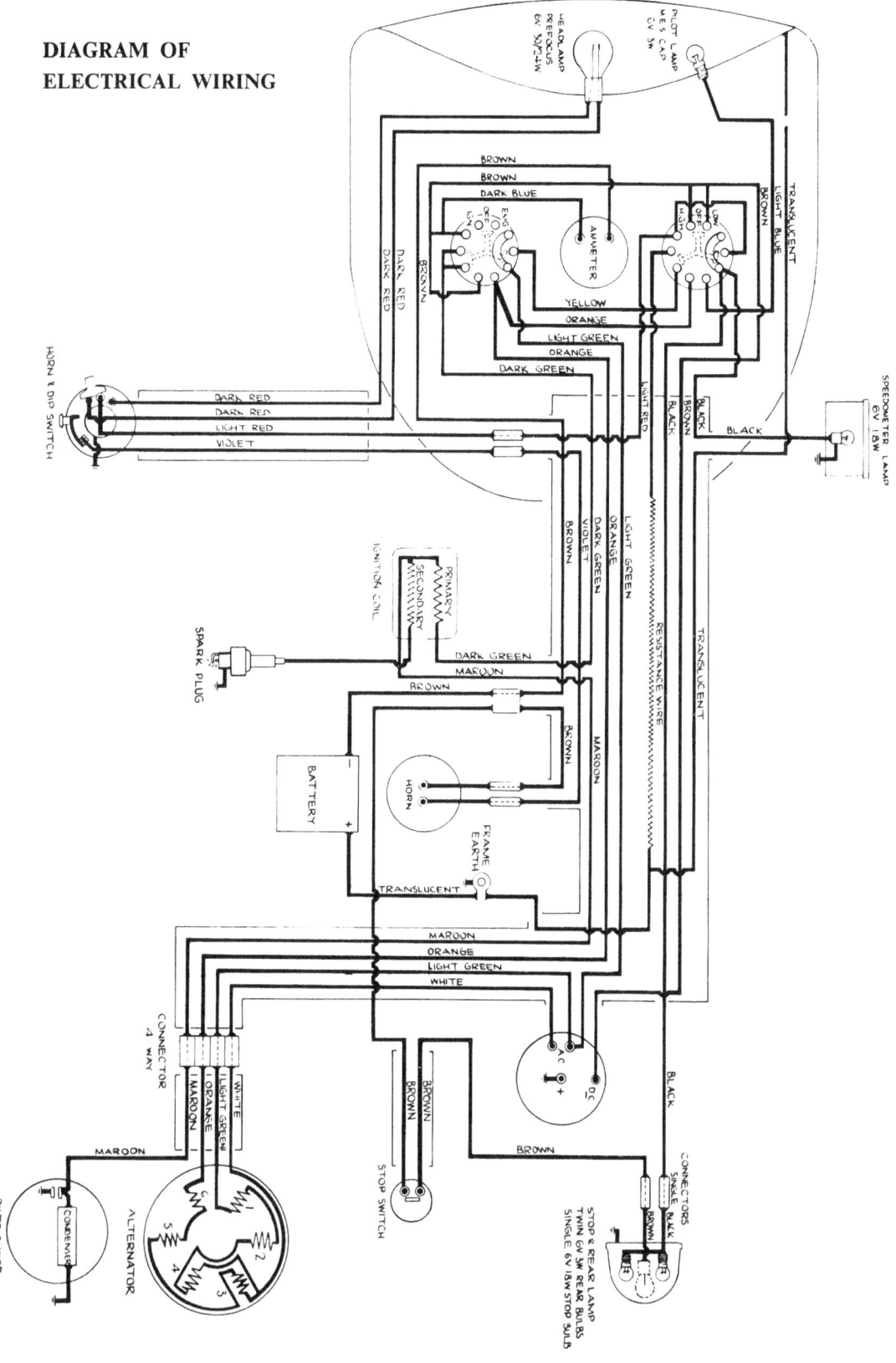

Fig. 70

ELECTRICAL WIRING DIAGRAM
for 650 Std. and de Luxe, 99 Std., de Luxe and S.S., 88 Std. and de Luxe

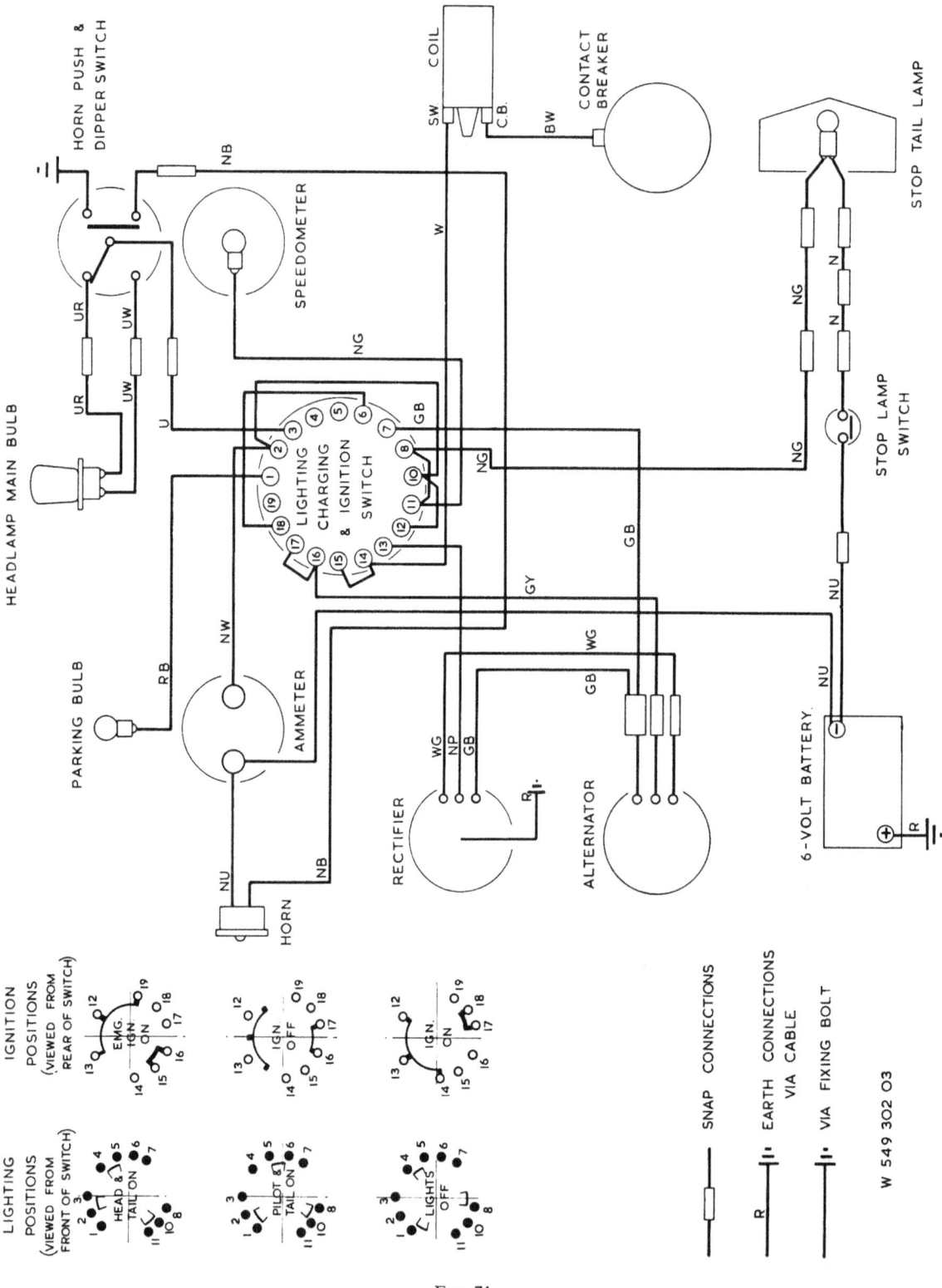

Fig. 71

ELECTRICAL WIRING DIAGRAM for models 500 S.S., 650 S.S. and 650 American

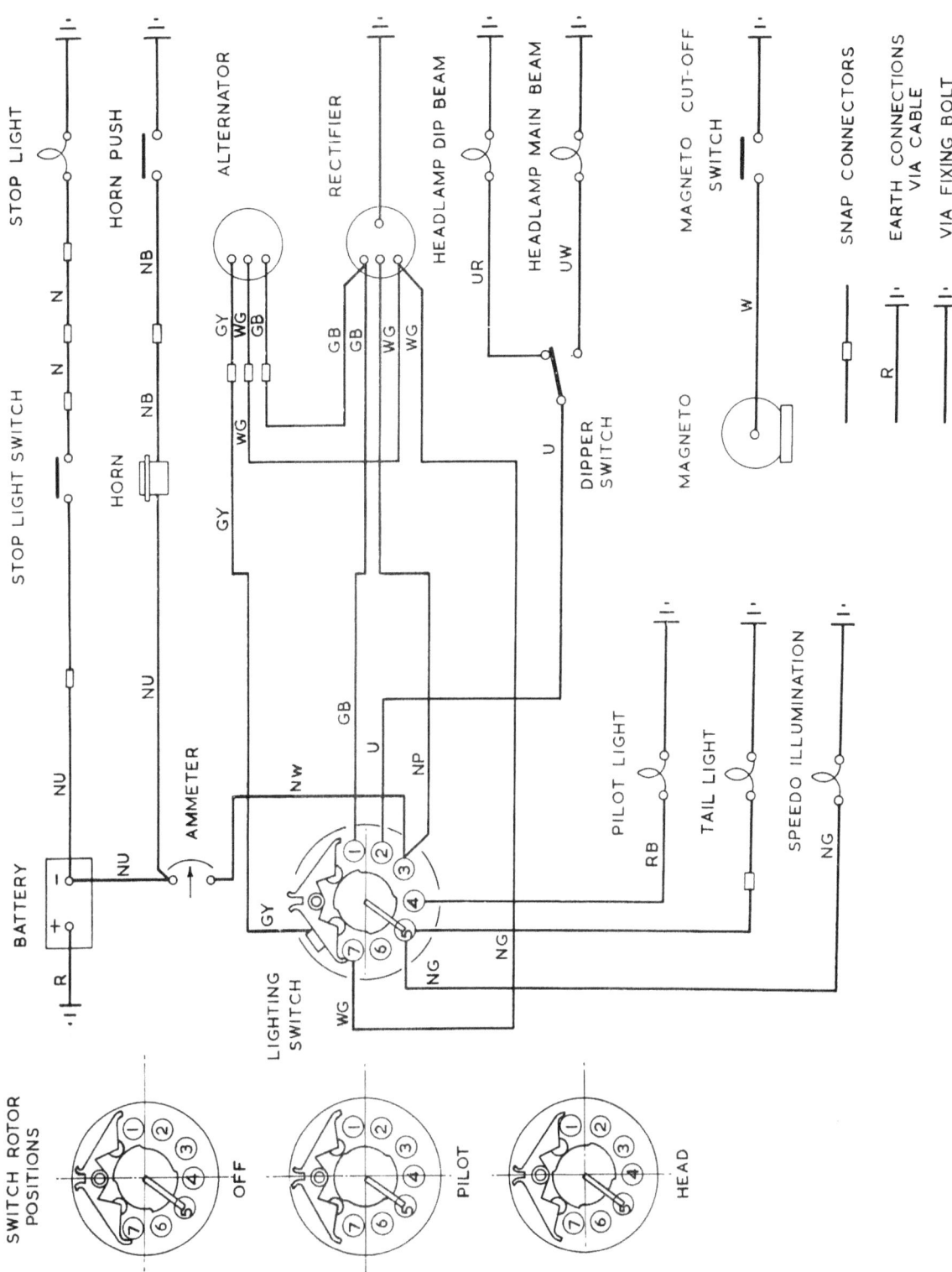

Fig. 72

ELECTRICAL WIRING DIAGRAM for Norton 88 S.S. and 500 cc. Twin
Magneto Ignition 12 volt 1964

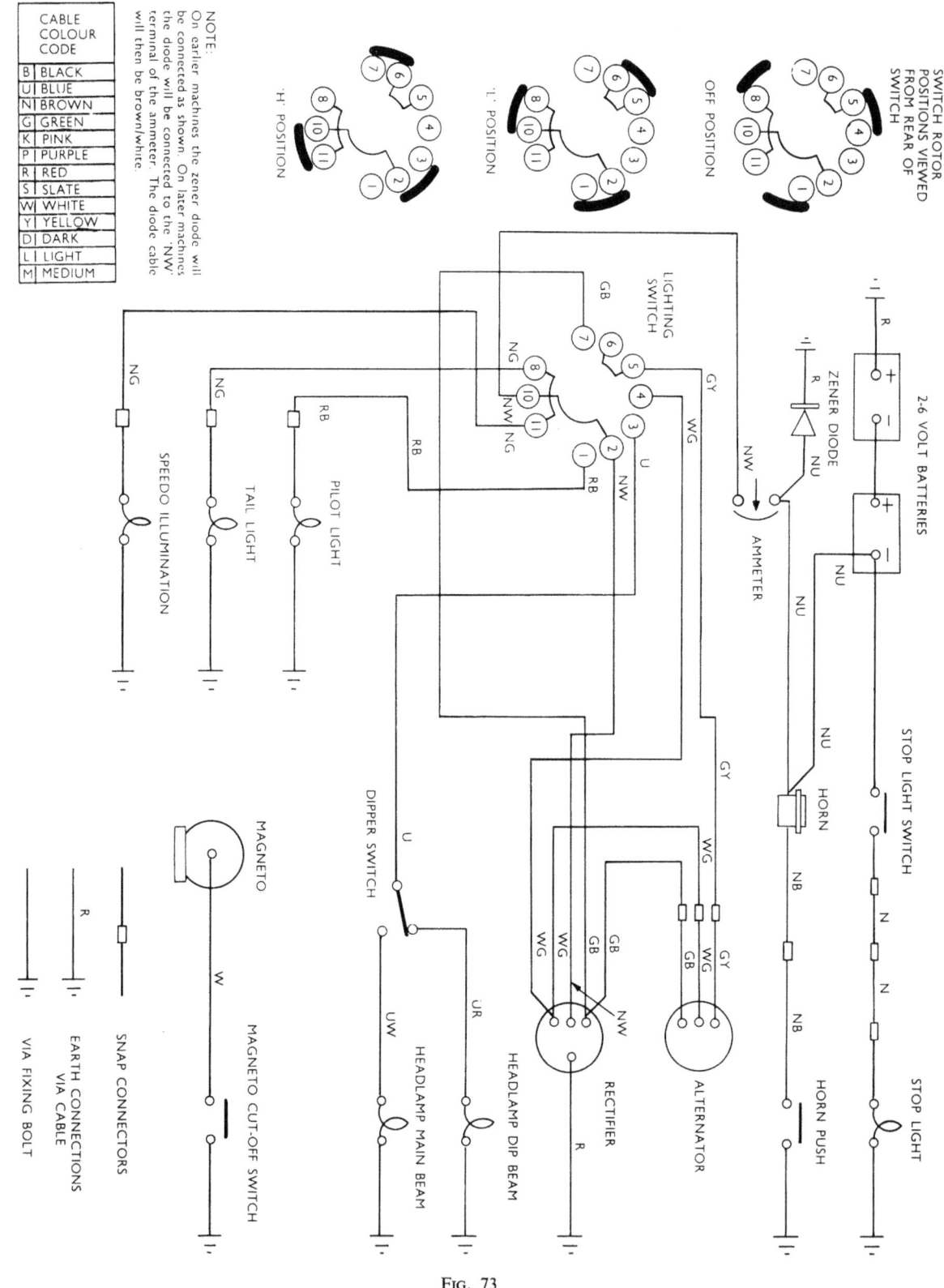

Fig. 73

ELECTRICAL WIRING DIAGRAM for Norton Atlas 750 cc. and 650 cc. Manxman (Export) 650 S.S. and 650 cc. Twin Magneto Ignition 12 volt 1964

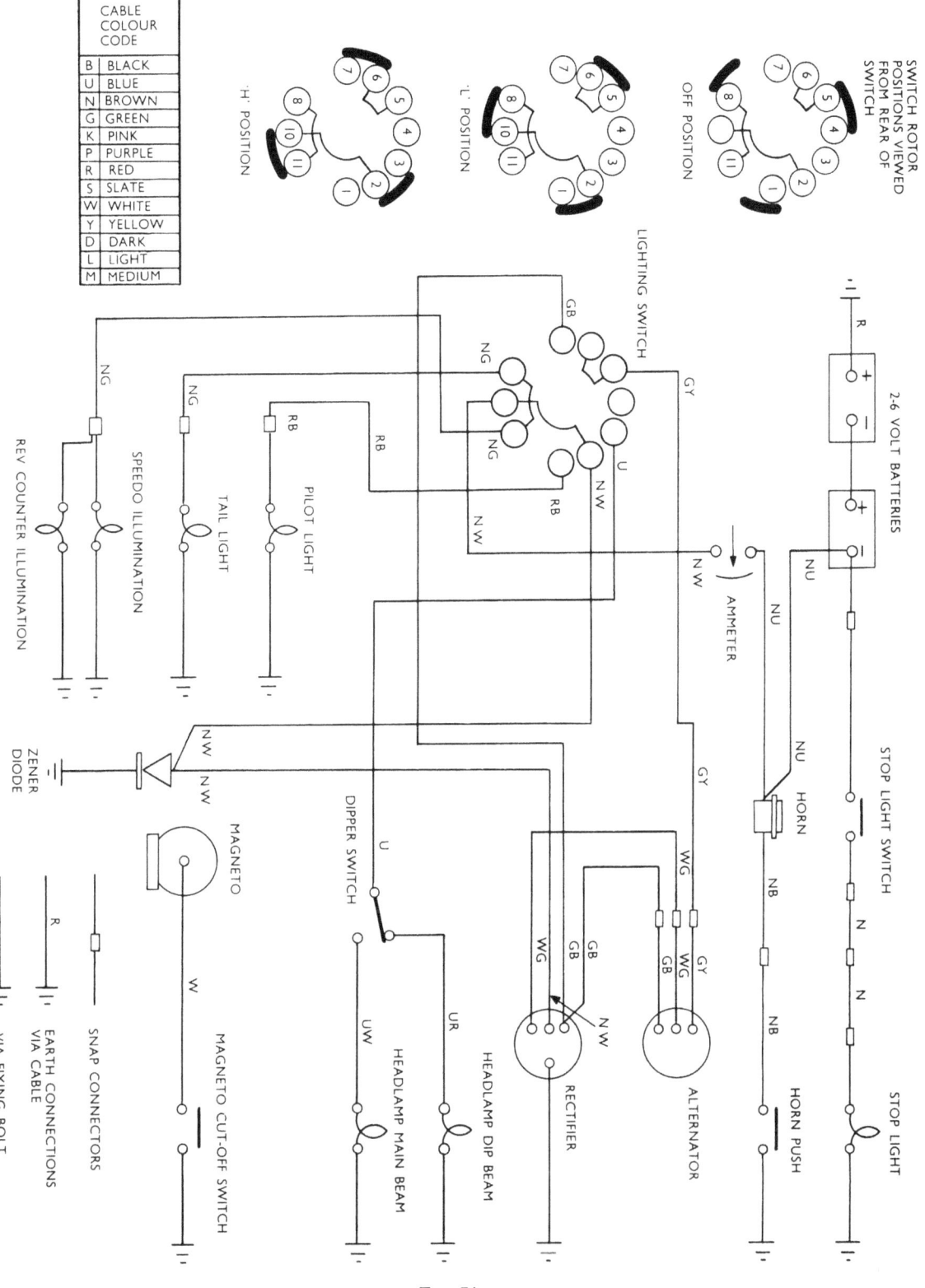

Fig. 74

Technical Data

	Lightweight Twins	Heavyweight Twins	
Cylinder barrel			
Finished bore size	2.5999″/2.5989″	2.6786″/2.6780″	2.8758″/2.8750″
Tappet bore size	.7505″/.7495″	1.1875″/1.1865″	1.1875″/1.1865
Tappet guide bore	.439″/.438″	Guides not used	Guides not used
Inlet valve			
Head diameter	1.172″	1.406″	1.500″
Stem diameter	.2795″/.2787″	.310″/.309″	.310″/.309″
Exhaust valve			
Head diameter	1.031″	1.312″	1.312″
Stem diameter	.2795″/.2787″	.310″/.309″	.310″/.309″
Valve guides			
(In. & Ex.) bore size	.2827″/.2820″	.3145″/.3135″	.3145″/.3135″
Piston pin			
O/dia.	.6868″/.6866″	.6868″/.6866″	.6868″/.6866″
Small end			
Bore of bush			
Bore of Con. Rod	.6878″/.6873″	.6878″/.6873″	.6878″/.6873″
Small end (no bush fitted)			
Piston ring end gap			
Compression	(.010″ 018″)	.014″/.009″	.014″/.009″
Oil scraper	.008 (.007″ 012″)	.014″/.009″	.014″/.009″
Rocker spindles			
O/Dia.	.499″/.498″	.499″/.4985″	.499″/.4985″
Rockers			
Bore dia.	.5003″/.4998″	.5003″/.4998″	.5003″/.4998″
Push rods			
Overall length inlet	3.400″	8.194″	8.194″
Overall length exhaust	3.400″	7.351″	7.351″
Valve springs			
Free length—inner	1.437″	1.531″	1.531″
Free length—outer	1.515″	1.700″	1.700″
Crankshaft			
Journal dia. D.S.	1.1815″/1.1812″	1.1815″/1.1812″	1.1812″/1.1812″
Journal dia. T.S.	1.1812″/1.1807″	1.1812″/1.1807″	1.1812″/1.1807″
Journal dia big end	1.5005″/1.5000″	1.7505″/1.7500″	1.7500″/1.7500″
Camshaft			
Bearing Dia.	.9365″/.9360″	.874″/.8735″ .8735″/.873″	.874″/.8735″ .8735″/.873″
Bore of bushes	.9383″/.9378″	.875″/.8745″	.875″/.8745″
Main bearings			
Driving side	Hoffmann— L.4621 (V3) 30 × 72 × 19mm	R33OL— (3 DOT) 30 × 72 × 19	R33OL— (3 DOT) 30 × 72 × 19mm
Timing side	Hoffman— N.6866 (V2) 30 × 72 × 19mm	MJ30— 30 × 72 × 19	MJ30— 30 × 72 × 19mm

Technical Data

GEAR BOX (HEAVYWEIGHT MODELS)

Mainshaft diameter	(Clutch End)	.8105″	.8095″
Mainshaft diameter	(Kickstart End)	.6248″	.6244″
Mainshaft Bearing	SKF-RLS5	$\tfrac{5}{8}″ \times 1\tfrac{9}{16}″ \times \tfrac{7}{16}″$	
Layshaft Bearing	SKF-6203	17 m/m × 40 m/m × 12 m/m	
Layshaft diameter	(Clutch End)	.6692″	.6687″
Layshaft diameter	(Kickstart End)	.6855″	.6845″
Sleeve gear bearing	situ (O/D)	1.2500″	1.2495″
Sleeve gear bush	(O/D)	.906″	.9055″
Sleeve gear bush—reamed in situ		.81325″	.81200″
Layshaft Bush—bare diameter		.6875″	.6865″

WHEELS

Front, left side bearing	(Hoffman 177)	17 m/m × 40 m/m × 12 m/m
Front, right side bearing	(Hoffman 117DR)	17 m/m × 40 m/m × 16 m/m
Rear, left side bearing	(Hoffman 117DR)	17 m/m × 40 m/m × 16 m/m
Rear, right side bearing	(Hoffman 117)	17 m/m × 40 m/m × 12 m/m

GEAR BOX DATA LIGHTWEIGHT TWINS (AFTER 106838)

Mainshaft, diameter, Clutch End	.7495″	.7490″
Mainshaft, diameter, Kickstarter End	.6248″	.6244″
Layshaft, diameter, Clutch End	.6248″	.6244″
Layshaft, diameter, Kickstarter End	.6235″	.6230″
Sleeve Gear, outside diameter	1.1807″	1.1802″ bearing situ
Sleeve Gear Bush, internal diameter (in situ)	.7515″	.7505″

Sleeve Gear Ball Bearing
 RMLJ 30
 Hoffman 130   62 m/m × 30 m/m × 16 m/m
 SKF 6206

Mainshaft ball bearing RLS 5 $1\tfrac{9}{16}″$ o/d × $\tfrac{5}{8}″$ bore × $\tfrac{9}{16}″$

Layshaft Bush, internal diameter (in situ)	.6263″	.6258″
Kickstart shaft bush (in situ)	.6258″	.6245″
Cam spindle bush (in situ)	.6263″	.6258″

	048147	Sleeve Gear, with bush	30 teeth
	048146	Gear, third, on mainshaft	27 teeth
	048145	Gear, second, on mainshaft	23 teeth
	048144	Gear, first, on mainshaft	17 teeth
	048261	Gear, fixed, on layshaft	21 teeth
	048145	Gear, third, on layshaft	23 teeth
	048146	Gear, second, on layshaft	27 teeth
048154		Gear, first, on layshaft, bushed	32 teeth

Technical Data

	Jubilee	Navigator	Electra	Heavyweight twins
Ignition timing				
Full advance....	32 degs	24 degs	30 degs	32 degs
Rocker clearance (cold)				
Inlet	0.004"	0.004"	0.006"	0.006"
Exhaust	0.006"	0.066"	0.008"	0.008"
Contact gap				
Full separation	0.012"	0.012"	0.012/0.015"	0.012/0.015"
Spark plug gap	0.020/0.022"	0.020/0.022"	0.020/0.022"	0.020/0.022"
Engine sprocket				**G15CS**
Normal	22 teeth	22 teeth	22 teeth	23 teeth 21 teeth

Chain sizes

Front	$\tfrac{3}{8}''$ duplex 66 pitches		$\tfrac{1}{2}'' \times .305 \times 75$ rollers
Rear	$\tfrac{1}{2}'' \times .305'' \times 121$ rollers	$\tfrac{1}{2}'' \times .305'' \times 121$ rollers	$\tfrac{5}{8}'' \times \tfrac{1}{4}'' \times 97$ rollers
Rear—G15 CS	$\tfrac{3}{8}'' \times \tfrac{5}{8}'' \times 97$ links		

Gear ratios

	Jubilee	Navigator	Electra
Top	6.76	5.72	4.53
Third	8.23	6.98	5.52
Second	11.34	9.62	7.57
First	18.18	15.4	11.6

Gear ratios G15 CS

Top	4.96
Third	6.03
Second	8.40
First	12.65

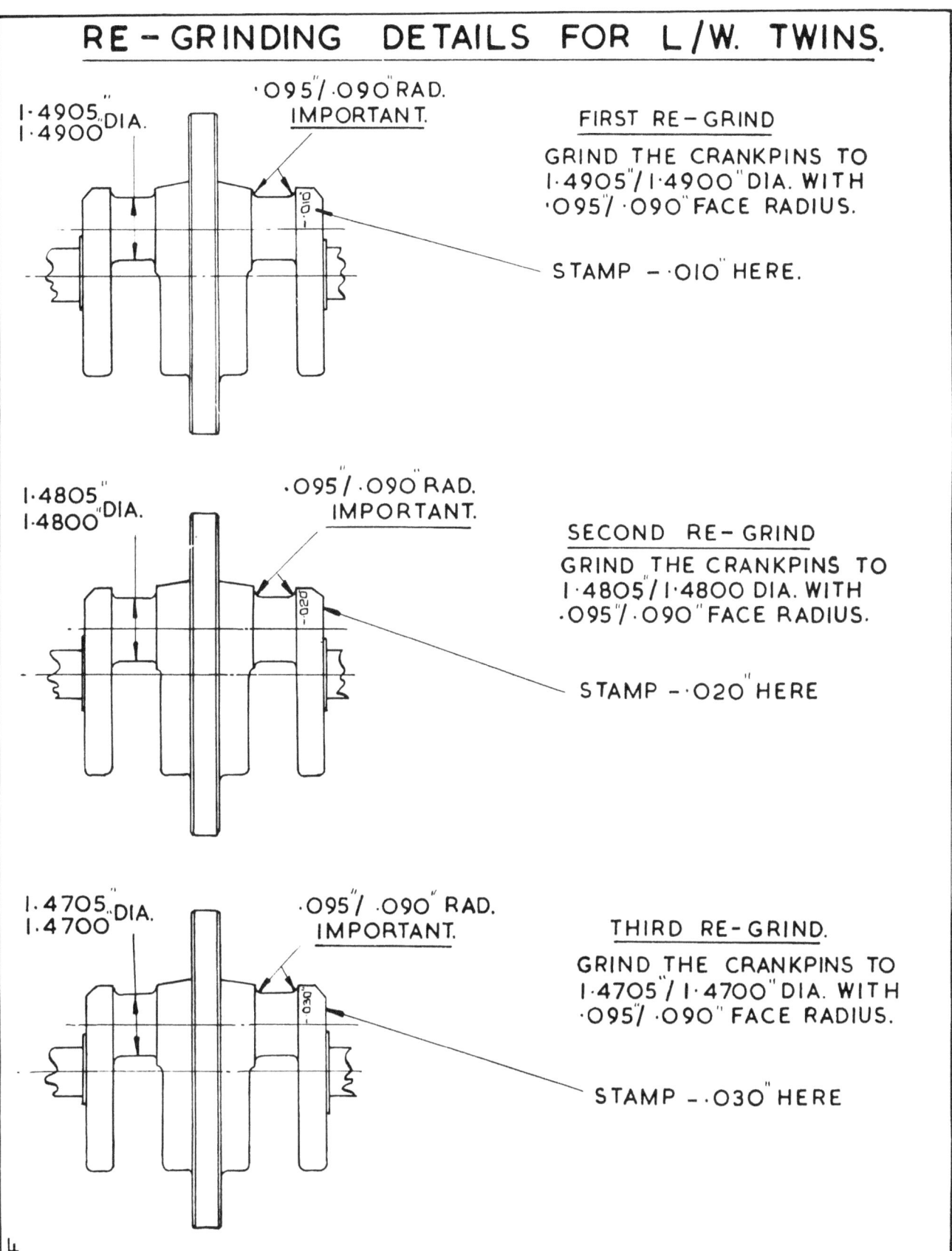

RE-GRINDING DETAILS FOR 500 TWINS

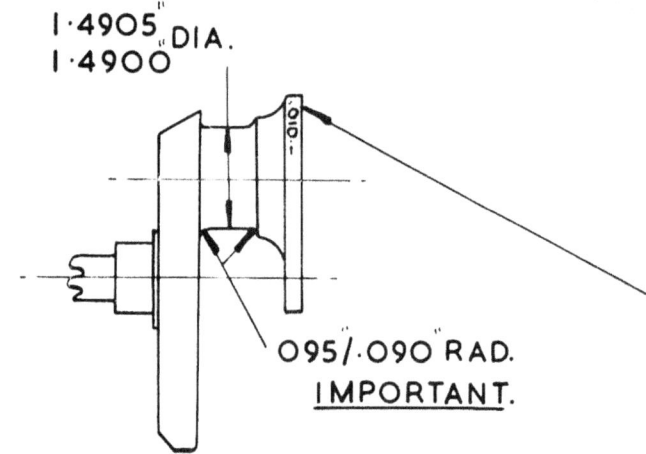

FIRST RE-GRIND.
GRIND THE CRANKPINS TO 1·4905"/1·4900" DIA. WITH ·095"/·090" FACE RADIUS.

STAMP —·010" HERE.

·095"/·090" RAD. IMPORTANT.

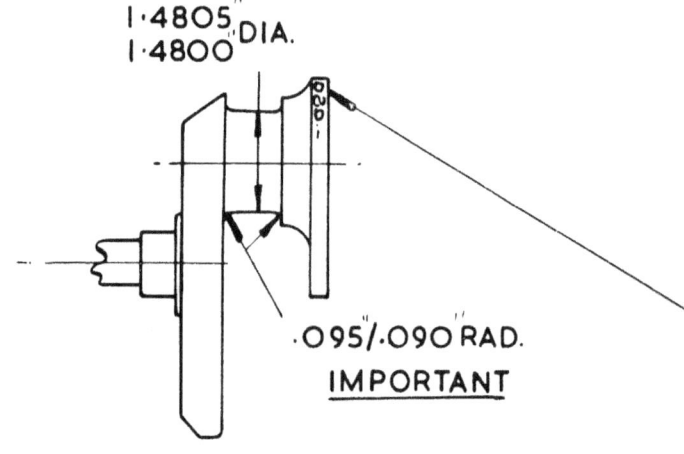

SECOND RE-GRIND.
GRIND THE CRANKPINS TO 1·4805"/1·4800" DIA. WITH ·095"/·090" FACE RADIUS.

STAMP —·020" HERE.

·095"/·090" RAD. IMPORTANT

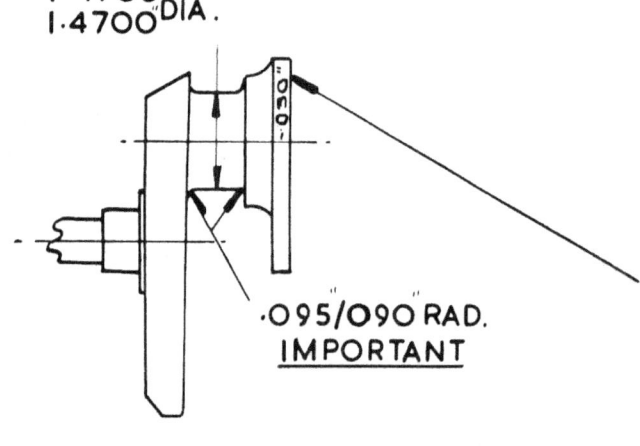

THIRD RE-GRIND.
GRIND THE CRANKPINS TO 1·4705"/1·4700" DIA. WITH ·095"/·090" FACE RADIUS.

STAMP —·030" HERE.

·095"/·090" RAD. IMPORTANT

RE-GRINDING DETAILS FOR 650 & 750 TWINS

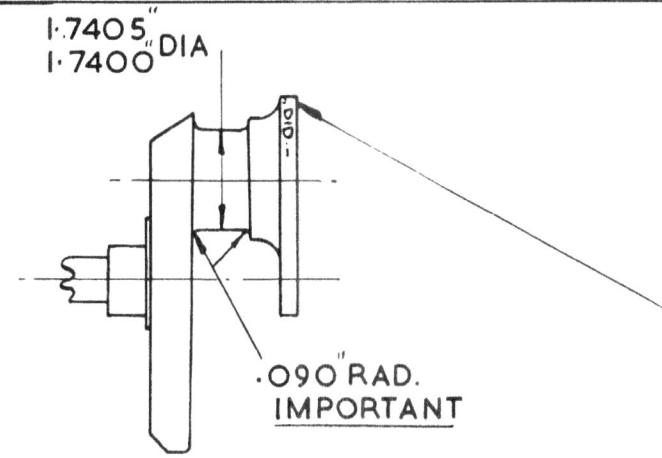

FIRST RE-GRIND

GRIND THE CRANKPIN TO 1·7405"/1·7400" DIA. WITH ·090" FACE RADIUS.

STAMP -·010" HERE.

·090" RAD. IMPORTANT

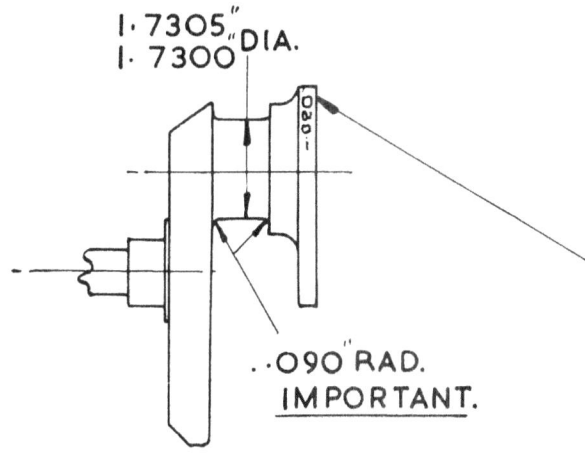

SECOND RE-GRIND

GRIND THE CRANKPIN TO 1·7305"/1·7300" DIA. WITH ·090" FACE RADIUS.

STAMP -·020" HERE.

·090" RAD. IMPORTANT.

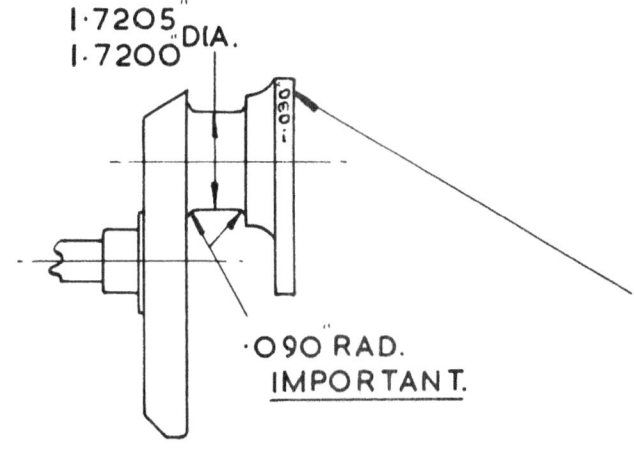

THIRD RE-GRIND

GRIND THE CRANKPIN TO 1·7205"/1·7200" DIA WITH ·090" FACE RADIUS.

STAMP -·030" HERE.

·090" RAD. IMPORTANT.

NOTES

COMMANDO WORKSHOP MANUAL

1968-1970 (Introduced 1967)
Commando MK1 (First production machine February 1968)
Fastback (Introduced March 1969)
S Type (Introduced March 1969)
R Type (Introduced March 1969)
Workshop Manual 06-3062

NORTON VILLIERS LIMITED
NORTON MATCHLESS DIVISION
LONDON S.E. 18.

Index

	Page
Alternator	46
Battery, Lucas	50
Brake adjustment, front	42
Brake adjustment, rear	43
Brakes, dismantling and assembly	43
Brake drum, removal	40
Carburetter service	45
Chain adjustment	32
Chain, primary adjustment	32
Chain, rear adjustment	32
Clutch	30
Clutch cable adjustment	31
Contact breaker	27, 48
Connecting rods, removal	22
Connecting rods, assembling	22
Crankcase bearings	24
Crankcase release valve	7
Crankcase separation	19
Crankshaft	22
Cylinder, removal	11
Cylinder, refitting	13
Cylinder barrel, removal	12
Cylinder head, removal	11
Cylinder head, refitting	14
Decarbonising	11
Electrical service, Lucas	45
Electrical wiring diagrams	47, 51
Engine Diagram	9
Engine, dismantling	19
Engine, assembly	24
Engine, service	11
Engine, removal	17
Frame	36
Forks, dismantling	34
Forks, front, assembling	36
Gearbox	28
Hubs, dismantling and assembling	41-42

	Page
Ignition timing	26
Kickstarter, dismantling	30
Lubrication	6, 7 & 8
Oil pressure	8
Oil pump	7
Oil seal, crankcase, driving side	24
Oil seal, pump	8
Oil seal, pump, checking	22
Oil seal, replacement	8
Oil seal, timing cover	8, 22
Pistons, fitting	13
Pistons, removal and fitting	13
Piston rings	13
Piston rings, fitting	13
Pressure relief valve	7
Rectifier	49
Regrinding details	23
Rocker adjustment, push rod clearance	14
Rocker ball end	13
Rockers, removal	12
Roller bearings	20
Shaft, intermediate	22
Steering lock	36
Sump filter	24
Swinging arm	39
Tappets	12
Technical data	5
Timing, adjustment	27
Valves	10, 11
Valves, removal	11
Valves, refitting	12
Valve grinding	11, 23
Valve guides, removal and refitting	12
Wheel balancing	42
Wheel, front, removal and refitting	40
Wheel, rear, removal	40
Zener diode charge control	48

INTRODUCTION

THIS manual has been compiled as a practical guide to enable owners who are competent to undertake major overhauls and dealers' service staff completely to service Norton Commando models. Technical data is included to enable the operator to check parts for wear against normal dimensions.

Where instruments for measuring engine and gearbox parts are available, reference to the technical data should be made to determine if replacement is necessary, or otherwise.

Torque wrenches should be used during assembly, particularly on stressed parts such as connecting rod bolts. A table of torque wrench approved settings is included in technical data.

Routine maintenance and normal running adjustments are detailed in the Riders' Handbook issued with each new Norton Commando motorcycle.

Technical Data

Engine Number	Stamped on crankcase
Gearbox Number	Stamped on gearcase
Frame Number	Stamped on left side head lug
Cylinder bore (finished size)	2.8750"/2.8758" (73.025mm/73.045mm)
Stroke	3.503" (89mm)
Capacity	45.5 cu. in. (745cc)
Compression ratio	8.9 to 1
Ignition timing	28° B.T.D.C. (full advance)
Spark plug	N6Y
Spark plug gap	.023"-.028"
Contact breaker gap	.014"/.016"
Tappet clearance (cold) inlet	.006"
Tappet clearance (cold) exhaust	.008"
Valve spring free length (inner)	1.531"
Valve spring free length (outer)	1.700"
Piston ring gap (compression ring)	.013"
Push rod length assembled (inlet)	8.130"/8.166"
Push rod length assembled (exh'st)	7.285"/7.321"
Valve length (head to stem) Inlet	4.069"
Valve stem diameter (inlet)	.3095"/.3105"
Valve length (head to stem) exhaust	4.020"
Valve stem diameter (exhaust)	.3095"/.3105"
Rocker shaft diameter	.4985"/.4998"
Wrist pin diameter	.6868"/.6866"
Crankshaft journal diameter (drive side)	1.1815"/1.1812"
Crankshaft journal diameter (timing side)	1.1807"/1.1812"
Crankshaft journal diameter (con rod)	1.7505"/1.7500"
Camshaft bearing diameter (drive side)	.874"/.8735"
Camshaft bearing diameter (timing side)	.8735"/.8730"
Camshaft bush (bore size)	.875"/.8745"
Main roller bearing (drive side) single dot	30mm × 72mm × 19mm
Main ball single dot bearing (timing tide)	30mm × 72mm × 19mm
Intermediate shaft diameter	.5615"/.5610"
Intermediate gear (bush diameter)	.5627"/.5620"

GEARBOX

Mainshaft diameter (clutch end)	.8105"/.8095"
Mainshaft diameter (kickstart end)	.6248"/.6244"
Mainshaft ball bearing	5/8" × 1 9/16" × 7/16"
Layshaft bearing	17mm × 40mm × 12mm
Layshaft diameter (clutch end)	.6692"/.6687"
Layshaft diameter (kickstart end)	.6855"/.6845"
Sleeve gear bush (OD)	.906"/.9053"
Sleeve gear bush (reamed *in situ*)	.81325"/.81200"
Layshaft bush (bore diameter)	.6875"/.6865"
Clutch bearing	35mm × 62mm × 14mm

SPROCKETS

Engine	26 teeth
Clutch	57 teeth
Final drive (gearbox)	21 teeth or 19 teeth
Rear wheel	42 teeth

CHAIN SIZES

Front chain endless (triplex)	3/8" × .225" (92 pitches)
Rear chain (21 teeth sprocket)	5/8" × .380" (99 pitches)
Camshaft chain	3/8" × .225" (38 pitches)
Ignition chain	3/8" × .155" (42 rollers)
Rear chain (19 teeth sprocket)	5/8" × .380" (98 pitches)

CARBURETTER SETTINGS

Choke diameter	1.180"
Main jet size	220
Pilot jet size	25
Needle jet size	.106"
Throttle slide	3
Needle location	central notch

WHEEL BEARINGS

Left side front bearing	17mm × 40mm × 12mm
Right side front bearing	17mm × 40mm × 16mm
Left side rear bearing	17mm × 40mm × 16mm
Right side rear bearing	17mm × 40mm × 12mm

TORQUE WRENCH SETTINGS

Cylinder head bolts and nuts 3/8"	360 inch lbs.
Cylinder head bolts 5/16" (2)	240 inch lbs.
All cylinder base nuts	240 inch lbs.
Con rod	300 inch lbs.
Rocker shaft cover plate bolt	100 inch lbs.
Gearbox inner cover nuts	140 inch lbs.
Cam chain tensioner nuts	180 inch lbs.
Oil pump stud nuts	180 inch lbs.
Banjo bolts	180 inch lbs.
Engine mounting bolts	300 inch lbs.
Alternator studs	120 inch lbs.

GEAR RATIOS

(21 teeth gearbox sprocket)	4.38 5.35 7.45 11.2
(19 teeth gearbox sprocket)	4.84 5.9 8.25 12.4

INTERNAL RATIOS   1:1 1.22:1 1.7:1 2.56:1

CAPACITIES

Gas tank	3.25 Imperial gallons (3.9 U.S. gallons) (14.7 litres)
Oil tank	5 Imperial pints (6 U.S. pints) (2.8 litres)
Gearbox	1 Imperial pint (1.2 U.S. pints) (.57 litre)
Primary chaincase	200 c.c (7 fluid ozs.)
Front forks	150 c.c (each leg)

Recommended Lubricants

Efficient lubrication is of vital importance and it is false economy to use cheap grades of oil. When buying oils or grease it is advisable to specify the brand as well as the grade and, as an additional precaution, to buy from sealed containers.

ENGINE

Ambient temperature above 50°F. (10°C.) use S.A.E. 20/50 or straight S.A.E. 50.
Ambient temperature above 32°F. (0°C.) use S.A.E. 20/50 or straight S.A.E. 30.
Ambient temperature below 32°F. (0°C.) use S.A.E. 10/30 or straight S.A.E. 20.
The following brands are recommended:

Mobiloil	Energol	Shell
Castrol	Essolube	Regent Advanced Havoline

GEARBOX

Ambient temperature above 32°F. (0°C.) S.A.E. 50 or GX 90 Mobilube.
Ambient temperature below 32°F. (0°C.) S.A.E. 30.

WHEEL HUB AND FRAME PARTS

Mobilgrease MP	Energrease C3	Shell Retinax A or C.D.
Castrolease LM	Regent Marfax Multipurpose	ESSO Multipurpose

TELEDRAULIC FRONT FORKS

Mobiloil Arctic (S.A.E. 20)	Energol (S.A.E. 20)	Shell X-100 Motor Oil 20/20W (S.A.E. 20)
Castrolite (S.A.E. 10W-30)	Essolube 20 (S.A.E. 20)	Regent S.A.E. 20

REAR CHAINS

Mobilgrease MP	Energrease A.O.	Regent Marfax Multipurpose
Esso Fluid Grease	Castrolease Grease Graphited	Shell Retinax A or C.D.

Lubrication System

Lubrication system

Oil flows by gravity from the oil tank, assisted by suction from the oil feed pump, via a coarse mesh oil filter in the oil feed pipe—at the oil tank end—to the oil pump.

Oil after passing through the feed pump, is forced under pressure to the engine, through a drilling in the timing cover to the crankshaft. A by-pass from the main oil feed conveys oil to the top part of the engine to lubricate moving parts in the cylinder head.

Oil from the cylinder head, drains by gravity, to the crankcase—via an oil passage drilled in the cylinder barrel—to a pre-determined oil level in the timing chest, to lubricate the two chains. The overspill drains to the sump portion of the crankcase.

Oil accumulated in the sump is returned to the oil tank—after passing through the filter contained in the sump drain plug—under the influence of the oil return pump.

Oil pressure relief valve

The pressure relief—or blow off—valve is mounted in the timing cover, adjacent to the cylinder head oil feed union. The valve consists of a spring loaded steel sleeve which is pre-set at the factory with packing discs to enable the valve to lift at 45/55 lbs. per square inch. Oil escaping from the valve is diverted back to the oil feed side of the pump. This valve does not require routine attention.

Crankcase release valve

The release valve is housed in the drive side crankcase, actuated by the camshaft. The valve is timed and ported to release positive pressure from the crankcase caused by piston displacement. The valve consists of the following parts:—

  (1) Stationary plate (below the camshaft bush).
  (2) Rotary plate (actuated by the camshaft).
  (3) Spring to keep the rotary plate in contact with the stationary plate.

The oil pump

The gear type pump dismantled is shown in Figure 1. The oil return side of the pump can be identified by the wider gears which have twice the pumping capacity of the oil feed side of the pump, designed to keep the sump free from excess oil. Providing clean oil is continually circulating—when the engine is running—the pump cannot become deranged.

Checking the oil pump

To remove the oil pump refer to paragraph 'Dismantling the engine'. When rotating the oil pump by hand, the gears should rotate freely. A tendency to partially jam indicates the presence of foreign matter in the gear teeth. To remedy, dismantle the pump for cleaning as described elsewhere. Check the pump for end float—by pulling and pushing on

FIG. 1 *The Oil Pump*

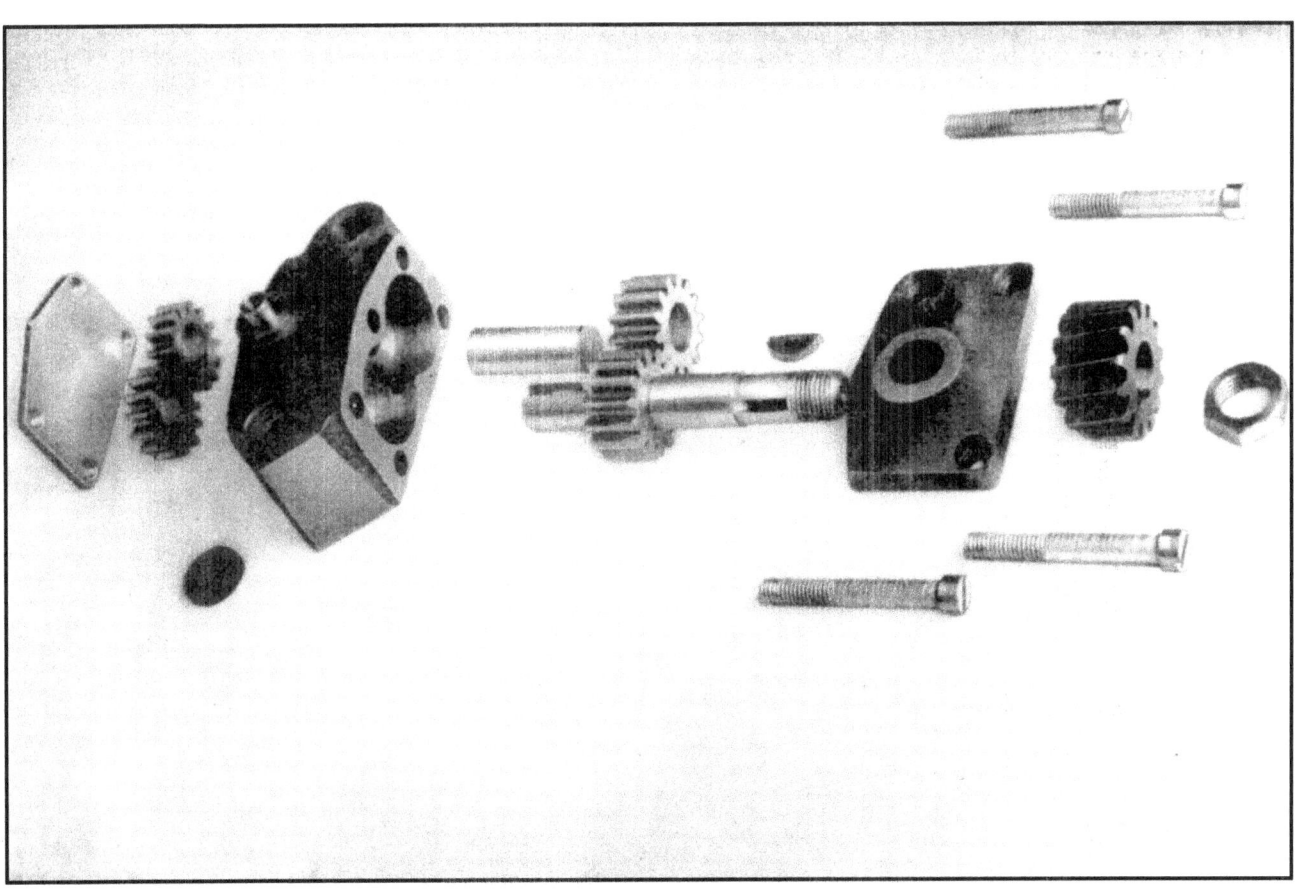

the drive spindle (end float should be NIL) check the four pump plate screws for security. When end float is manifest to any noticeable extent, the efficiency of the pump will be adversely affected and the unit should be returned to the dealer for service.

Before refitting the pump, check the face of the pump body, where it abuts against the crankcase, by using a straight edge on this face across the two stud holes. A slight bow in the pump body face will create an air leak, which will adversely affect the pick up of oil from the sump. To rectify, the pump body should be rubbed down on a surface plate—until it is perfectly flat—then ensure that the pump interior is scrupulously clean and free from abrasive.

Dismantling the oil pump

An examination of the pump will show that the two end plates are either flush, or slightly below the pump body. It follows that if one—or both plates are proud of the pump body after assembly—an air tight joint between the pump and the crankcase cannot be made.

With the worm drive removed (this is not essential)
Remove four pump body screws.
Remove the brass end plate.
Remove the iron plate with shaft and drive key—the drive pinion is usually a close fit on the shaft—a light tap with a brass drift will dislodge the pinion.
Remove the idler shaft from feed side.
Remove the return idler pinion.
Remove the two drive pinions.

Assemble the pump in reverse sequence and note the small radius on the oil return gear should face the inside of the pump body.

The oil pump seal

The conical shaped oil seal (see Figure 1), made from oil and heat resisting material, is located on the oil pump body by a steel ferrule—which is a press fit. If the conical shaped seal is deformed, it should be discarded and a replacement used Part No. T.272, to prevent oil, under pressure, leaking between the seal and the concave face in the timing cover, thus curtailing the oil delivery to the crankshaft.

If the oil seal is normal, when the timing cover is in position, pressure on the seal should move the timing cover away from the crankcase, making a gap approximately .010". If this pressure does not exist, fit a new seal, alternatively use shim washers—between the seal and the body—to obtain the desired pressure.

Timing cover oil seal

Oil under pressure from the oil feed pump, passes through the steel ferrule in the pump body—which locates the conical oil seal—through a drilled oil passage in the timing cover entering a cavity which houses the oil seal encircling the plain portion of the timing side crankshaft. The slight restriction caused by the close fitting connecting rod bearings, builds up pressure in the cavity, making the oil seal more effective. If, after considerable mileage, the seal is worn, or deformed—during the process of refitting the timing cover—the seal should be replaced (Part No. 048023).

To replace the oil seal

Take out the circlip—prise out the seal; gently heat the cover, press home the new seal with the METAL BACKING OUTWARDS. Refit the circlip. Apply a small amount of clean oil on the plain portion of the crankshaft to facilitate entry.

Checking oil pressure

A pressure gauge with a scale reading of 0 to 100 lbs. per square inch, can be attached to the timing cover at the point where the union for the cylinder head oil feed pipe is attached. The recorded pressure should be between 45 to 55 lbs. per square inch, when the oil is at normal running temperature.

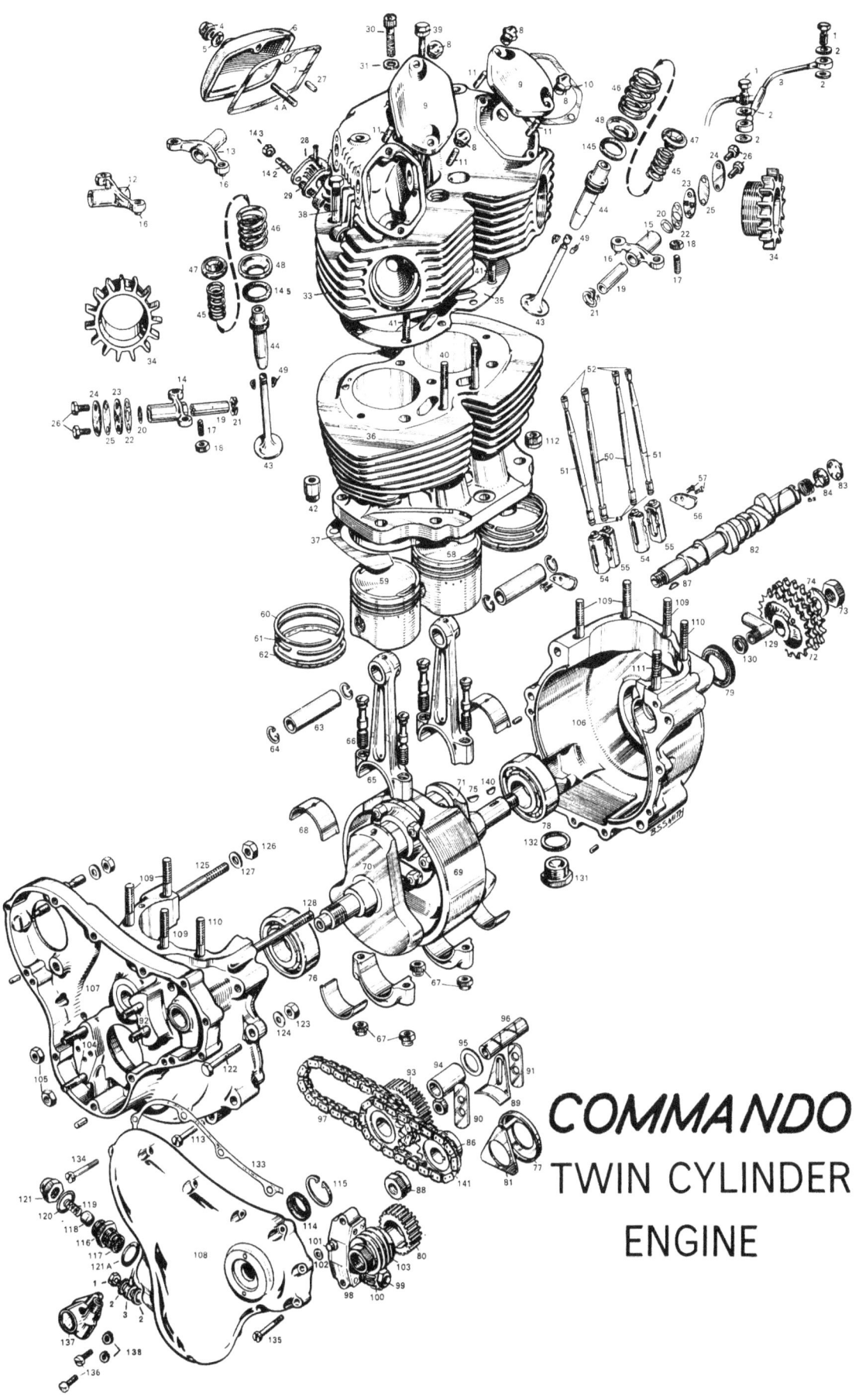

COMMANDO
TWIN CYLINDER ENGINE

No.	Description	No.	Description
1	Banjo bolt for oil feed pipe.	74	Washer for rotor.
2	Washer for banjo bolt.	75	Key for engine sprocket.
3	Rocker feed pipe assembly.	76	Mainshaft bearing, timing side.
4	Domed nut for rear cap.	77	Sealing washer, timing side bearing.
4A	Stud for rear cap.	78	Mainshaft roller bearing, driving side.
5	Washer for domed nut.	79	Driving side shaft oil seal.
6	Rocker box cap (rear).	80	Half time pinion.
7	Sealing washer for rear cap.	81	Backing plate for pinion.
8	Nut for rocker box front cap stud.	82	Camshaft.
9	Rocker box cap (front).	83	Stationary plate, camshaft breather.
10	Sealing washer for front cap.	84	Rotary plate, timing breather.
11	Stud for front cap.	85	Spring for breather.
12	Rocker inlet, right hand.	86	Camshaft sprocket.
13	Rocker inlet, left hand.	87	Key for sprocket.
14	Rocker exhaust, right hand.	88	Nut for sprocket and rev.-counter drive.
15	Rocker exhaust, left hand.	89	Chain tensioner slipper.
16	Rocker ball end.	90	Plate for chain tensioner (thick).
17	Rocker adjuster.	91	Plate for chain tensioner (thin).
18	Nut for adjuster.	92	Stud for chain tensioner.
19	Rocker shaft.	93	Intermediate gear, with sprocket.
20	Thrust washer for shaft.	94	Bush for intermediate gear.
21	Spring washer for shaft.	95	Washer for intermediate gear.
22	Joint washer for shaft.	96	Spindle for intermediate gear.
23	Locking plate for shaft.	97	Driving chain for ignition.
24	Retaining plate for shaft.	98	Oil pump assembly.
25	Joint washer for plate.	99	Nut for oil pump spindle.
26	Bolt for shaft retaining plate.	100	Worm gear wheel (on pump).
27	Dowel for rocker box cap (rear).	101	Feed bush for pump.
28	Inlet manifold.	102	Sealing washer for feed bush.
29	Allen bolt manifold to head.	103	Pump driving worm (on mainshaft).
30	Allen bolt for head steady plate.	104	Stud, oil pump to crankcase.
31	Washer for bolt.	105	Nut for stud.
33	Cylinder head, with valve guides.	106	Crankcase, driving side only.
34	Finned locking nut for exhaust pipe.	107	Crankcase, timing side only.
35	Gasket cylinder head to barrel.	108	Timing cover (for rev.-counter fixing).
36	Cylinder barrel.	109	Crankcase cylinder base stud.
37	Washer, cylinder base to crankcase.	110	Crankcase cylinder base stud $\frac{5}{16}$" diameter.
38	Cylinder head bolt (long).	111	Crankcase cylinder base stud $\frac{3}{8}$" diameter.
39	Cylinder head bolt (short).	112	Nut, cylinder base stud $\frac{3}{8}$".
40	Stud, cylinder barrel to head.	113	Screw, timing to driving side crankcase sump.
41	Stud, cylinder head to barrel.	114	Mainshaft oil seal, in timing cover.
42	Nut, cylinder head to barrel stud.	115	Circlip, mainshaft oil seal.
43	Valve, exhaust.	116	Pressure release body (only).
44	Valve guide, inlet or exhaust.	117	Wire gauze complete.
45	Valve spring, inner.	118	Pressure release piston.
46	Valve spring, outer.	119	Pressure release spring.
47	Valve spring, top cap.	120	Pressure release union nut washer.
48	Valve spring, bottom collar.	121	Pressure release body nut.
49	Valve collet.	121A	Washer for pressure release union.
50	Push rod complete, inlet.	122	Crankcase bolt (short).
51	Push rod complete, exhaust.	123	Nut for bolt.
52	Push rod, top end.	124	Washer for bolt.
53	Push rod, bottom end.	125	Crankcase top stud (rear).
54	Tappet, right hand.	126	Nut for stud.
55	Tappet, left hand.	127	Washer for stud.
56	Tappet location plate.	128	Crankcase top stud (front).
57	Screw for location plate.	129	Elbow for crankcase breather pipe.
58	Piston complete, left hand.	130	Nut for crankcase breather elbow.
59	Piston complete, right hand.	131	Crankcase oil sump filter body.
60	Piston ring, compression, top, chrome.	132	C and A washer, filter body.
61	Piston ring, compression, bottom, plain.	133	Timing cover gasket.
62	Piston ring, scraper.	134	Timing cover screw (long).
63	Gudgeon pin.	135	Timing cover screw (short).
64	Circlip for gudgeon pin.	136	Fixing screw, revolution counter drive.
65	Connecting rod.	137	Gearbox revolution counter drive.
66	Big end cap bolt.	138	Washer for fixing screw.
67	Nut for cap bolt.	140	Key for alternator rotor.
68	Big end bearing shell, lower and upper.	141	Driving chain for camshaft.
69	Flywheel.	142	Stud, inlet manifold to carburetter.
70	Crankshaft, timing side.	143	Nut for stud.
71	Crankshaft, driving side.	144	Washer for stud.
72	Engine sprocket, 26 teeth.	145	Heat resisting washer.
73	Retaining nut for rotor.		

Engine Service

Models after Engine No. 131257 March 1969 onwards - with camshaft driven contact breaker points (see page 52)

Decarbonising the engine

There is no stipulated mileage when the engine should be decarbonised, the necessity to undertake this work is usually indicated by a gradual loss of power accompanied with an increase in petrol consumption. If the engine performance has not deteriorated, the petrol consumption is normal, no useful purpose is served by removing the cylinder head.

The only risk, by running the engine for prolonged intervals between decarbonising, is the possibility of exhaust valve burning. This is caused by separation of the additives—used in modern fuels—on combustion which builds up on the valve and becomes trapped between the valve and the valve seat in the cylinder head. Gas leakage past the valve when on its seat is responsible for the valve burning. Before removing the cylinder head check for derangement;

Rocker clearance.
Contact breaker gap.
Ignition timing.
Throttle cables for lost motion.
Try also the effect of two new spark plugs.

Removing the cylinder head

Have available the following equipment:—

(A) Decoke gasket set Part Number 060911.
(B) Socket wrench (ring spanner) for $\frac{3}{8}''$ Whitworth form.
(C) Socket wrench (ring spanner) for $\frac{5}{16}''$ Whitworth form.
(D) 'C' spanner for exhaust pipe finned nuts—Part Number SHU/29.
(E) Tubular box key $\frac{1}{4}''$ Whitworth form.
(F) Open end spanner $\frac{7}{16}''$ Whitworth form.
(G) Allen key size $\frac{3}{32}''$.
(H) Feeler gauge .006″ and .008″.

To remove cylinder head

1. Remove rider's seat by releasing the two captive knurled knobs—retained by a pin passing through the boss. Raise the seat to clear the two fixing brackets and draw backwards, clear of the machine.
2. Disconnect the two fuel pipes at the tank end.
3. Take out the two front gas tank fixing bolts, remove the rubber ring securing the rear end of the gas tank.
4. With care—to avoid damage—carefully lift and remove the tank clear of the machine.
5. Remove both spark plugs, right and left exhaust pipes, leaving the mufflers in position. Use the 'C' spanner to unscrew the finned nuts, slacken the muffler clip bolt securing the muffler to the exhaust pipe.
6. Remove the cylinder head oil feed pipe—two banjo pins—take care of the washers used.
7. Remove cylinder head torque bracket—three bolts passing through the bracket—three Allen screws securing plate to cylinder head.
8. Remove both rocker covers.
9. Remove four Allen screws fixing the two carburetter manifolds—take away both carburetters.
10. Remove five nuts below the cylinder head, five bolts on the top of the cylinder head. The cylinder head can now be separated from the cylinder barrel. If difficulty exists, a light blow with a soft-faced mallet, under the exhaust ports for the cylinder head, will cause the cylinder head to separate from the cylinder.
11. Lift the cylinder head—to clear the push rods—then it can be taken away from the engine.

Dismantling the cylinder head

With the cylinder head removed, it is preferable to remove all carbon formed on both valve heads also the sphere of the cylinder head, before the valves are taken out of the head. The intention is to prevent carbon chippings entering the recess in the ports, where the valve guides are situated, which can be difficult to dislodge.

Valve check

It can be decided if the valve seatings are gas tight, or otherwise, before the valves are taken out of the head by:

Wiping the sphere of the head until it is dry.
Stand the head with the exhaust ports vertical.
Nearly fill both ports with gasoline and leave standing for a short while.
If the seatings are sound, gasoline will not leak past the valves.

Deal with the inlet valves in a similar manner, with care to wipe the head dry, before filling gasoline into the ports. It is worthwhile making this check *after* the valves have been ground to verify the seatings are gas tight.

Removing the valves

Take out the stud for the inlet rocker cover. Use a proprietary valve spring compressor tool to compress the valve springs, then remove the valve keepers (collets), identify the location of each valve so that they can be refitted in their original position. Carbon on the valve stem and throat of the valve is removed with a knife—use fine emery or abrasive cloth on the stem sparingly. Use the abrasive longitudinally, the same way as the valve operates.

The valve stem diameter can be measured for wear and checked against the normal dimensions given in technical data.

Valve grinding

Valve grinding should be kept to a minimum, the valve seat should be refaced if badly pitted. Most dealers have suitable equipment for this purpose. The seat angle is 45°.

Excessive grinding will result in destroying the seat angle of the valve, also on the seating in the cylinder head, so preventing a satisfactory gas seal.

A short length of close fitting rubber hose pressed over the valve stem can be used to turn the valve during the process of grinding. Do not use a rotary motion—which will form continuous lines on the seatings—turn the valve 180° each way until a matt surface is seen on both the valve and seat in the cylinder head. Avoid depositing grinding paste on the valve stem which can cause a lapping process when the engine is running. Pass a piece of fluff-proof rag through the valve guides, after valve grinding has been completed.

Valve springs

Heat-insulating washers are used between the valve spring seat and the cylinder head to prevent heat transference from the cylinder head to the valve springs. It is desirable to check the free length of all valve springs against the measurement given in technical data. If the free length of any spring is below $\frac{1}{16}''$ the normal length the spring should be discarded and replaced. Part Number 22839 (inner) 22838 (outer).

All springs are "rated"; the two close coils should abut against the bottom valve spring seat.

Loss of valve spring pressure—due to the springs partially collapsing—will adversely affect maximum R.P.M.

Valve guides

The four valve guides are dimensionally, and materially, identical. They are a force fit in the cylinder head, an attempt to drive out the guide from the cylinder head without pre-heating will impair the interference fit of the guide in the head, as a result of scruffing. There is also the attendant risk of breaking the guide. The head should be pre-heated by placing it on a hot plate or in a domestic oven to a temperature up to, and not exceeding 200° Centigrade. A valve guide drift can be made to the dimensions shown in Figure 2 which can be used for both valve guide fitting and removal.

Refitting the valve guides

The cylinder head must be pre-heated as described for valve guide removal, for reasons already explained. To enable the guide to enter the valve guide hole in the cylinder head, parallel to the bore, insert the valve through the port, hold it firmly against its seat in the cylinder head, then pass the guide over the valve stem protruding and press home as far as possible. Using the valve guide drift, drive the guide home so that the flange on the guide abuts against the cylinder head. The valve seat in the cylinder head should now be concentric with the axis of the valve guide bore, which will obviate the necessity to re-cut the valve seat in the cylinder head.

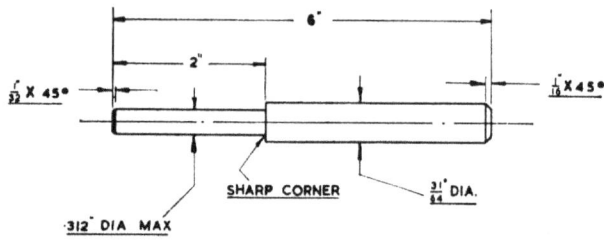

DRIFT FOR REMOVING VALVE GUIDES T 2011

MAT^L: MILD STEEL

FIG. 2

Refitting the valves

Should it be necessary to replace any of the four valves on the Commando engine, it is essential that correct replacements are used. The valves used are similar in appearance to those fitted to earlier models, but the overall length of both the inlet and exhaust valves, are dissimilar to those used on earlier engines. The Part Number for the inlet valve is 25501, the exhaust 25500. Replacement valves should be checked for overall length against the dimensions given in technical data, to ensure the correct type are fitted. Apply some clean engine oil to the valve stem before fitting—ensure the heat resisting washer is in place—assemble the valve springs with top and bottom collars, then compress the springs. A little grease applied to the valve stem (where the keepers, or collets, are located) will retain them whilst the spring pressure is being released.

Removing the cylinder barrel

When decarbonising, the cylinder should not be disturbed, without good reason. If the oil consumption is normal, it can be assumed that the cylinder bore and piston rings are in good order.

With both pistons on the top of the stroke, carbon formed on the piston crowns can be removed by using a cheap six inch steel rule, or scraper.

There is an annular gap between the top land on the piston and the cylinder barrel. Carbon chippings can collect in this space, which are difficult to extract without the use of an air line.

These chippings, if not removed, can become trapped between the valves and the seatings in the cylinder head when the engine is first run after refitting the cylinder head. Without an air line the chippings can be removed by:

Turn the engine until the pistons are about half an inch down the stroke.

With the index finger, press a small quantity of clean grease into the gap between the top land of the piston and the cylinder barrel.

Turn the engine in an opposite direction past top centre of the stroke until the pistons are about half an inch down the stroke. A ring of grease with carbon chippings embedded will form in the cylinder bore, which can be easily removed.

Repeat this process to ensure all carbon from the piston has been removed.

Nine nuts secure the cylinder to the crankcase; as these nuts are unscrewed the cylinder must be raised to enable the nuts to clear the base studs.

Before the cylinder is taken off, lift it sufficiently to enable some clean rag to be inserted into the aperture in the crankcase—under the pistons—thus safeguarding the possibility of a broken portion of a piston ring falling into the sump.

Removing the tappets

The tappets are located in the lower part of the cylinder barrel—retained by four 2 BA screws (two to each plate) passing through a separating plate for each tappet.

To remove the tappet sever the securing wire for the plate retaining screws—remove the screws.

The tappets are machined in pairs and must be refitted in the same order as removed, they do not inter-change.

Before refitting the tappets, apply a little clean oil and ensure the bevelled edges are side-by-side facing the front of the engine. Inadvertent reversal will restrict oil drainage, also prevent lubrication. Firmly tighten the plate retaining screws and secure with steel wire linking the two screws.

Removing the rockers

The spindles supporting the rockers are a close interference press fit in the cylinder head. The assembly sequence of the retaining plate for the spindles is shown in Figure 3. The interference fit of the spindles will be reduced by expansion after heating the head. A draw bolt $\frac{5}{16}$" diameter with 26 T.P.I. together with a short length of steel tube with a bore diameter of over .499" (spindle diameter) can be used to draw out each spindle. With this bolt inserted in the steel tube—screwed into the rocker spindle will extract the spindle, as the bolt is tightened. Take out the rockers; do not misplace the shim washer .015" thick.

The spindle should be smooth when the rocker operates. Any roughness, or blemish, should be removed by the use of fine abrasive strip where the rocker operates—*not* at the spindle ends.

Removing the rocker ball end

The ball end in each rocker is a parallel interference fit in the rocker. To remove the ball end, support the end of the rocker, use a drift to extract the ball end. It will be observed that there is a drilling in the rocker to convey oil from the rocker spindle to lubricate the ball end and push rod cup. Check drilling for obstruction. The ball end should be fully spherical with a mirror-like finish.

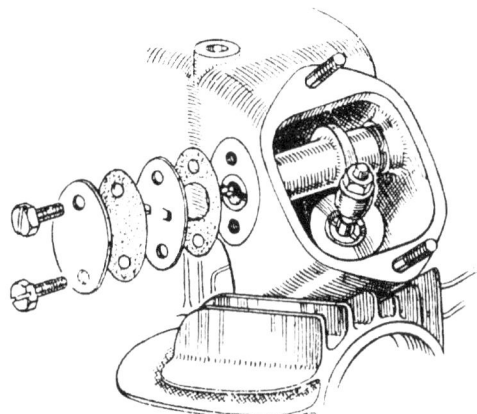

FIG. 3 *Rocker—removal*

Fitting the ball end

The oil hole in the ball end must register with the oil drilling in the rocker. For easy location, with a pencil scribe a line along—and across—the oil hole.

Insert the ball end with the scribed line in register with the oil drilling and press home as far as possible.

Refitting the rockers

The correct location of the rocker spindle is with the oil hole facing *away* from the centre of the cylinder head. The slot at the end of the spindle is horizontal—to engage with both tags on the spindle locating plate (Figure 3).

Assemble in the following order:—
1. Shim washer
2. Rocker
3. Spring washer
4. Press home the rocker spindle
5. Oval paper gasket
6. Oval plate with tags engaged in spindle slot
7. Paper gasket
8. Oval plain plate
9. Two fixing bolts.

Note: An oil leak can develop if the end of the rocker spindle is not just below the gasket face on the cylinder head.

Removing the pistons

The gudgeon (wrist) pin is a close press fit in the piston bosses, an attempt to drive out this pin without applying heat will distort the piston skirt.

Use a pair of pin pointed pliers to compress and extract the outside gudgeon (wrist) pin circlip. Heat can be applied with the use of an electric iron placed on the piston crown. Alternatively, use some rag soaked in very hot water, on the piston, which should cause the piston to expand sufficiently to enable the pin to be pushed out of the piston. Should the pin resist removal do not use force—use a sharp pointed scraper, or pen knife to remove a burr or carbon deposit alongside the circlip recess.

Fitting piston rings

The scraper or oil control piston ring originally fitted has been selected as the most suitable for the Commando engine (Part Number 06.0954.) Non-regular rings should not be fitted as a substitute.

Fit the oil control ring in the following sequence:—
1. Wind one of the two thin rails over the piston, position the rail clear, and slightly below the lower ring groove.
2. Fit the corrugated expander ring in the lower groove—with care that both ends abut—*the ends must not overlap*. The two ends are coloured which should be visible, if correctly positioned.
3. Move the thin rail previously fitted up, and into the ring groove, starting at the butt joint of the expander ring—to prevent overlapping. The rail is located on the stepped part of the expander ring.
4. Fit the remaining rail, from the top part of the piston, into the ring groove, locate it on the other stepped part of the expander ring. The ring gap on the two rails and the expander rings are equi-spaced round the piston (120° apart).
5. Fit the plain ring, which is taper faced and marked Top—for location—into the middle ring groove.
6. Fit the top ring, which is chromium plated and cargraph treated, into the top ring groove.

Note: The red coating on this ring must not be removed.

Fitting the pistons

The pistons are "handed" and the location in the engine is stamped on the piston crowns viz: LH EXHAUST. The additional mark A or B is for piston grading. Heat the pistons, as described for removal—apply clean engine oil on the pin before insertion. Fit the circlip with a rotary motion—check to make sure it is correctly located. If the circlip has become deformed during the process of removal, discard it and fit a replacement Part Number 23276.

Engine push rods

Push rods used in the Commando engine—like the valves—are similar in appearance to those used on earlier type engines, but are dissimilar in length. If replacements are used, the overall length should be checked against the dimensions given in technical data. The correct Part Number for inlet push rod is 25515; the exhaust is 25516.

This part of the engine is usually trouble free. If on examination one or more push rods are found to be bent the cause can be due to:—

(A) The engine has been run with excessive rocker clearance, allowing the ball end on the rocker to make contact with the rim of the cup end of the push rod. The crippling load, under this condition would bend the push rod.

(B) Non-regular valve springs have been supplied or fitted in error—the springs becoming coil bound when the valve is at full lift causing the push rod to bend.

Refitting the cylinder

To avoid piston ring breakage during the process of fitting the cylinder, piston ring clamps are essential, particularly to ensure entry into the cylinder of the thin rails for the oil control ring. These clamps are inexpensive and are shown in position in Figure 4. To support both pistons, a plate used on the crankcase and below the piston skirts is illustrated

FIG. 4
Piston Ring Clamp assembled

also. This tool can be made from a piece of stout plywood, its use, together with the piston ring clamps will enable the cylinder to be fitted with comparative ease.

It is essential to use a new cylinder base gasket, to safeguard against oil leakage, also subsequent attention to the engine. Remove every trace of the old gasket adhering to the cylinder and crankcase face. Check the crankcase face for bruises, or burrs; flatten with a fine oil stone. Place the new gasket on the crankcase (jointing compound is not used) put the piston support plate in position. Take up the cylinder—engage both pistons square with the bore—a sharp downwards press will enable both pistons to enter the cylinder and dislodge the piston ring clamps, which can be un-linked and taken away with the piston support plate. Raise the cylinder slightly to fit the cylinder base stud nuts, which must be tightened diagonally, NOT one side at a time.

Refitting the cylinder head

With both pistons on the top of the stroke place a new cylinder head gasket on the cylinder, put the cylinder head onto the cylinder barrel.

Take up the four push rods—the inlet are the two longest rods, used in the midway position.

Tilt the cylinder head backwards (see Figure 5) to enable the push rods to enter the tunnels cast in the cylinder barrel.

Starting from the left, fit one short push rod (exhaust) one long push rod (inlet centre position).

The second long push rod (centre position).

Finally the remaining short push rod (exhaust).

Ensure all push rods are located in the cupped portion in the tappets.

To enable the four push rods to engage with the ball end on the rockers, the cylinder is raised approximately ¼" and supported in this position. The two short cylinder head sleeve nuts (used below both exhaust ports) placed horizontally in between the cylinder head and cylinder barrel will act as a support.

Locate the push rods with the rocker ball ends if difficulty exists; use a short length of stout wire to manipulate the rods into position.

Take away the two sleeve nuts—used to support the cylinder head—lower the cylinder head into position.

Refit the cylinder head holding down bolts and nuts; tighten in the sequence shown in Figure 6. See technical data for torque loading figures.

Rocker adjustment

Have available .006" and .008" feeler gauges. The correct clearance between the rocker and end of the valve is .006" for the inlet, .008" for the exhaust—this adjustment is made with the engine cold.

The engine must be positioned so that the tappet in the cylinder is clear of the quietening curve on the camshaft.

Deal with the right side inlet valve first by:—

Turning the engine until the *left* side inlet valve is fully open.

Releasing the right side inlet rocker adjuster bolt lock nut.

With a spanner on the square part of this bolt unscrew it a few turns until there is clearance between the bolt and the valve end.

Place the .006" feeler gauge on the valve end.

Screw down the adjuster bolt until it just "nips" the feeler gauge.

Tighten the adjuster bolt locknut.

If the clearance is correct the gauge should just slide through the gap formed by the valve and adjuster bolt.

Turn the engine again until the *right* side inlet valve is fully open.

Deal with the left side inlet valve in a similar manner.

FIG. 5 *Fitting Cylinder Head*

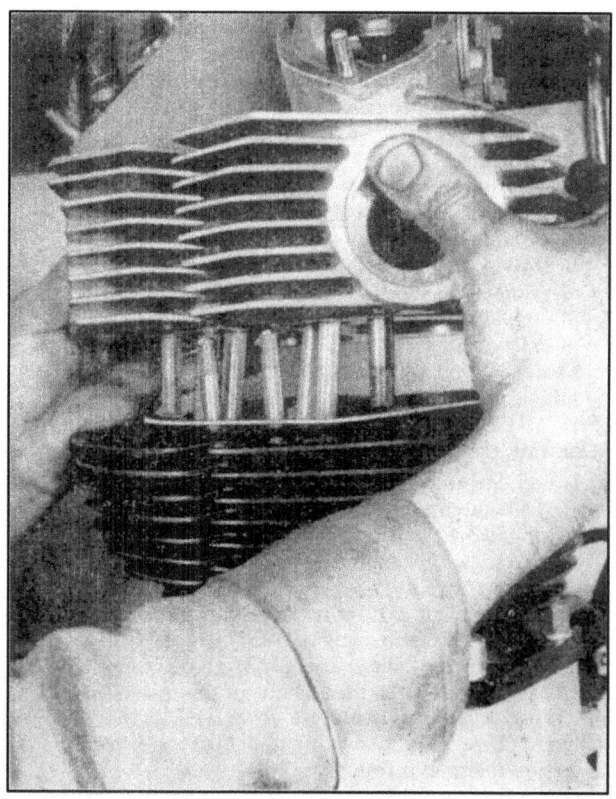

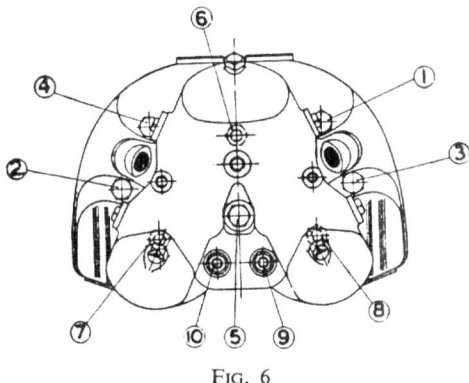

Fig. 6

Order of tightening down Cylinder Head nuts and bolts

Use the same procedure for the exhaust rockers with .008" feeler gauge for correct clearance.

Recheck the clearance after the adjuster bolt lock nut has been tightened.

Apply clean oil in the push rod cups.

Refit the rocker covers.

Note: If the rocker cover gaskets are renewed, jointing compound is not necessary.

Fit and firmly tighten the torque stay plate.

Put back the exhaust pipes, with other parts removed in the reverse order described for removal.

Road test the machine sufficiently far enough to enable the engine to reach its normal running temperature.

When the engine has cooled down after test, retorque all the cylinder head bolts and nuts.

Check and reset the rocker clearance.

Special precaution

After road test, firmly and positively retighten the two exhaust pipe finned nuts.

Engine Overhaul

If, after considerable mileage, attention to the lower part of the engine is necessary, the engine can be removed from the frame leaving the gearbox in position.

Special tools

In addition to the usual workshop tools the following special tools are required to dismantle the clutch and engine.

(A) Compressor tool for diaphragm clutch Part No. 06-0999.
(B) Engine drive sprocket and clutch hub extractor tool Part No. 06-0941.
(C) Camshaft sprocket extractor Part No. EST 12.
(D) Small timing pinion extractor Part No. ET 2003.
(E) Piston ring clamps.

FIG. 7 *Timing Pinion tool in use (ET 2003*

Fig. 8 *Clutch Tool in use*

Removing engine

Use the following sequence to take the engine out of the frame.

1. Release the two knurled knobs securing the seat, (the knobs are captive, retained by a pin through the boss), lift seat to clear the two slotted brackets and remove by pulling seat backwards.
2. Disconnect the two petrol pipes at tank end—take out two front tank fixing bolts—detach rubber securing rear end of tank and lift the tank clear of the frame.
3. Take out the four screws securing the top caps on each carburetter, and withdraw the throttle and air slides. (Attach these temporarily to the frame tube out of harm's way).
4. Detach the two spark plug covers attached to the high tension cables.
5. Remove the muffler clamp bolts securing exhaust pipes to each muffler, unscrew the two exhaust pipe finned nuts—take away both exhaust pipes.
6. Remove frame torque stay plates (three nuts for each plate) also three Allen screws securing plate to cylinder head.
7. Drain oil tank; disconnect both oil pipes at tank and engine end.
8. Take off gear shift lever.
9. Disconnect tachometer drive cable (engine end).
10. Remove battery cover; disconnect the positive battery wire (to avoid a short circuit). Disconnect by pulling out the two wires from the alternator and two wires for the contact breakers, attached to the fourway connector (located between the two rear engine plates).
11. Remove left side foot peg with brake pedal.
12. Use a tray below the primary chaincase (to catch oil), remove the central dome nut with washer—the outer portion of the chaincase can now be removed. This nut is ¾" across flats.
13. Remove stator for alternator—three nuts—with care, pull out the two wires attached to the alternator (ONE WIRE AT A TIME) through the rubber grommet in the back portion of the primary chaincase. Take off the three spacers on the alternator studs.
14. Remove sleeve nut (1 3/16" across flats) with lock washer securing rotor for the alternator. Take off the rotor, washer, spacer and woodruff key in the shaft. The rotor has a parallel bore—a tool is not required to extract.

17

15. The triplex primary chain is endless, in consequence the engine sprocket and clutch sprocket are removed simultaneously. Release the clutch push rod adjuster screw lock nut a few turns and take out the screw.
16. Take up the clutch diaphragm spring compressor tool Part No. 06-0999, screw in the central bolt for this tool into the diaphragm spring centre. Tighten the nut on the central bolt until the diaphragm spring is free to revolve in the clutch sprocket—and no further. Take out the circlip retaining the diaphragm spring from the recess in the clutch sprocket (a slot is machined in the end of the circlip to facilitate extraction). The diaphragm spring, with tool attached, can be taken out (see Figure 9.)
17. Fit the clutch hub tool 06-1015 over the clutch hub (to prevent it turning). Remove the nut and washer securing the clutch hub to the gear box mainshaft (a 14 mm spark plug spanner fits this nut).
18. Fit the engine sprocket extractor tool by entering the two outside bolts into the two screwed holes in the engine sprocket. Tighten the central bolt in the tool, a sharp blow with a hammer on the head of the central bolt will separate the sprocket from its shaft.
19. Usually the clutch hub with sprocket can be removed from the gearbox mainshaft without the use of an extractor tool. Where difficulty exists, use the engine sprocket extractor for this purpose.
20. The engine sprocket—clutch sprocket with chain can now be removed. Watch for the shim washers behind the clutch sprocket—used to adjust the chain line.
21. Three bolts secure the rear portion of the primary chaincase to the crankcase. Straighten the three tab washers securing the bolts—take out the three bolts—the chaincase can now be removed. Take off the gasket from the crankcase for the chaincase.
22. Take off the rubber tube attached to the elbow union on the drive side crankcase.
23. Detach the earth wire attached to the bottom crankcase stud on the left side of the crankcase.
24. Before the engine mounting plates are removed the engine must be supported under the crankcase to prevent the engine dropping down in between the lower frame tubes. A block of wood under the crankcase can be used or alternatively a steel rod under the crankcase and over the lower frame tubes will suffice.
25. Take off the self-locking nut from the bolt passing through the front engine mounting and the frame. Withdraw the bolt from the right side of the frame. Remove the front engine mounting assembled complete by moving the assembly downwards to clear the frame tubes.
26. Remove the three studs passing through the rear engine plates and crankcase. With the engine support mentioned in paragraph 24 removed, the engine, together with both carburetters attached can be lifted out of the frame from the right side of the machine. The air filter to carburetter rubber connection will come away as the engine is taken out of the frame.

FIG. 10. *Removing Engine Sprocket*

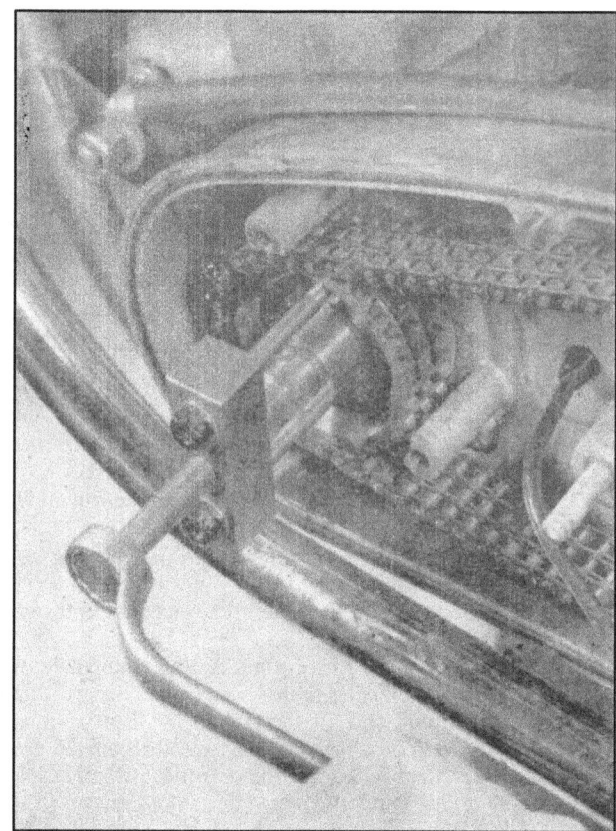

FIG. 9 *Clutch diaphragm removed*

Dismantling the Engine

Have available complete gasket set 060910. Wash down the crankcase exterior with a solvent, particularly the bottom part of the crankcase, where road grit can accumulate, to avoid fouling the work bench. Take out the crankcase sump plug to drain oil. It is preferable to dismantle the timing gear before removing the cylinder head, spark plugs and cylinder barrel, to protect both pistons and to provide resistance by compression during the process of removing parts used in the timing side of the engine.

Dismantle the engine in the following sequence:—

1. Remove the timing cover (12 screws). A light tap with a soft-faced mallet on one side of the cover whilst pulling on the tachometer drive will enable the cover to separate from the crankcase.
2. Remove the oil pump (two nuts). The pump can be pulled off the two fixing studs. Do not misplace the conical rubber seal attached to the pump.
3. Remove the oil pump worm nut LEFT HAND THREAD.
4. Remove camshaft chain tension slipper (two nuts), take off the outside plate (thick one), the tension slipper then the thin plate.
5. Remove nut securing camshaft sprocket; use extractor tool Part No. EST.12 to extract the sprocket from the camshaft. Use a suitable distance piece between the central bolt and the end of the camshaft. The camshaft sprocket has a parallel bore.
6. Tap out, with a suitable punch, the spring pin passing through the ignition chain sprocket boss and the shaft for the distributor.
7. Take off the camshaft sprocket and chain together, the intermediate gear pinion, and ignition chain with its sprocket. Pinch the top and bottom run of the camshaft chain during removal and wire the top and bottom run of the chain together (see Figure 14) which will avoid disturbing the valve timing when refitting. Watch for the thrust washer behind intermediate pinion.
8. Remove small timing pinion from timing side crankshaft —use extractor tool ET.2003. Take out the pinion key, the star-shaped thrust washer and steel oil seal.
9. Remove the cylinder head, cylinder barrel and both pistons as detailed in chapter "Engine Service".

Separating the crankcase

The ignition distributor can be left on the timing side part of the crankcase when the two halves of the crankcase are separated. To remove the distributor assembly, remove one bolt from inside the crankcase and the two stud nuts outside. The distributor complete with gasket can then be removed.

Separate the crankcase by:—

1. Removing all the studs passing through the crankcase and the two cheese-headed screws from the lower part of the crankcase.
2. Take up the crankcase assembly with both hands, with the drive side crankshaft pointing to the bench. The act of thumping the assembly with the drive side shaft against the bench, will cause the drive side part of the crankcase to separate, leaving the inner member of the roller bearing on the crankshaft.
3. Take out the camshaft, the spring and rotary release valve plate. The inner member of the timing side ball bearing is a close fit on the timing side crankshaft. To protect the end of the shaft and to prevent the entry

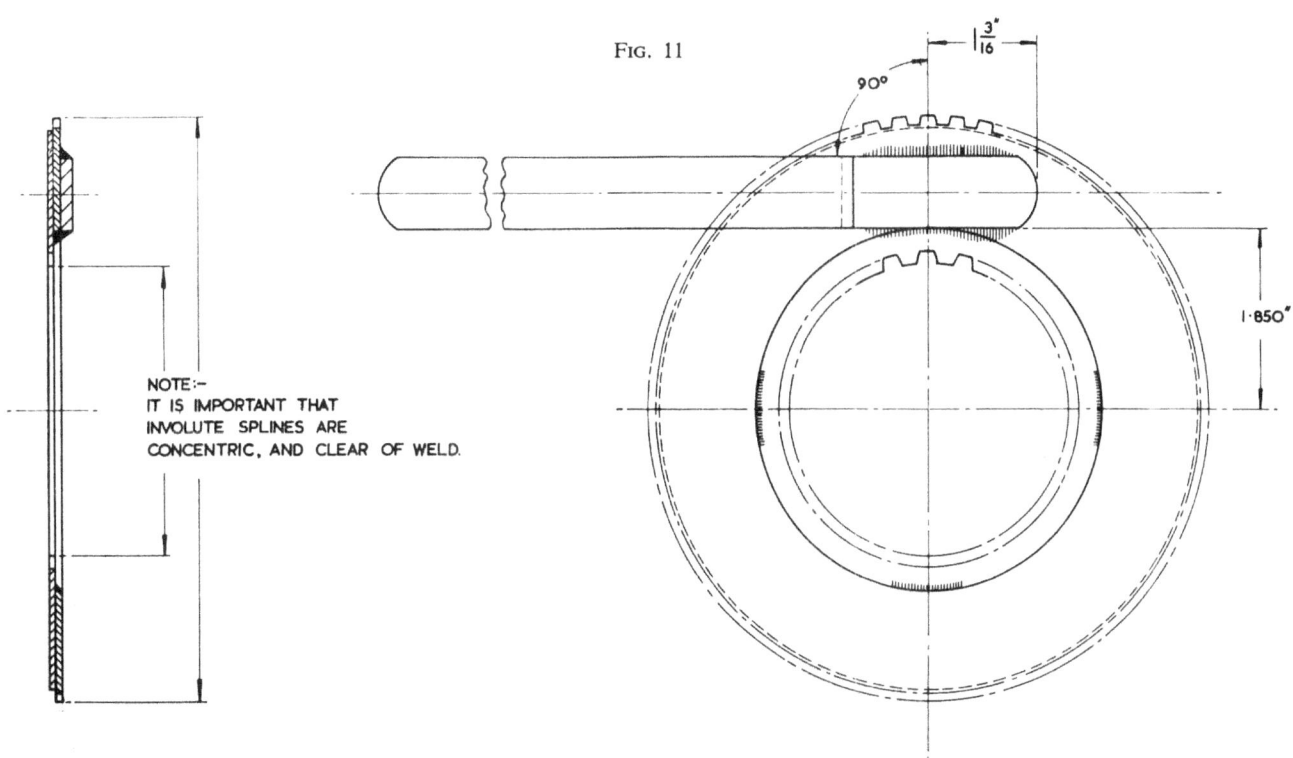

FIG. 11

CLUTCH HUB TOOL 06-1015

of foreign matter into the oil passage drilled in the crankshaft, a sleeve tool as shown in Figure 13 should be used. This tool and the method of forcing the crankshaft out of the ball bearing is shown in Figure 12 which is self explanatory.

Removing the roller bearing

The inner member is a close fit on the shaft which is vitally important.

The roller path can be examined for wear or damage by taking out one roller. Use a stout pair of pliers to grip each side of the roller, when a sharp upward jerk of the pliers will extract the roller.

Check and examine the entire diameter of the roller path, through the aperture made when the roller is removed.

The inner member can be removed with the use of two sharp edge wedges placed each side of the steel sleeve and crankshaft which will move the bearing member sufficiently far enough to enable a regular claw-type extractor to be used for final removal.

Removing the roller bearing sleeve

To remove the bearing sleeve, the drive side crankcase must be heated, by using a domestic oven or hot plate to a temperature of approximately 200° Centigrade. With crankcase in this condition, the action of dropping the crankcase on to a flat wood bench (to avoid bruising the crankcase face) will dislodge the bearing sleeve.

Fig. 13

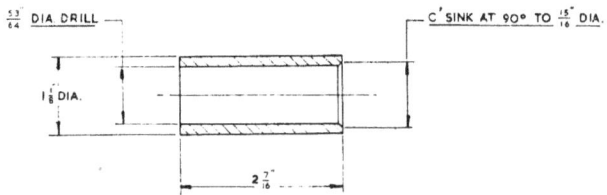

CRANKSHAFT REMOVING SLEEVE

Removing the ball bearing

Heat the crankcase as described for removing the roller bearing sleeve, using the same method of removal, taking care that the intermediate pinion shaft does not move.

Fig. 12 *Removing the Crankshaft*

Fig. 14 *Retaining Valve Timing*

Fig. 15 *The Crankshaft*

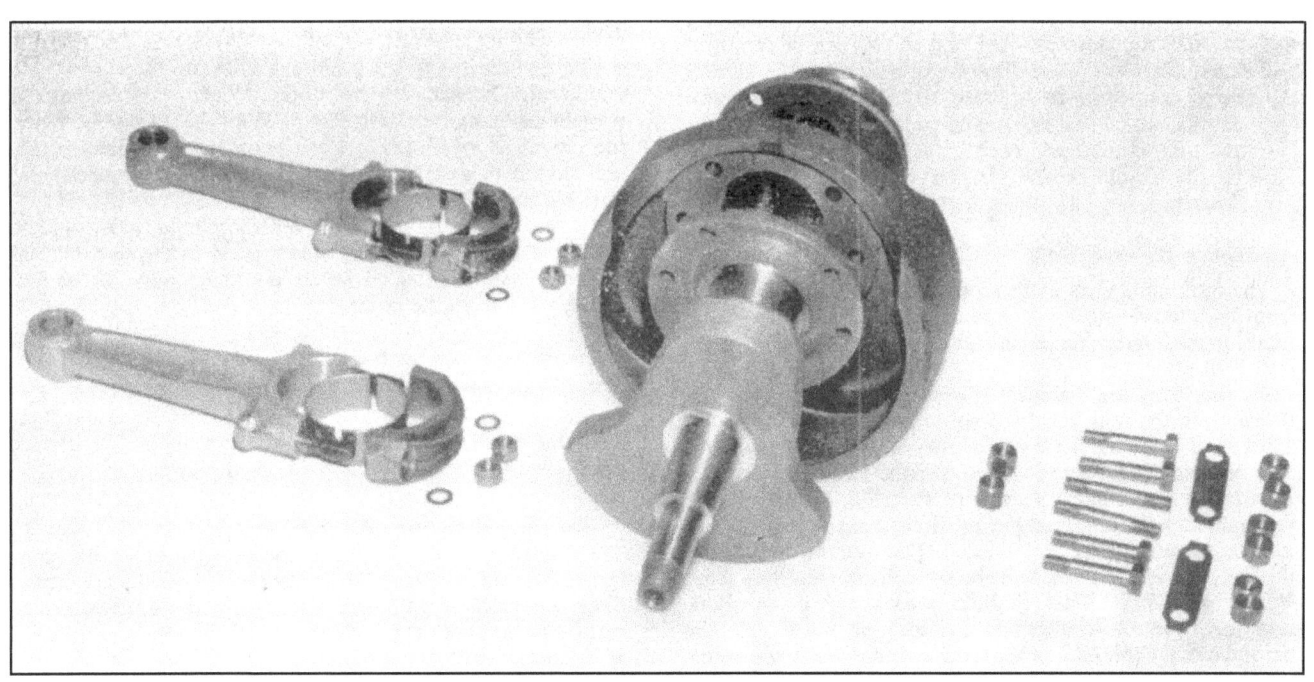

The Crankshaft

Removing the connecting rods

Remove the two self-locking nuts holding the connecting rod; a sharp jerk away from the crankshaft will separate the detachable cap from the connecting rod. If the cap jams half way up the studs, tap it back and repeat the process. With the detachable cap removed, it will be observed there is an oblique mark on the cap which registers with a similar mark on the connecting rod to indicate the correct location for the detachable cap when it is refitted. The caps do not interchange as they are machined *in situ* with the connecting rod. The connecting rod bearing shells can be taken out without difficulty.

The crankshaft

The crankshaft journals, where the connecting rods operate, are not prone to wear even after considerable mileage, providing clean oil of the correct viscosity has been continually circulating when the engine is running. There is a cavity in both crankshaft cheeks, where sludge and foreign matter can collect, which must be removed by cleaning when the crankshaft is serviced.

The journals must be perfectly smooth. Score marks, due to contaminated oil circulating, should be removed by re-grinding.

Maximum permissive ovality, before re-grinding is .001″. The normal dimensions are given in technical data.

Dimensions for re-grinding in three stages are shown on page 23.

Note: It is vitally important to restore the radius on each journal after re-grinding. The journals must have a mirror-like finish, by lapping with the finest grade abrasive tape obtainable.

Dismantling the crankshaft

1. Mark the flywheel to identify its position for reassembly in its original position.
2. Straighten the two tab washers, take off the nuts for the two studs. Remove four nuts for the bolts passing through the assembly—the end cheeks can be removed from the flywheel as illustrated. Extreme care should be taken to avoid bruising the faces on the crank cheeks, which will affect true running when the crankshaft is reassembled. The oil passages and the cavities in the crank cheeks can be cleaned as previously described.

Assembling the crankshaft

The four bolts used in the crankshaft assembly are made from high tensile steel which must not be replaced by bolts made from inferior material. The Part No. for these bolts is T.2033.

As the bolts are "peened" by a centre pop punch the threads for the nuts can become damaged during removal. The use of new nuts for this vital part of the engine is therefore recommended. The Part No. for the two long top nuts is 23280—the six short nuts have Part No. T.2031. If the two tab washers are damaged by straightening they should also be replaced (Part No. T.2032). The faces on both crank cheeks, also the flywheel, must be perfectly flat and free from bruises or blemish. Pass the bolts through the crank cheek into the flywheel—engaged in the locating dowel. Fit the second crank cheek and fit the tab washers to the lower studs.

Assemble the fixing nuts, tighten them diagonally, then deal with each nut in turn and make sure they are very, very tight. Turn back the tab washer, "peen" with a centre punch the remainder of the nuts.

Fitting the connecting rods

Undersize shells for the connecting rods are available, for use when the crankshaft journals have been reground. The connecting rods and caps must not be filed to absorb movement. When the maximum permissible ovality on the journals has been reached, the journals must be reground to restore concentricity.

Before assembling the connecting rods, check the bolt holes in each connecting rod for swarf or particles of metal that can become trapped under the head of the bolts retaining the detachable caps. Fit the shells to both connecting rods; assemble connecting rods with the small oil holes facing away from the centre of the crankshaft.

Use new self-locking nuts Part No. 23253, tighten with a torque wrench set to 25 ft. lbs. Use a Wesco oil gun to force clean engine oil through the crankshaft until the oil emerges each side of the connecting rods.

Checking oil pump seal

Before assembling the engine, and fitting the timing chains with sprockets, verify that the conical oil seal, on the oil pump, is effective by:—

1. Temporarily fitting to the crankcase the oil pump, securing the pump with the two stud nuts.
2. Put the timing cover into position, push it home and release. If the conical oil seal is effective it will push the timing cover away, leaving a gap of approximately .010″ between the cover and the crankcase. If the seal is not effective replace it with a new one, Part No. T.272. Shim washers, used behind the seal and the pump body can be used, providing the conical portion is not deformed or damaged.

Timing cover oil seal

The seal encircling the plain extension on the timing side crankshaft—housed in the timing cover—is designed to prevent oil leakage under pressure from the oil pump. When the engine is overhauled, after considerable mileage, this seal should be examined. If doubt exists use a replacement, Part No. 048023.

To remove the oil seal, take out the circlip, prise out the seal—gently heat the timing cover, press in the new oil seal *with the metal backing outwards*, the sharp edge of the seal facing away from the cover.

Intermediate pinion shaft

The shaft for the intermediate pinion is a close press fit in the crankcase. A circlip at the inner end prevents the shaft from moving inwards towards the crankshaft. To remove the shaft, heat the crankcase, pull out the shaft.

Fitting the intermediate pinion shaft

The shaft has a small hole in one end, the other end has a large hole and is slotted. To fit the shaft, heat the crankcase, insert the shaft, small end inwards with the oil hole drilled central in the shaft at 6 o'clock, press home the shaft until it is in contact with the circlip.

Re-grinding dimensions Commando crankshaft

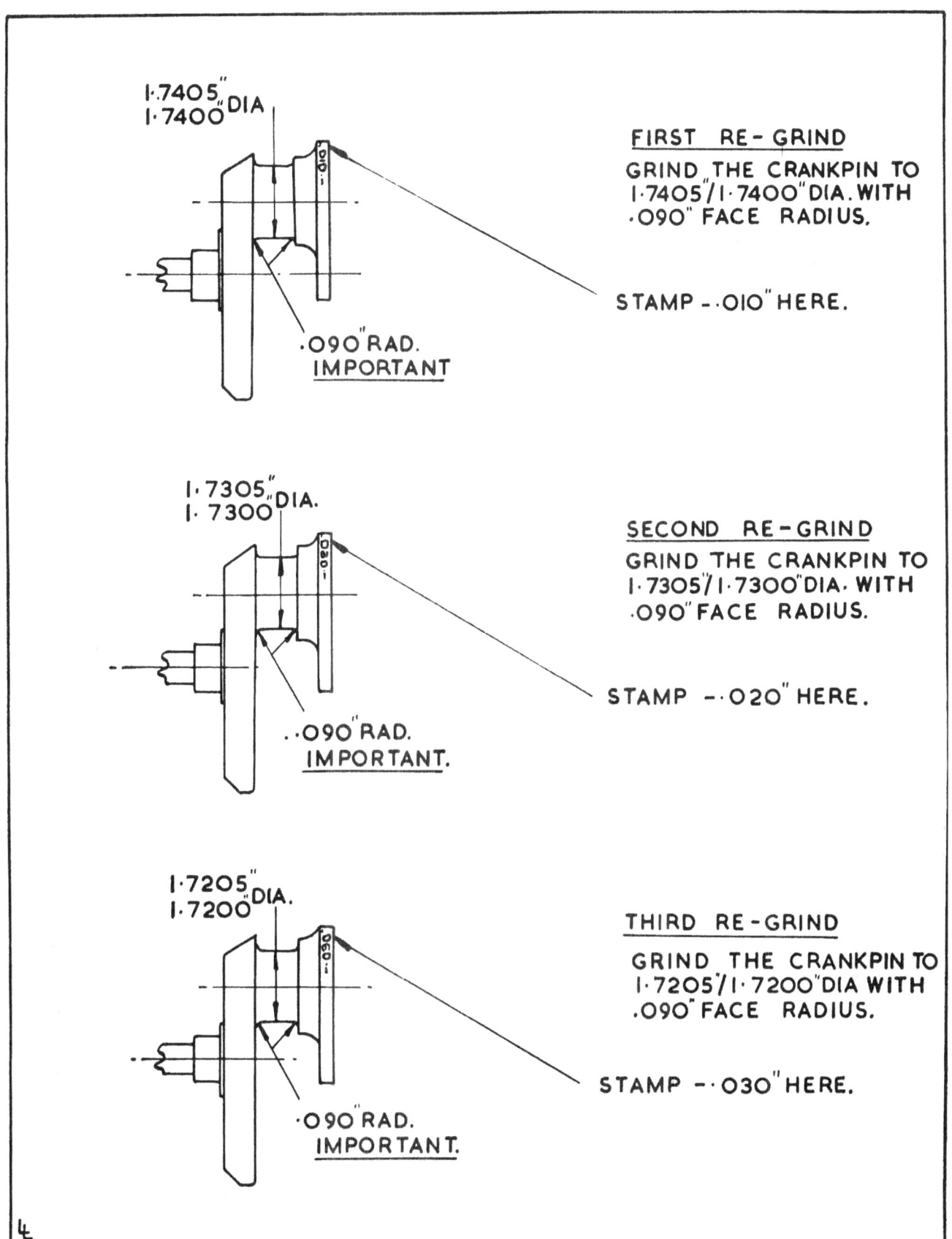

The driving side crankcase oil seal

A worn oil seal in this part of the engine will allow oil from the crankcase to be discharged into the primary chaincase.

To replace, the seal can be pressed out from inside the crankcase; the new seal, Part No. T.2187, is pressed into the crankcase, with the sharp edge inwards viz: the widest aperture facing outwards.

The sump filter

The crankcase drain plug incorporates a corrugated shaped gauze, to filter oil returned from the crankcase sump to the oil pump. To dismantle the filter take out the circlip, the metal washer, the gauze; also the interior of the plug can be cleaned.

A $\frac{7}{8}''$ Whitworth hexagon spanner is used to tighten firmly the sump filter plug.

Assembling the engine

Cleanliness in working is an important factor to get the best results. Every moving part in the engine must be treated with clean oil before assembly. It is an advantage to treat highly stressed parts, such as the camshaft and tappets, with a coating of non-scruffing material such as molybdenum disulphide. Clean the face joint on the timing and driving side crankcase. Remove all traces of jointing compound used previously. Use a fine oil stone to remove burrs or bruises that can prevent an oil tight joint.

Fitting the driving side bearing

When a new bearing is fitted it is most important that a correct replacement is used. The bearing is of the single "dot" type, Part No. 17824; a substitute should not be fitted.

FIG. 16 *Extracting the Camshaft*

The inner member for the roller bearing is a press fit on the crankshaft, it is immaterial which way the bearing is fitted as there is a radius on both sides of the inner member. With the crankshaft suitably supported, an arbour press is used to press the bearing member fully home on the crankshaft. Heat the crankcase—to fit the roller bearing sleeve—as described in paragraph "Dismantling the engine", insert the sleeve square with the bearing housing in the crankcase and press home before the crankcase temperature falls.

Fitting the timing side bearing

A single "dot" ball bearing Part No. 17822 must be used. Heat the crankcase as described in paragraph "Dismantling the engine". Insert the bearing squarely with the bore, then press home.

Assembling the crankcase

1. Take up the drive side crankcase, apply clean oil on the roller bearing, assemble the case on to the roller bearing with the connecting rods positioned as shown in Figure 16.
2. Invert the crankshaft with case, insert the rotary plate for the crankcase release with the two projections pointing outwards, followed by the spring. Engage the camshaft with the two projections on the rotary plate as shown in Figure 16. When the camshaft is correctly positioned it should move up and down, with finger pressure on the end of the camshaft, under the influence of the spring.
3. Apply a thin coating of non-flaking jointing compound to the joint face for the drive side crankcase, particularly on the bottom part of the crankcase, where oil can leak by gravity.
4. Take up the timing side crankcase, refit the distributor if removed, apply some oil to the ball bearing, then pass the crankcase over the projecting crankshaft and camshaft. The crankcase bearing will go on to the crankshaft bearing more easily if the crankcase is gently heated.
5. Fit the crankcase uniting bolts—the two cheese-headed screws at the lower part of the crankcase, then tighten.

FIG. 17 *Rod supporting Connecting Rods*

6. Assemble in the following order:—
   Oil seal dished washer.
   Star shaped pinion plate.
   Key for the small pinion in crankshaft.
   Small timing pinion, with care not to dislodge the key.
   Thrust washer on the intermediate pinion shaft.
7. Rotate crankshaft until the mark on the small timing pinion is at 12 o'clock. Take up the two timing chains with the intermediate gear, sever the wire on the chain, assemble the pinion with both chains in the crankcase with the mark on the intermediate gear pinion in register with the mark on the small timing pinion. The intermediate pinion is marked with white paint for easy identification. Assemble ignition chain, sprocket and spring pin.

Note: If the camshaft drive chain has been removed, or replaced, the camshaft sprocket and intermediate gear must be correctly located. Six outer plates on the camshaft chain should separate the mark on the intermediate gear and the mark on the camshaft pinion (see Figure 18 which shows the two sprockets correctly located).

8. To prevent the crankshaft rotating during the process of tightening the nut for the camshaft pinion and the oil pump worm drive nut, a bar is inserted through both connecting rods as shown in Figure 17. Fit and tighten the camshaft sprocket nut. Fit the oil pump worm drive nut LEFT HAND THREAD. A cutaway timing cover—for dealers' service staff use—is useful to support the intermediate pinion shaft whilst tightening the camshaft pinion sprocket nut, also to enable the ignition and camshaft chain to be adjusted correctly. The cutaway cover is shown in Figure 19.

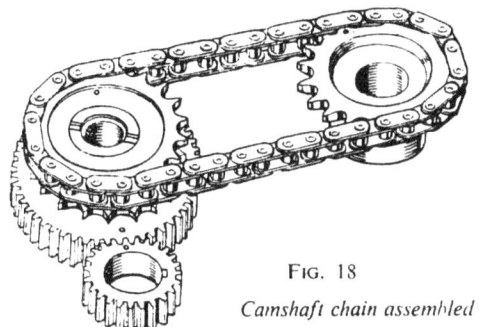

FIG. 18
Camshaft chain assembled

9. Apply sparingly a thin coating of jointing compound on the pump body face, where it abuts against the crankcase. Fit the oil pump, run down the two nuts evenly—not one at a time—tighten the nuts (see torque spanner settings).

FIG. 15 *Cut-Away Timing Cover*

10. Fit one of the two camshaft driving chain tensioner plates, with the longest portion from the bolt hole downwards, then the slipper, followed by the second tensioner plate; put back the two slipper fixing nuts loosely.
11. Adjust the camshaft driving chain by moving the slipper, leaving $\frac{1}{16}''$ up and down movement (slack) in the top run of the chain, tighten the tensioner plate nuts. (See torque spanner settings).
12. Adjust the ignition timing chain by releasing the two stud nuts, one bolt fixing the distributor. Turn the distributor body, leaving $\frac{1}{16}''$ up and down movement (slack) in the top run of the chain. Retighten the nuts and in particular the bolt inside the timing cover with its lock washer, which must be securely tightened.
13. Refit both pistons, cylinder barrel with cylinder head in the reverse sequence described in chapter "Engine Service". It is also possible to assemble the cylinder head, with push rods in the cylinder, to be fitted to the crankcase as a sub-unit, the cylinder head bolts can be torqued when the cylinder has been bolted to the crankcase.
14. Use a new gasket, fit the timing cover—six long and six short screws—the long screws are situated on the left of the centre of the cover.
15. The engine can now be reinstalled in the frame.

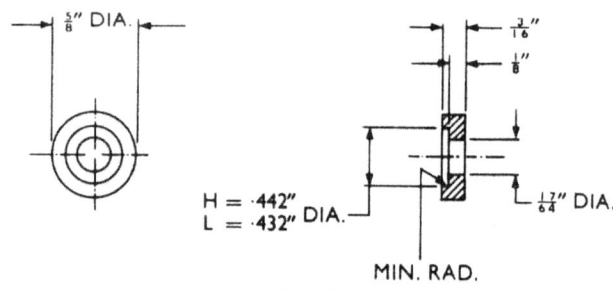

FIG. 21.
Locking Washer for Auto-Advance and Retard Unit

2. Support the engine (as described in paragraph 24 "Engine overhaul"), fit the front engine mounting complete, insert the fixing bolt, tighten self-locking nut with wrench set to 300 in./lbs. Tighten the nuts on the three rear engine mounting studs.
3. Continue the assembly in the reverse sequence described in chapter "Engine overhaul". Set the rocker adjustment as already described.

Primary chain alignment

After engine overhaul, before assembling the clutch and engine sprocket, check the chain line by placing a straight edge on both the engine and clutch sprocket. Correct alignment must be established, by using shim washers placed over the gearbox mainshaft, before the clutch and engine sprockets are finally assembled.

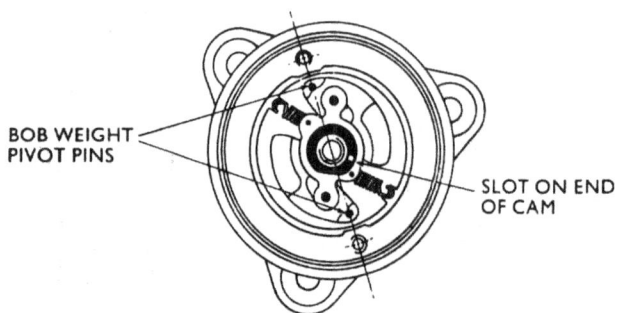

FIG. 20 *Contact Breaker location (approximate)*

Refitting engine

1. Introduce the engine into the frame from the right side of the machine. Fit the three studs and nuts passing through the rear engine mounting and the crankcase.

Setting ignition timing

The ignition timing can be either set, or checked with the engine stationary, or with the engine running at 2,000 revs. per minute, with the use of a stroboscope.

A line marking on the rotor for the alternator is made during manufacture to register when the pistons are on the top dead centre of the stroke.

Adjacent to this marking, a degree plate with a two degree scale reading is attached to the outer portion of the primary chaincase.

Normally the LEFT contact breaker set in the distributor (to which a yellow and black wire is attached) is used for ignition on the DRIVE SIDE cylinder.

The contact breaker gap must be checked and adjusted for each cylinder, before the ignition timing is either reset, or adjusted.

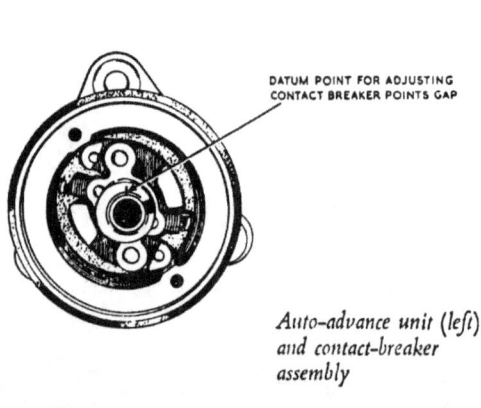

Auto-advance unit (left) and contact-breaker assembly

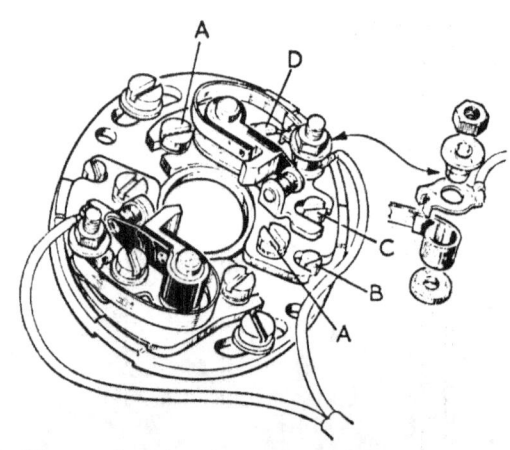

FIG. 22

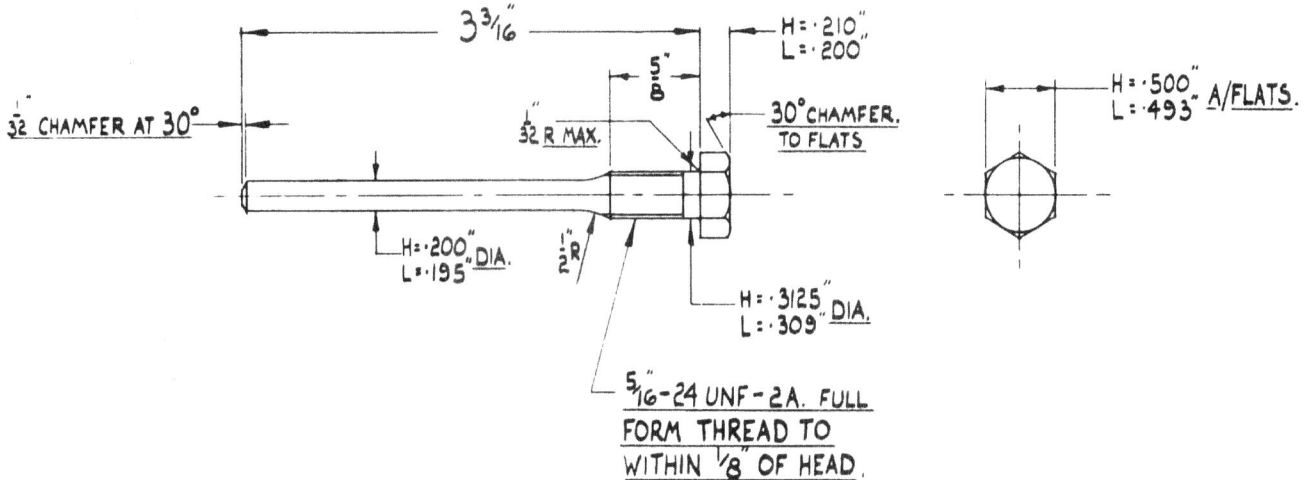

Fig. 23 *Extractor Bolt for Auto-Advance and Retard Unit*

The contact breaker Type 6CA

The contact breaker assembly is shown in Figure 22. A separate contact set on a moveable mounting plate is used for each cylinder, thus making it possible to accurately set the ignition timing on either cylinder.

Both contact breaker sets are mounted on a circular base plate, secured by two cheese-headed screws passing through slotted holes. The two screws should be central in the slotted holes when assembled.

A datum mark is made on the face of the cam, used to obtain a uniform contact breaker gap for each cylinder, when adjustment is made.

The cam is a taper fit on the distributor shaft and is retained by the central fixing bolt.

Adjusting the contact breaker gap

This adjustment must be made when the nylon heel on the contact breaker is in line with the datum mark on the cam. The normal contact breaker gap is .014" to .016". If adjustment is necessary:—

1. Release the contact breaker plate screw (D) Figure 22.
2. Manipulate the eccentric adjusting screw (C) until the contact breaker gap is correct.
3. Tighten the plate screw (D).
4. Then deal with the opposite contact breaker in a similar manner.

To reset ignition timing

1. Take off the inlet valve rocker cover.
2. Rotate engine until the DRIVE SIDE inlet rocker goes down and returns—the drive side piston is now on the firing stroke.
3. Take out the central bolt in the contact breaker assembly —use the draw bolt Part No. 06-0934 to extract the contact breaker cam assembly from the distributor shaft. Take off inspection cap on chaincase.
4. Position the engine with the mark on the rotor to register with 28 degrees on the timing scale. (Each line represents two degrees).
5. Position the contact breaker cam as shown in Figure 20 which is an approximate setting.

6. To lock the auto advance unit in the fully advanced position, use a washer for the central cam fixing bolt with a hole in the washer sufficiently large enough to clear the cam post projecting and to bear on the cam itself. Turn the cam to the full advance position and tighten the bolt. A special washer for workshop use is shown in Figure 21 together with its dimensions.

Checking ignition timing (engine stationary)

1. Use a low wattage 12 volt bulb and holder with a short length of wire soldered to the bulb holder body. Attach a second length of wire to the bulb connection. Connect one wire to the left contact breaker spring, the remaining wire to a convenient earth point on the engine.
2. Turn the ignition switch. If the timing is correct the bulb should light when the mark on the rotor registers with 28 degrees on the timing plate.

To adjust ignition timing

1. If the required adjustment is slight, release slightly the two contact breaker plate securing screws (A) and rotate the eccentric screw (B) so that the lamp bulb will light at 28 degrees when the engine is moved.
2. Retighten the two contact breaker plate securing screws (A).
3. If the adjustment required is considerable, release the two screws passing through the slotted plate and make the adjustment by moving the complete assembly.
4. Rotate the engine forward 180 degrees to make the same adjustment on the opposite cylinder.
5. Take out the central bolt—remove the temporary washer used—fit the regular washers and tighten the central cam fixing bolt. For contact breaker and auto advance unit maintenance see "Electrical Section".

Check ignition timing (engine running)

1. Attach the strobe lamp to the engine, in accordance with the lamp maker's instructions.
2. Take off the inspection cover from the primary chaincase. Remove the contact breaker cover.
3. Run the engine at 2,000 r.p.m. with the strobe lamp in position; the marking on the rotor should register with 28 degrees on the indicator plate if the timing is correct.

4. To **advance** or retard the ignition timing, refer to paragraph "To adjust ignition timing" (1) to manipulate the eccentric screw B to obtain the correct timing.
5. Check timing on opposite cylinder.

Valve timing

No useful purpose will be served by deviating from the valve timing established when the engine is first assembled by the factory, for, if an improved engine performance could be obtained—by an alteration to the valve timing—such alteration would be incorporated during initial engine assembly at the factory.

If so desired, the valve timing can be checked by:—

1. Mounting a degree plate on the drive side crankshaft, where the rotor for the alternator is fitted.
2. Using a pointer attached to the engine to register the top dead centre position of the engine—to record the degree when the valve opens or closes.
3. Increase the rocker clearance on all four valves to give a clearance of .016".
4. Use a .003" feeler gauge between the valve end and the rocker to register when the valves start to open or close. The mean valve timing figures taken from a number of engines is as follows:—
   Inlet valve opens 50° before top dead centre.
   Inlet valve closes 74° after bottom dead centre.
   Exhaust valve opens 82° before bottom dead centre.
   Exhaust valve closes 42° after top dead centre.
   Reset rocker clearance to .006" inlet valves—.008" exhaust valves.

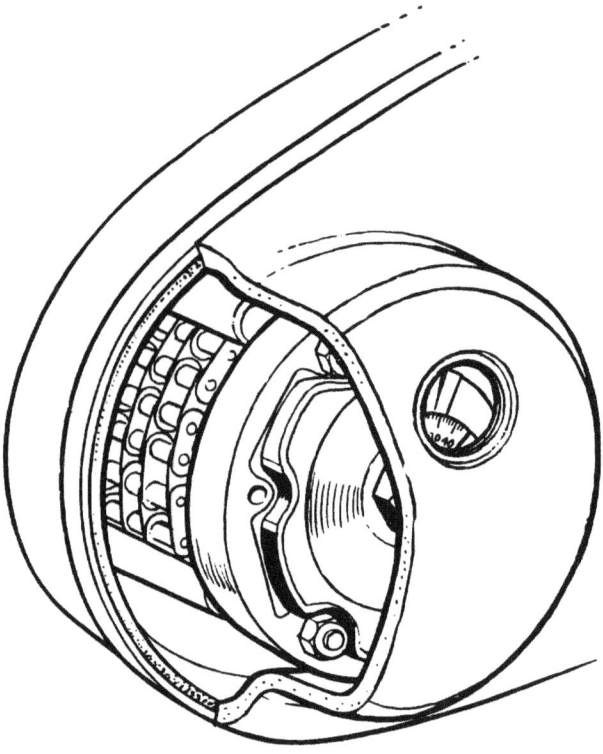

FIG. 24 *Timing Degree Plate*

The Gearbox

Dismantling the gearbox

To dismantle the gearbox, with the gearbox casing in the frame, have available the special tool to remove the clutch and engine sprocket outlined in the chapter "Engine overhaul". For access to the gearbox internals, proceed by:—

(A) Remove the outer portion primary chaincase and engine sprocket as detailed in paragraphs 15 to 20, chapter "Engine overhaul".
(B) Remove the steel sleeve on the mainshaft (use two screwdrivers) to expose the circlip encircling the mainshaft—take out the circlip.

The figures in parenthesis against the ensuing instructions refer to Figure 25.

Removing the outer cover

Remove the drain plug (15) to drain oil.
Remove the inspection cap (66) take off the clutch cable.
Remove the bolt for gear shift indicator, leave the pedal on.
Remove the kickstart crank bolt (90), take off the crank.
Remove the five cheese-headed screws fixing cover (68).
Remove the cover by pulling off, using the gear shift pedal.

Removing the inner cover (47)

Remove the ratchet plate and spindle (5).
Remove the clutch operating arm and roller (82).
Remove the lock ring (80), take away the body and ball.
Remove the mainshaft nut (74).
Remove the seven nuts fixing the cover (89).
Remove the cover, tap the edge and pull off (47).

Removing the internals

Remove the low gear pinion on mainshaft (39).
Remove the striker fork spindle (25) by unscrewing.
Remove the two striker forks (33 and 34).
Remove the clutch push rod (21).
Remove the mainshaft with the gears on it (11).
Remove the layshaft gears (12).

Removing the sleeve gear (23)

Remove the screw fixing the lock plate (4).
Remove the sleeve gear sprocket nut (5), *left hand thread*.
Remove the sprocket (6) from the splines.
Remove the distance piece, behind sprocket.
Remove the gear from the bearing (17).

Removing the cam plate (26)

Remove the dome nut (20) take out the plunger and spring.
Remove the two bolts (28 and 29).
Remove the cam plate and quadrant (26).

Removing the gear bushes

Remove the bushes by pressing out—note location first the bushes are brittle (oilite) use care in fitting. Size *in situ*, 0.81325"—0.81200".

Removing the main bearing (17)

Remove the oil seal (16) by prising out.
Remove the bearing by warming the case and press out.

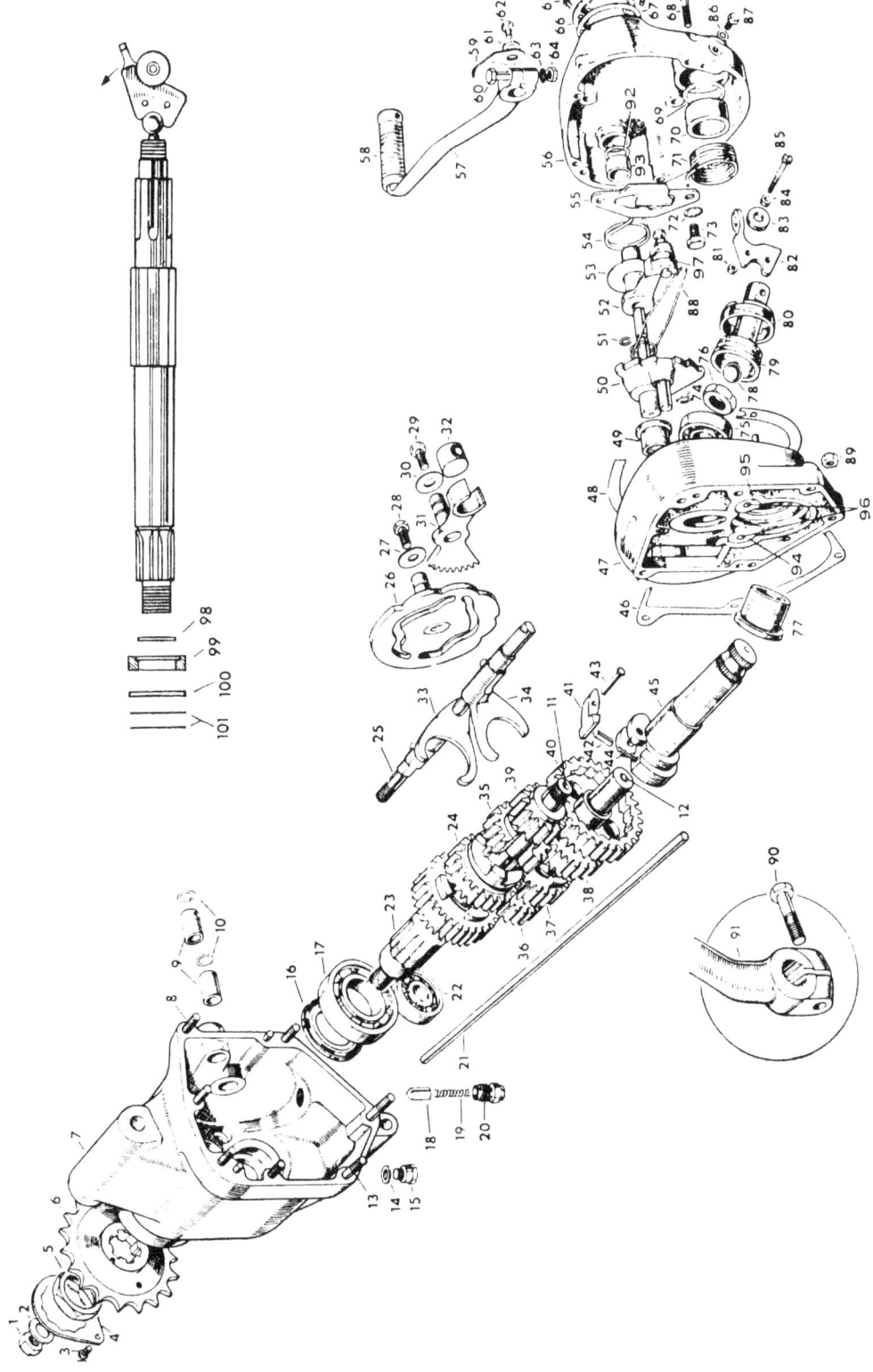

Fig. 25 *The Gearbox*

Removing the bushes

Remove the kickstart bush (77) by warming the cover, pressing out from the *outside*; ream new bush to 0.6875" to 0.6865".

Remove the footchange spindle bush—it has a blind hole; heat the cover, screw a coarse threaded tap into the bush and pull out.

Assembling the gearbox

Fit the main gear bearing (17), heat the case.

Fit the sleeve gear (23) the distance piece and seal (16).

Fit the sleeve gear sprocket and nut—this must be very firmly tightened.

Fit the lock plate and its screw.

Fitting the cam plate

This plate must be correctly positioned to index the four gears.

Fit the quadrant (31) with bolt and washer. Lift the lever portion of quadrant, with radius on lever to be in line with the top stud for the cover (top gear).

Insert cam plate so that the first two teeth in the quadrant are visible through the slot in the cam plate—then fit the bolt and washer (27 and 28).

Fitting the internals

Fit the mainshaft with the third gear (24) on shaft.

Fit the second gear (35) with striker fork (33) in the slot in the pinion.

Fit the projection on striker fork in cam plate.

Fit the first gear (39).

Fit the layshaft assembled with gear (36) gear (37) gear (38) with the other striker fork in (38) engage projection in cam plate, insert the layshaft in its bush.

Line up the two holes in both striker forks, insert the spindle (25) and screw home.

Fit the first gear (40).

To complete the assembly

Put back the roller (32), line up to take foot shift spindle. Use new gasket and fit the inner cover. Before tightening the body lock ring (80), position the lever (82) so that it is in line with the clutch cable entry to give a straight pull. Refill one pint of S.A.E. 50 oil.

FIG. 26 *Gear shift Pedal Spring*

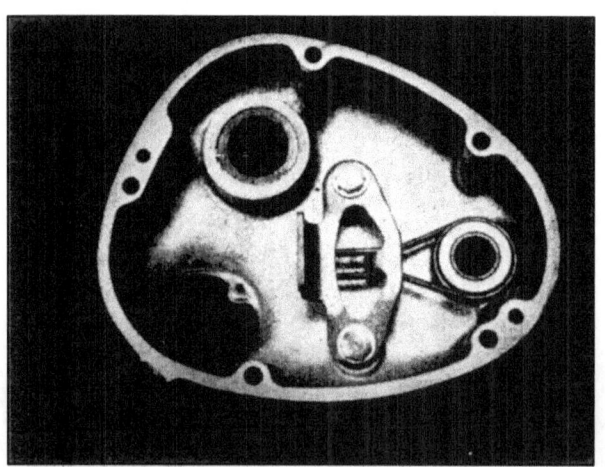

Replacing the gear shift spring

Take off the outer cover (56) then the quadrant (50) with the pawl spring behind it. Tap out the gearshift sleeve (52), washer (53). Take out two bolts (73), remove plate. The spring assembled is shown in Figure 29.

Replacing the kickstarter spring

1. Remove the gearbox outer cover (56), the inner gearbox cover (47) as described in paragraph "Dismantling the gearbox".
2. Detach the kickstarter return spring from the gearbox cover and from the kickstarter shaft. (Use a tool like a button hook for this operation).
3. Fit the kickstarter spring with the hole in the shaft at 12 o'clock engaged in the end—that is turned down vertically—into the hole in the shaft.
4. Using the tool suggested, hooked in the opposite end of the spring, pull the spring sufficiently for the end to engage with the locating hole drilled in the cover.
5. Replace the inner and outer covers. Refill with one pint of S.A.E. 50 oil.

Removing the gearbox

The gearbox assembly can only be removed when the engine is taken out of the frame.

Disconnect the rear chain, take out the top and bottom gearbox fixing bolts, turn the assembly anti-clockwise (from kickstarter side). The gearbox can then be removed from the rear engine mounting.

Replacing gearbox outer cover

Use a new gasket for the outer cover, Part No. 040055. If the gear shift pawl spring has been removed, or replaced, the spring must be correctly positioned to enable the gears to be selected as the spring is not reversible. An examination of this spring will show that one leg of the spring is straight, the other spring leg is cranked.

The correct spring location is with the straight leg of the spring in the uppermost position. Position both spring legs on each edge of the rocking pawl as shown in Figure 29.

The clutch

The diaphragm clutch in a dismantled form is shown in Figure 27. The assembly sequence is self-explanatory, the clutch needs no adjustment other than to maintain free movement between the clutch operating push rod and the operating lever inside the gearbox cover (see paragraph "Clutch cable adjustment"). As the clutch plate friction inserts tend to settle down—this has the effect of absorbing the free movement of the clutch operating mechanism, which can result in the clutch ceasing to grip, by reason of relieving pressure on the diaphragm spring.

FIG. 27 *Clutch assembly*

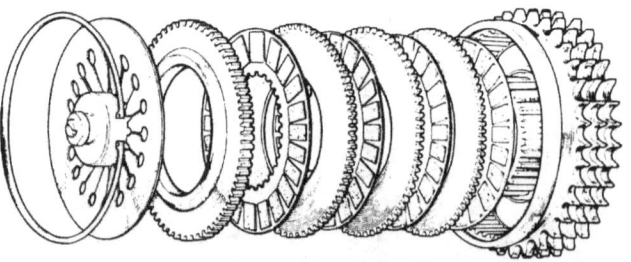

Fig. 28 *Clutch Bearing dismantled*

The clutch bearing

The clutch hub runs on a journal bearing which is a close fit in the clutch sprocket, located by circlip.

To remove the clutch bearing

1. Take out the circlip retaining the clutch hub with sleeve extension (the smallest of the two circlips).
2. Press out the clutch hub.
3. Take out the circlip for the bearing (the largest of the two circlips).

Fig. 29 *Gear shift Pawl Spring*

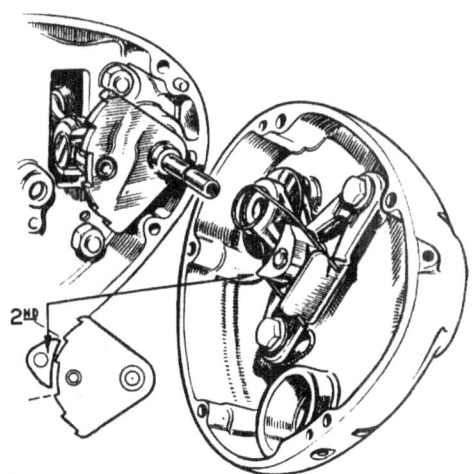

4. Press out the bearing from inside the clutch sprocket.

Refitting the clutch bearing

Apply a little anti-centrifuge grease on the bearing—refit the parts removed in the reverse order described for removal.

Clutch cable adjustment

To enable the clutch to function satisfactorily, it is important that the correct amount of free play in between the clutch operating mechanism is maintained. The principle used for operating the clutch is shown in Figure 25.

To adjust clutch cable

1. Run back the clutch cable adjuster lock nut, screw down as far as possible the clutch cable adjuster, at the handlebar end of the clutch cable.
2. Take off the large inspection cap on the primary chaincase.
3. Release the nut locking the slotted push rod adjusting screw, in the boss for the diaphragm spring.
4. Screw in gently the slotted adjusting screw until contact with the clutch push rod can be felt—unscrew the adjusting screw one quarter of a turn.
5. With care that the adjusting screw does not move, retighten the adjusting screw lock nut—use a screwdriver to hold the adjusting screw with a ring spanner to tighten the lock nut.
6. Unscrew the clutch cable adjuster leaving $\frac{1}{16}''$ to $\frac{1}{4}''$ free movement between the inner and outer casing for the clutch cable—tighten the cable adjuster lock nut.

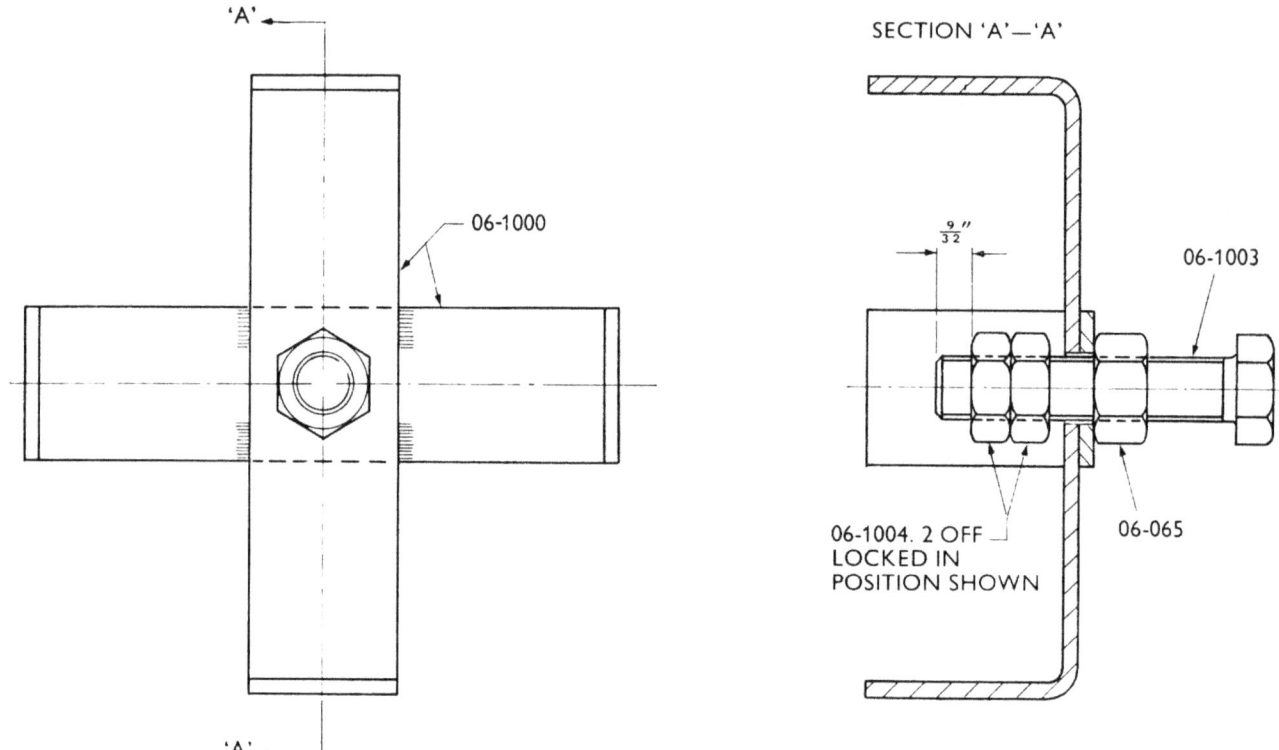

Fig. 30 *Workshop Clutch Diaphragm Tool*

Chain Adjustment

To adjust primary chain

The gearbox is fitted in the rear engine support mounting by two bolts passing through the engine mounting plates and the gearbox casing. On releasing the nut for the top gearbox fixing bolt the gearbox can pivot on the bottom bolt, thus allowing the primary chain tension to be adjusted. To adjust the primary chain:—

1. Remove the central inspection cap from the primary chaincase.
2. Release the nut for the top gearbox fixing bolt.
3. Unscrew several turns the *front* nut on the chain adjusting bolt to pull the gearbox backwards (located on the right side of the rear engine mounting).
4. Tighten the *rear* nut on the chain adjuster bolt slowly, until the primary chain is just tight—which can be felt with the index finger through the inspection cap aperture.
5. Unscrew several turns the *rear* nut on the adjuster bolt then tighten the *front* adjuster bolt nut a trifle at a time until the chain whip is ⅜" in the centre run of the chain.
6. Tighten the rear adjuster bolt nut firmly. Rotate the engine to check the chain tension in more than one position. Tighten the top gearbox fixing bolt nut.

It is important to first adjust the chain tight, so that the final adjustment is to move the gearbox forwards to prevent the gearbox moving when changing into a higher gear.

Note: Moving the gearbox from its original position will affect the tension of the rear chain, which should be corrected.

Rear chain adjustment

1. Release slightly the rear wheel spindle nuts.
2. Release the adjuster lock nuts, move the two chain adjuster bolts an equal amount to either tighten or slacken the chain until there is ¾" whip in the bottom run of the chain.
3. Tighten the chain adjuster lock nuts and wheel spindle nuts—then check chain adjustment in more than one place.

Fig. 31 *Chain Oiler Cartridge*

Removing the rear chain guard

1. Take out the front and lower fixing bolt. Release the bottom nut for the left side rear suspension unit.
2. Move the chain guard forward—to clear the rear attachment—raise the rear end to remove the guard.

Rear chain lubrication

The rear chain is positively lubricated by oil by-passed from oil returning from the engine. A plastic hose connected to a 'T' piece on the oil tank conveys oil to the rear chain via a felt cartridge—to act as a restrictor. The plastic hose terminates close to the rear chain.

A clip to locate the plastic hose is attached to the rear chain guard fixing bolt. The location of the felt cartridge is shown in Figure 31.

The primary chaincase

The outer portion of the primary chaincase is retained by a nut for the central fixing bolt. By removing the fixing nut the outer portion of the chaincase can be removed.

The oil sealing band

The rubber sealing band is located in a channel cast in the rear portion of the primary chaincase; the sealing band can be removed by prising it out of the channel.

Rear portion primary chaincase

The rear portion of the primary chaincase is attached to the drive side crankcase by three bolts with tab washers to secure the bolts. The engine sprocket, together with the clutch, must be taken off for access to the three fixing bolts. The tab washers must be turned back after refitting the bolts.

A sliding oil seal surrounding the gearbox mainshaft is incorporated in the rear portion of the chaincase. The seal consists of two steel discs with a felt sealing washer interposed.

The steel discs are not detachable, being spot welded during assembly. The felt oil seal can be removed by prising it out—to fit a replacement.

Front Forks

Lubrication (The figures in parenthesis refer to Figure 33).

For routine maintenance, refer to riders handbook. Use one of the recommended grades of S.A.E. 20 oil shown in the table of lubricants.

Steering head adjustment

If movement develops in the steering head bearings and is not corrected promptly, vibration will be produced, and damage to these bearings will inevitably occur. Usually, movement in these bearings can be detected when the front brake is applied. Additionally, the bearings can be checked for movement by:—

1. Raising the front wheel clear of the ground as shown in Figure 34. Place the fingers of the left hand on the point where the handlebar lug meets the top part of the frame head lug.
2. Grasp the extreme end of the front fender with the right hand, lift the entire assembly up and down, when movement will be felt by the left hand.
3. To adjust the bearing; to eliminate movement, release both fork tube clamping nuts (28) release slightly the fork crown and column nut (37).
4. With a thin open-end spanner, tighten a trifle at a time the fork head race adjusting nut until all movement is taken up, without friction on the bearings.
5. Tighten the column nut (37). the two clamping nuts (28).

To drain the front forks

A container to catch oil drained, should be placed under one of the front fork legs with the machine on the central stand.

1. Take out one of the two cheese-headed drain screws and washers at the bottom of the fork leg—take the machine off the central stand.
2. Apply the front brake—to stop the machine moving forwards—work the forks up and down to eject the oil. Repeat the process for the other leg.
3. Put the machine on the central stand and refit the two cheese headed drain screws with washers.

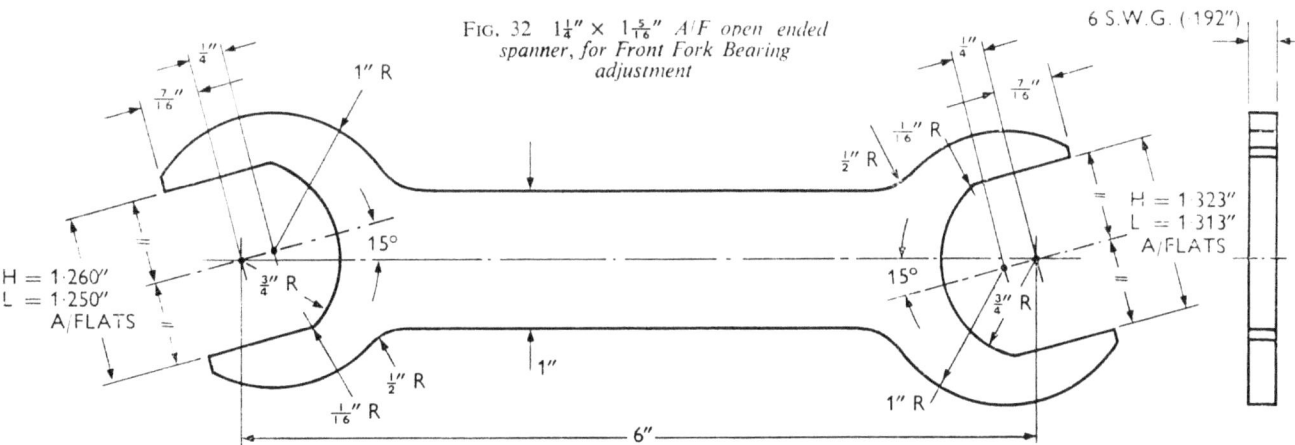

FIG. 32 $1\frac{1}{4}'' \times 1\frac{5}{16}''$ A/F open ended spanner, for Front Fork Bearing adjustment

4. Remove the two top fork tube bolts (34). Raise the front wheel—to expose the front fork springs—use a wooden box, or block of wood under the front wheel for support.
5. Detach both damper rods from the front fork top bolts (34), use two spanners, set aside the tachometer and speedometer in their covers.
6. Remove the support for the front wheel to allow the forks to fully extend, fill 150 cc of S.A.E. 20 oil to each fork tube. As the air space between the spring and the fork tube is small, the oil should be filled slowly to avoid overspill.
7. Refit the damper rods to the top bolts—firmly tighten the lock nuts.

Dismantling the front forks

The front forks can be dismantled, for examination of the damper mechanism or fork springs—leaving the steering column, handlebar lug and attachments in position. The fork legs can also be removed individually.

FRONT FORK ASSEMBLY

1 Fork main tube.
2 Main tube bush.
3 Main tube bottom bush.
4 Main tube bottom bush circlip.
5 Fork slider left hand.
6 Fork slider right hand.
7 Fork end drain plug.
8 Washer for plug.
9 Oil damper tube.
10 Oil damper rod.
11 Oil damper tube bolt.
12 Washer for bolt.
13 Washer for tube.
14 Nut for rod top.
15 Nut for rod bottom.
16 Damper tube cap.
17 Piston locating peg.
18 Oil damper valve cup.
19 Oil damper valve cup slotted ring.
20 Main tube lock ring with cup.
21 Main spring.
22 Main spring locating bushes.
23 Spring cover tube.
24 Spring top cover tube securing plate.
25 Screws securing plate.
26 Crown lug complete with column.
27 Pinch stud for crown lug.
28 Nut for stud.
29 Dust cover.
30 Fork head race adjuster nut.
31 Top cover left hand.
32 Top cover right hand.
33 Main tube top cover ring.
34 Fork main tube filler and retaining plug.
35 Washer for plug.
36 Fork head clip.
37 Fork crown and column lock nut.

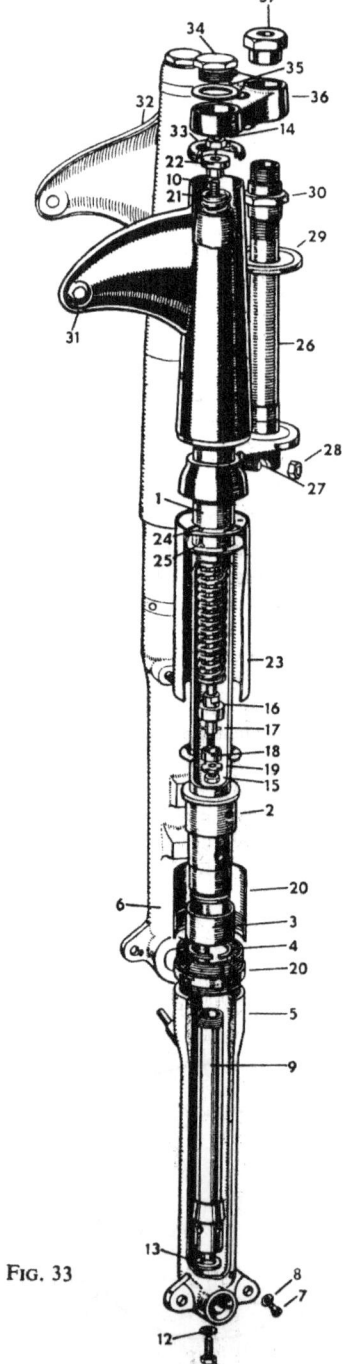

FIG. 33

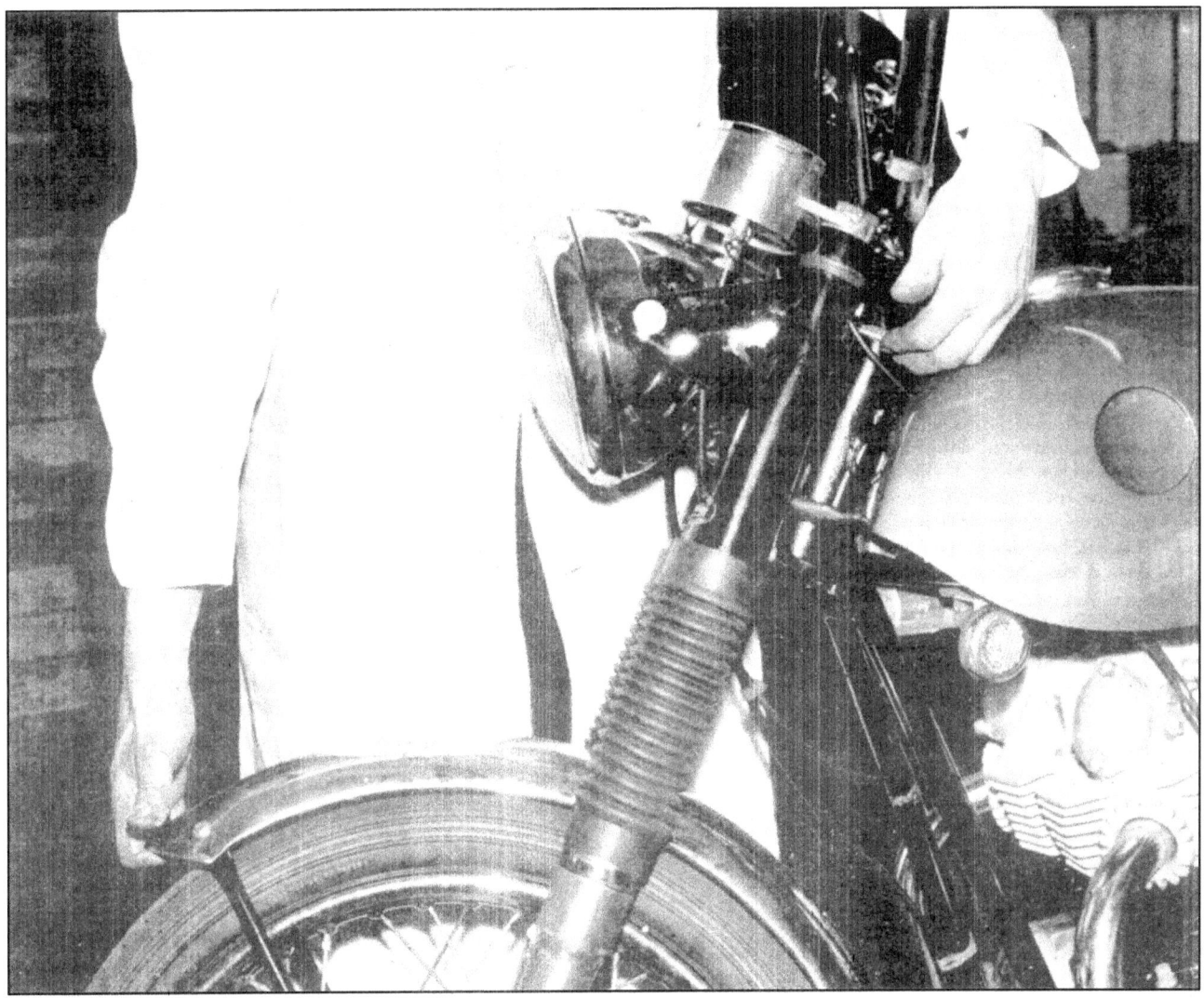

Fig. 34 *Checking Steering Head Bearings*

To remove one fork leg
1. Support the machine with a box under the engine, remove front wheel, detach the brake cable, take off the front fender with stays.
2. Release the fork tube clamp (28), take out the top fork bolt (34), lay aside the instrument secured by this bolt, detach the damper rod.
3. The inner fork tube has a taper on the end that engages with the handlebar lug, a sharp downwards jerk on the bottom slider should enable the fork tube to be extracted —if the fork tube does not come away—put back the top fork bolt only (34), screw in a few turns. A sharp blow with a soft-faced mallet will separate the fork tube from the top lug. The fork tube with slider and spring can be taken away from the front forks.

Dismantling fork inner tube
1. Remove the damper tube fixing bolt (11), unscrew the bottom screwed extension—take off the fork slider.
2. Take out the damper tube with spring, remove nut on top end of spring (14), unscrew the damper tube cap (16)—use a tommy bar inserted through the holes in the damper tube.
3. Remove the oil seal, sealing washer with flanged bush from the top taper end of the fork inner tube, if the oil seal is to be used again.
4. Remove the circlip (4), take off the fork tube steel bush.

Assembling the fork tube

Remove any trace of rust on the fork tube with abrasive tape. The portion of the fork tube (where the oil seal operates) must have a mirror-like finish—any roughness or blemish on the tube will damage the oil seal and make it ineffective. Put back the dismantled parts in the reverse order described for dismantling.

Removing forks as a unit
1. Remove the handlebars, the drive cables for tachometer and speedometer, the lamp wires for these instruments.
2. Remove the two fork tube top bolts (34), the tachometer and speedometer, support the front wheel with a box to expose the springs—disconnect both damper tubes.
3. Remove the fork crown column nut (37) with a soft-faced mallet. Give the underside of the handlebar lug (36) a few sharp blows to part it from the fork inner tubes.

4. Take off the headlamp—leave it suspended by the wiring loom, remove the front wheel. The forks can then be withdrawn through the frame. Watch for the 36 ¼" dia. ball bearings.

Removing steering head bearings

The bearing cups are a press fit in the frame lug. Use a short length of steel tubing through the head lug to drive out the cups—moving the steel tubing to alternate edges of the cup so that it will come out parallel with its housing.

Use a taper wedge or old screwdriver to remove the cone bearing on the fork column.

Reassembling the front forks

If the forks have been completely dismantled, the following precautions should be observed during assembly.

1. The fork inner tube must be clean and smooth, with clean oil applied before assembly.
2. The flanged bush should be a close free sliding fit—replace the bush if there is undue clearance between the bush and the fork inner tube.
3. The flanged bush, the paper washer and oil seal are passed over the fork inner tube from the top taper end.

Note: The oil seal is fitted with a spiral spring inside the seal towards the paper washer for the flanged bush.

4. The fork tube clamping nuts (28) must be firmly tightened.
5. Use some stiff grease on the cone bearing for the fork column—to retain the 18 ¼" diameter steel ball bearings. Use similar grease in the top bearing cup in the frame to retain the 18 ¼" diameter ball bearings during the process of refitting the front forks. Ensure the correct number of steel balls are used in both ball races.

Rear suspension units

These are sealed units. The damping fluid—filled during assembly—is sufficient for the serviceable life of the unit.

Each unit is adjustable to three positions by means of the 'C' spanner supplied in the rider's toolkit.

The soft, or normal position is when the segment, welded to the unit body is in contact with the topmost position of the cam face, viz. rotated to the limit in an anti-clockwise position—viewed from above the unit. Rotation, by use of the 'C' spanner in a clockwise direction pre-loads the spring into a stronger position. *Both* units must have identical adjustment.

A grating noise, audible when the units are moving can be rectified by:—

1. Remove the units—one at a time.
2. Compress the unit spring—take out the top split collar.
3. Remove the unit dust cover, apply some anti-centrifuge grease on the outside diameter of the spring, then reassemble.

Steering lock

The key-operated lock, which is a thief-proof device, is pressed into the front fork handlebar lug.

To remove, it can be driven out from the underneath portion of the lock.

A number is stamped on the lock base for identification.

The Frame (Registered design)

Removing the oil tank

The oil tank is located by a plain stud passing through a rubber grommet at the bottom of the oil tank. To remove the oil tank:—

1. Drain off the oil content—remove the two oil pipes connecting the oil tank to the engine.
2. Remove the rubber hose from the crankcase release valve where it joins the top left of the oil tank, remove the rubber hose for the oil tank vent pipe connected to the air filter on the top right of the tank.
3. Take out the two rubber-bonded studs securing the tank to the frame located at each side of the tank at the top. Move the tank outwards and up—to clear the lower locating stud.

Removing the air filter

To clean, or replace the air filter element:—

1. Remove cover for battery compartment by using a coin in the Rotolok catch, at the bottom of the cover.
2. Slide the cover in the direction of the front wheel to remove.
3. Take off the Zener diode from its mounting by releasing the Rotolok catch.
4. Remove two bolts clamping the air filter front and back plate—the filter element can be withdrawn downwards for removal.

Removing the rear mudguard

1. Take out the rear wheel.
2. Remove the self-locking nut securing the rear mudguard to the frame cross member.
3. Remove the bolt fixing the mudguard or the rear fairing bracket.
4. Remove bolt fixing mudguard to rear number plate, disconnect the two rear lamp cables from the connector.

Removing the rear fairing

The rear fairing is attached to the frame by the two top rear suspension bolts together with a bracket under the fairing connected to the rear frame loop.

1. Remove the two top bolts for the rear suspension units (the knurled discs are captive).
2. Remove the bolt for the rear loop clip bracket.
3. Disconnect the two rear lamp cables.

To remove the battery carrier

To take off the battery carrier, the following parts are dismantled, the methods for removing these sub units are described in the frame section of this manual.

1. Rear wheel.
2. Rear mudguard bottom fixing bolt.
3. Electric horn (disconnect two cables.)
4. Oil tank.

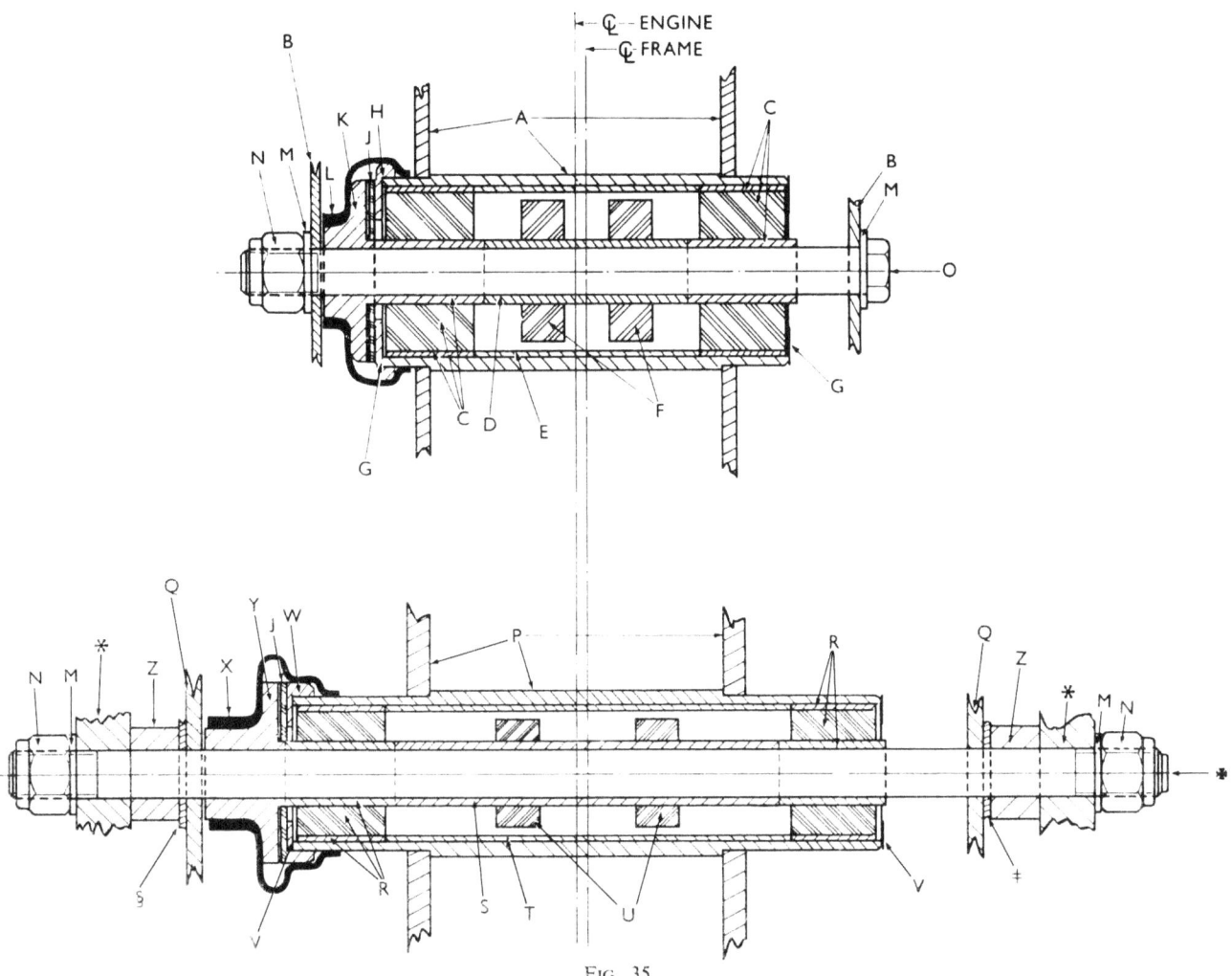

Fig. 35

A	06-0418	Front engine mounting assembled	1 off
B	06-0415	Frame front engine mounting plate	2 off
C	06-0421	Front engine mounting bush	2 off
D	06-0427	Metalastik spacer tube (front)	1 off
E	06-0771	Front engine mounting bearing spacer	1 off
F	06-0428	Front engine mounting rubber spacer	2 off
G	06-0686-9	Front engine mounting shim	as required
H	06-0684	Front engine mounting tube cap	1 each end—2 off
J	06-0578	Mounting plate shim (polyurethane)	1 each end—4 off
K	06-0422	Front mounting spacer (engine plates)	1 each end—2 off
L	06-0773	Front engine mounting gaiter	1 each end—2 off
M	000008	Washer	1 each end—4 off
N	06-0438	Nut	3 off
O	06-0423	Front engine mounting bolt	1 off
P	06-0424	Rear engine mounting assembled	1 off
Q	06-0414	Rear engine mounting plate (frame)	2 off
R	06-0432	Rear engine mounting bush	2 off
S	06-0434	Metalastik spacer tube (rear)	1 off
T	06-0772	Rear engine mounting bearing spacer	1 off
U	06-0435	Rear engine mounting rubber spacer	2 off
V	06-0775-8	Rear engine mounting shim	as required
W	06-0685	Rear engine mounting tube cap	1 each end—2 off
X	06-0774	Rear engine mounting gaiter	1 each end—2 off
Y	06-0436	Rear mounting spacer (engine plates)	1 each end—2 off
Z	06-0472	Spacer	1 each end—2 off
✱	06-0468	Footrest support plate	2 off
✠	06-0437	Rear engine mounting stud	1 off
‡	06-0831	Front support bracket R.H.	1 off
§	06-0832	Front support bracket L.H.	1 off

Fig. 36 *Front Engine Mounting Assembly*

5. The battery.
6. Air filter back plate (see footnote).
7. Condenser pack cables and earth wire.
8. Chain oiler cartridge clip and harness clip.
9. Zener diode (Rotolok).
10. Two wires for ignition switch.

The battery carrier platform is slotted at the front end. Take out the two rear bolts in the footrest plate—slacken the two front nuts—the battery carrier can be lifted at the rear end to remove.

Note: The tab washers on the air filter back plate must be turned back to prevent the bolts becoming detached.

Removing the side stand

The hinge pin is a press fit in the stand lug, located by a circlip at each end. Remove circlip, detach the stand spring—drift out the hinge pin to remove stand leg. Take out two bolts to remove stand bracket.

Removing the central stand

1. Disconnect the central stand return spring from the right side stand stop plate.
2. Take out the two central stand hinge bolts and nuts—the stand can be removed.

The front engine mounting

With the engine mounting bolt torqued to 25 ft. lbs. the total side play should be .020-.025″. If the normal side play is reduced, the mounting bush will not function.

Checking front engine mounting side play

If the combined side play measured on each side of the unit exceeds .025″, the shim washers should be exchanged.

If the engine plate portion of the assembly is moved and then released, the assembly should react by the elasticity of the engine mounting bush. If this reaction does not occur, the shim washers fitted are too thick and must be re-shimmed to give a total of .020-.025″ clearance. This is a vital adjustment, which must be effected accurately.

Checking rear engine mounting side play

The amount of side play, .010-.015″, for this mounting can also be checked with the unit assembled in the frame. The check should be made on the right side of the mounting by using the same method as described for checking the front mounting.

Fitting new shims for rear engine mounting

1. Take off the right side nut to the bolt passing through the engine mounting assembly.
2. Drive out the bolt sufficiently far enough to enable the spacer (K) and the cap (H) to be removed for access to the shim washer.

Fig. 37 *Rear Engine Mounting Assembly*

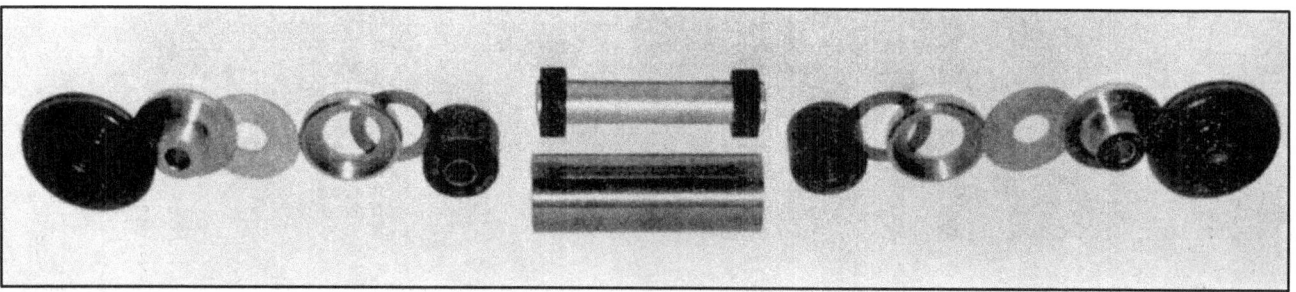

Fig. 38

3. Take out the existing shim washer—replace it with the shim washer selected.
4. Assemble the parts removed, drive back the mounting bolt—torque to 25 ft. lbs.—then recheck the side play—readjust if required.

Removing rear engine mounting (see also paragraph "Swinging Arm").

To service the rear engine mounting or to replace the mounting bushes the following dismantling is necessary:—

1. Remove engine (see chapter "Engine overhaul").
2. The oil tank.
3. The hinge spindle for the swinging arm.
4. The gearbox (see chapter "The gearbox").

Removing the engine mounting bush

To remove the engine mounting bush (C), and the two rubber spacers (F), an arbour press is used with a suitable mandrel inserted through the assembly. The method used is shown in Figure 38. With the engine mounting suitably located, the mandrel under pressure will press out the bushes and spacers as shown in the general arrangement drawing (Figure 35).

The swinging arm

The swinging arm pivots on two flanged bushes in both ends of the swinging arm supported by the swinging arm spindle, which passes through the rear engine mounting plate. To remove the spindle:—

1. Take out the screwed rod securing the two end plates for the swinging arm bushes.
2. Remove the lock bolt—central in the rear engine mounting—which secures the swinging arm spindle, which is threaded on the right side. Use a ½" UNF bolt to extract spindle, which must be removed to take off mounting.

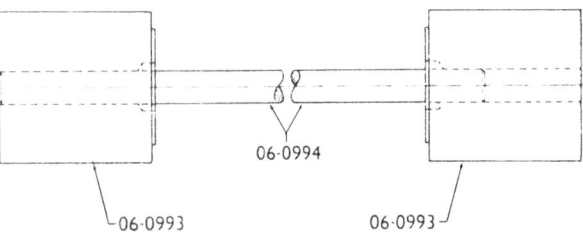

Fig. 39 *Assembling Tool complete (front engine mounting bushes)*

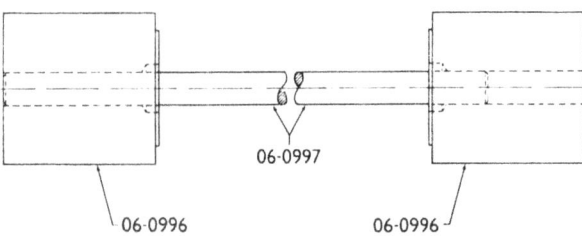

Fig. 40 *Assembling Tool complete (rear engine mounting bushes)*

To remove the swinging arm

With the pivot spindle removed take off:—

1. Rear wheel—disconnect the rear chain.
2. Rear brake.
3. Rear chain guard and chain oiler tube clip.
4. Two rear suspension unit bottom bolts. The swinging arm can be taken away from the frame.

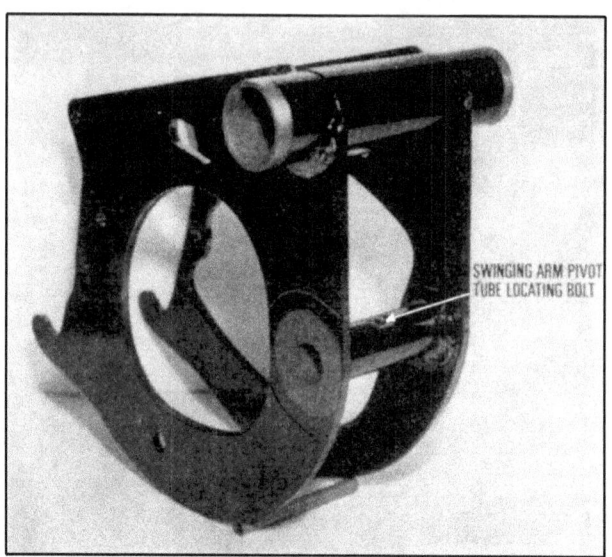

Fig. 41 *Rear Engine Mounting Plate*

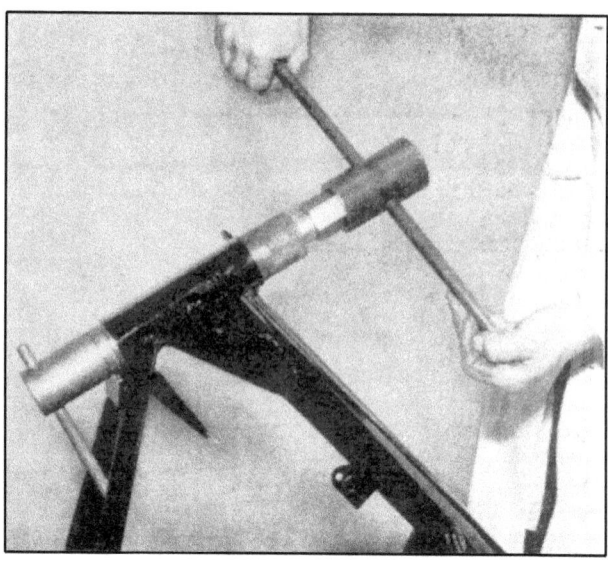

Fig. 42 *Fitting Frame Races*

The swinging arm bushes

The two flanged bushes, use an 'O' ring in the dust plate, also in the recess for the bush in its housing, as an oil seal. The bushes are a press fit; to remove, take out the two 'O' rings, support the end of the swinging arm—use an arbour press to remove both bushes.

Fitting the bushes

Place the dust plate over the bush with the recess for the 'O' ring facing inwards. Press in the bush.

Fit the large 'O' ring in the dust plate with the small 'O' ring in the bush recess for the swinging arm. New bushes do not require reaming after fitting.

Fitting the frame races

A draw bolt used to press home the top and bottom frame race is shown in Figure 42. All traces of enamel or foreign matter must be removed to enable both races to be positioned correctly in the frame housing.

Wheels and Brakes

Front wheel removal

With the machine on the central stand:—
1. Take out the split clip with clevis pin—unscrew the brake cable adjuster—remove the cable.
2. Take off the wheel spindle nut on the right side of the machine—release the left side fork slider pinch bolt.
3. Support the wheel with one hand—use a tommy bar through the hole drilled in the wheel spindle—pull out the spindle.

Refitting front wheel

1. Remove rust formed on the spindle—apply a little grease.
2. Put the wheel back in the fork with care to locate the brake plate in the brake torque stop.
3. Fit the wheel spindle (see the dust cover is in position), tighten the spindle nut. Tighten the slider pinch bolt.
4. Refit the brake operating cable.

Note: If the fork motion is stiff, after refitting the wheel, release the right side spindle nut up and down sharply to relieve side stress on the fork members, then retighten the spindle nut.

Removing rear wheel

The rear wheel is detachable from the brake drum and sprocket, secured by three extended nuts. With the rear wheel clear of the ground:—
1. Remove three rubber grommets (4) from the right side hub disc. Take off the three extended nuts (8).
2. Unscrew the wheel spindle (20), withdraw spindle through the hub.
3. Take away the distance piece (19); the speedometer drive (39) can be left attached to the drive cable.
4. Pull the wheel clear of the three driving studs (6) to remove.

Removing the rear brake drum

1. Disconnect the rear brake operating cable.
2. Remove the connecting links from the rear chain.
3. Remove nut for dummy spindle (22) with washer (21); take out the brake drum with brake plate assembled, from the fork ends.

Refitting rear wheel

Put back the rear wheel in the reverse order described for removal with the following precautions:—
(A) Before tightening the rear wheel spindle (20) ensure the two driving dogs in the speedometer drive (39) are properly engaged in the two slots in the hub bearing lock ring (14).

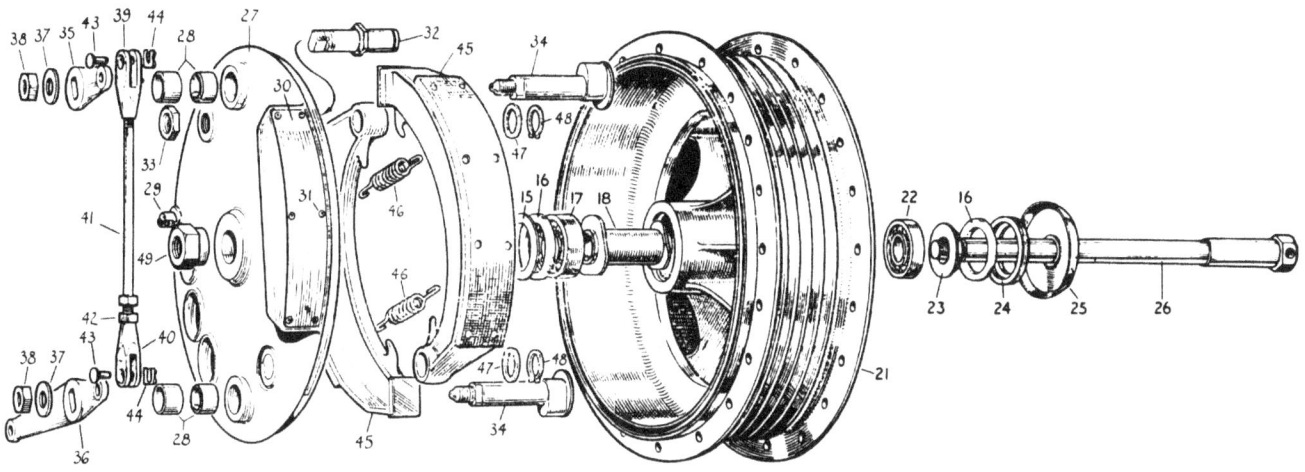

FIG. 43 *Front Hub*

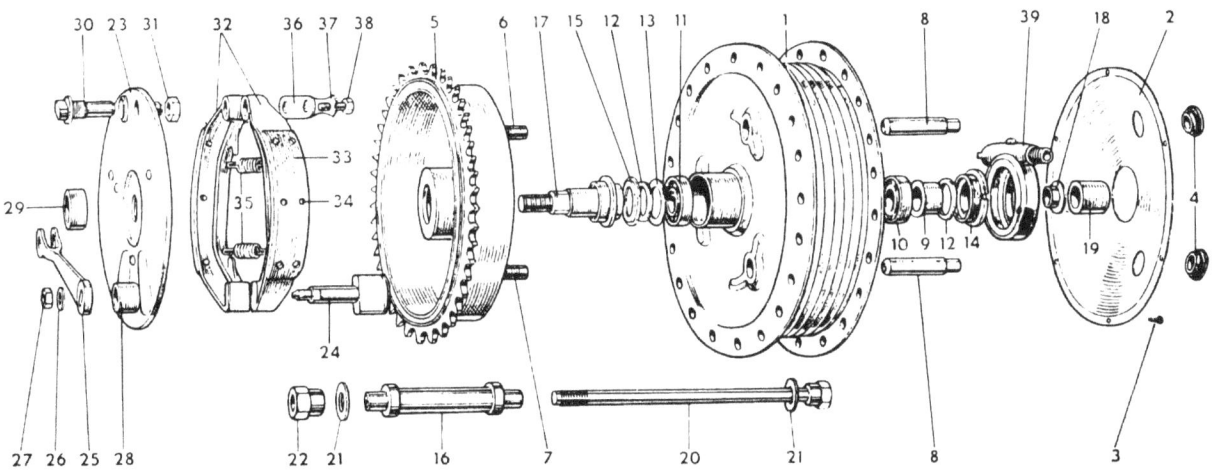

FIG. 44 *Rear Hub*

(B) Position the speedometer drive cable before finally tightening the wheel spindle.

Dismantling rear wheel hub

The wheel hub bearings are packed with grease during initial assembly. When the bearings are removed they should be cleaned and fresh grease applied (see table of lubricants). Further attention should not be required until 10,000 miles has been covered. With wheel removed to dismantle:—

1. Unscrew the hub bearing lock ring (14) LEFT HAND THREAD. Take out felt washer (12) distance piece (9).
2. Take up the rear wheel spindle (20), fit to it the washer (21) also the spacer (19).
3. Insert the wheel spindle with the washer and spacer on it, through the rear hub. A few sharp blows with a soft-faced mallet on the end of the spindle will move the bearing until it abuts against the reduced diameter in the hub.
4. Use a short length of steel tube with an outside diameter slightly smaller than the internal diameter of the bearing. Drift out the bearing (10).
5. Invert the wheel, then drift out the double row bearing, which will take with it the steel cup for the felt washer (15), the felt washer (12) and thin steel washer (13). Clean and grease the bearings.

Assembling the rear wheel hub

First, fit the single row bearing (10), then assemble parts removed in the reverse order described to dismantle. When assembled, "peen" the steel cup (15) against the hub with a suitable punch.

Dismantling front wheel hub

With the front wheel removed:—

1. Unscrew the hub lock ring (24) right hand thread. Use a peg spanner or pin punch if a spanner is not available. Should the lock ring be difficult to remove, use gentle heat on the hub in the vicinity of the lock ring.
2. Remove felt washer (16) the spacer (23). Use the front wheel spindle as a drift by passing the spindle through the wheel hub from the brake side.
3. A few gentle blows on the end of the wheel spindle with

a soft-faced mallet will drive the double row bearing (18) into the hub and, at the same time, push out the single row bearing (22). Any further attempt to drive the double row bearing in the hub can damage the spacer tube between the two bearings.

4. Take out the wheel spindle, invert the wheel again, insert the wheel spindle through the hub, position the spindle central in the spacing tube—then drift out the double row bearing—ejecting the large steel washer, the felt washer and the thin steel washer.

Assembling front hub

Clean and repack bearings with fresh grease; use one of the recommended lubricants.

1. Press home the single row bearing into the left side of the hub followed by the distance washer (flat side against the bearing), then the felt washer and lock ring.
2. Fit the distance tube into the hub (small end first) until it abuts against the bearing, already fitted.
3. Fit the double row bearing—with care that the bearing starts square in the hub—use the wheel spindle to drive the bearing home, until it abuts against the distance tube.
4. Fit the thin steel washer (the smallest of the two), the felt washer and finally the large washer. Lightly "peen" the washer with a centre punch alongside the wheel hub.

Wheel balancing

Should it so happen that the wheels are out of balance—due to variation in the construction of the tyre and inner tube—this can have an adverse effect on road holding at high road speed particularly in the case of the front wheel. It is not possible to balance the wheel in its normal position by reason of friction caused by the oil seals for the hub bearings.

To accurately balance the wheel:—
1. Remove it from the frame.
2. Obtain a steel rod, together with two unlubricated ball bearings (to reduce friction).
3. Mount the wheel—with the rod through the hub supported by the two bearings, on a stand—two wooden boxes will do. A workshop stand for this service is shown in Figure 45.

If the wheel is correctly balanced, it should remain stationary in any position. If out of balance the heaviest part of the wheel—usually where the tyre valve is used—will slowly come to a standstill at the bottom of the circumference (6 o'clock).

Counter balance weights to attach to the wheel spokes are available. As an alternative, strips of lead sheet attached to the wheel spokes can be used. Secure the lead strips with adhesive tape, with a coating of jointing compound to seal.

Front brake adjustment

Adjustment, to compensate for cable stretch and brake lining wear, can be made by unscrewing the brake cable adjusters located at the handlebar end of the brake cable, also on the front brake plate.

The brake link rod is preset at the factory. The rod length should not be altered unless the brake shoes are serviced.

To reset the link rod

1. Release the lock nut on the link rod, take out the top clevis pin and retaining clip.

FIG. 45 *Balancing the Road Wheels*

FIG. 46 *Front Brake assembled*

2. With the assistance of a second person, apply pressure on both brake expander levers to press the brake shoes hard against the brake drum.
3. Whilst maintaining this pressure, adjust the brake rod length, so that the top clevis pin will enter the yoke end on the link rod. Fit the clip and tighten the lock nut on the link rod.
4. Manipulate the cable adjuster so that the wheel will spin freely, with a minimum of movement in the operating lever.

Centralising the brake shoes

1. Release the front wheel spindle nut.
2. Apply pressure on the front brake operating lever. Maintain the pressure, then tighten the spindle nut. Reset the cable adjuster if required.

Front brake air scoops

The air scoops on the front brake plate are intentionally sealed off by blanking plates. Where prevailing conditions permit, for additional cooling, the blanking plates fore and aft can be removed.
1. Remove eight screws retaining the blanking plates and wire mesh. Discard the blanking plates. Use suitable washer under screw heads to secure the wire mesh.

Rear brake adjustment

The rear brake is cable operated in conjunction with the Commando frame design. Under no circumstances must this operation be altered to rod operation. Adjustment is effected by the use of the brake cable adjuster nut at the brake expander lever end.

Centralising the brake shoes

Release the rear wheel spindle nuts on the brake side. Press on the brake operating pedal, maintain the pressure and retighten the wheel spindle nuts. This will ensure that both brake shoes make simultaneous contact with the brake drum, and permit a close adjustment with freedom from brake binding.

The front brake

After a very considerable mileage, continual adjustment will cause the brake expander cams to occupy a position whereby the available leverage is considerably reduced, with a loss of brake efficiency. It is at this stage the brake shoes, or brake shoe linings should be replaced to restore brake efficiency.

Removing the brake shoes

1. With the brake plate removed from the wheel, hold the brake plate in a smooth-jaw vice clamped on the slotted brake cable stop.
2. Remove the two circlips for the pivot pins.
3. Use a pair of pliers—or mole wrench—extend the brake shoe spring to clear its anchorage on the brake shoe.

Refitting the brake shoes

Check the two expanders for free movement, use a grease gun on the two nipples, wipe off surplus grease.

With the brake plate held in the vice:—
Refit the two brake shoes, the two circlips. Attach a shoe spring to the projection on the brake shoe, grip the free end of the spring with pliers or a mole wrench. Extend the spring sufficiently to engage the loop on the spring with its anchorage.

Dismantling the rear brake

To remove the brake shoes with the brake plate removed:—
1. Hold the brake plate in a smooth-jaw vice clamped on the torque lug, take off the nut and washer (26-27), remove the expander lever (25).
2. Use a screwdriver placed between the loop on the brake shoe spring and the hole in the brake shoe for the spring—a slight thump with the palm of the hand will dislodge the spring. Deal with the remaining brake shoe spring in a similar manner.
3. Straighten the tab washer (37) at both ends—remove the two fixing bolts (38), take off the tie plate (36), remove the brake shoes.
4. Remove the expander cam (24), remove traces of rust with abrasive tape so that the spindle for the cam works freely in the bush. Apply a smear of clean grease for assembly later.

Removing the cam expander bush

The bush for the expander cam spindle is detachable from the brake plate. To remove, take off the lock nut, unscrew the bush. The bush, Part No. E.5082, should be replaced if the movement between the expander spindle and the bush is excessive.

Assembling the rear brake

With the brake plate held in a vice as described previously:—
1. Put back both brake shoes the tie plate, tab washers and bolts; turn up the ends of the tab washer.
2. To fit the brake shoe springs, anchor the end of the spring furthest away from the operator. Use a length of stout string in the free end of the spring—expand the spring with one hand—guide the spring into its anchorage with the free hand. A thin blade screwdriver can also be used for this purpose.
3. Finally fit the expander lever.

FIG. 47 *Fitting Brake Shoe Spring*

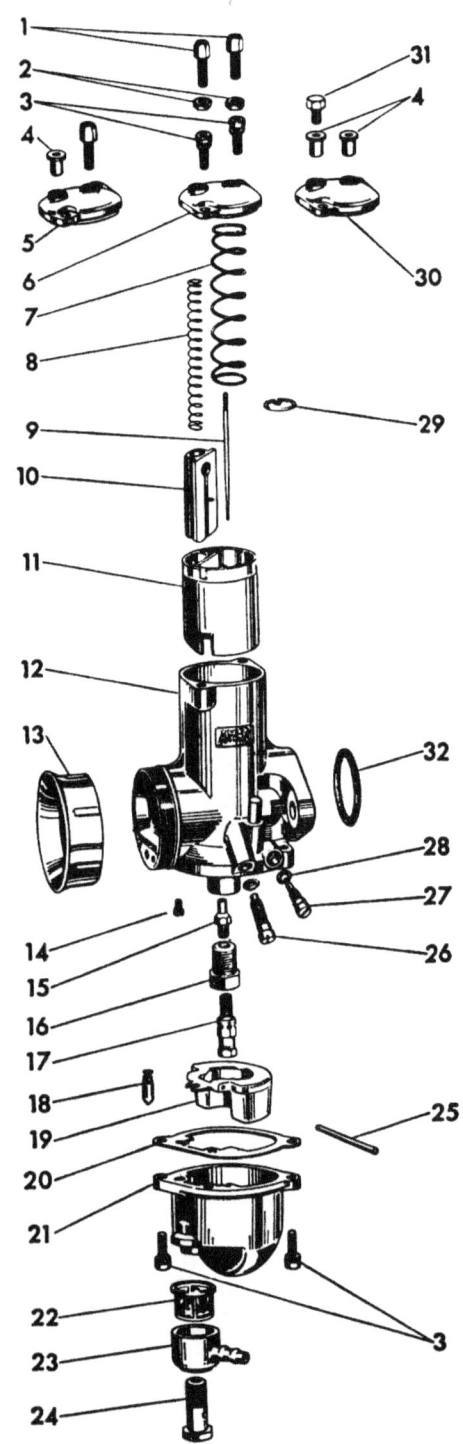

Amal concentric carburettor

1. Cable adjuster
2. Cable-adjuster locknut
3. Float-chamber and mixing-chamber-top securing screws
4. Cable ferrules
5. Mixing-chamber top for adjuster and ferrule
6. Mixing-chamber top (standard)
7. Throttle-valve spring
8. Air-valve spring
9. Throttle needle
10. Air valve
11. Throttle valve
12. Carburettor body and tickler assembly
13. Air-intake tube
14. Pilot jet
15. Needle jet
16. Jet holder
17. Main jet
18. Float needle
19. Float
20. Float-chamber washer
21. Float-chamber body
22. Filter
23. Banjo union
24. Banjo bolt
25. Float spindle
26. Throttle-stop adjusting screw
27. Pilot-air adjusting screw
28. 'O' Rings
29. Needle clip
30. Mixing-chamber top for two ferrules
31. Plug for mixing-chamber top
32. 'O' ring for flange sealing

Carburetters

Amal twin concentric type 930 carburetters are used for the Commando engine.

The carburetter settings given in the technical data have been determined to give maximum performance, with progressive acceleration, using the normal exhaust system and air filter.

The carburetter settings are satisfactory for machines operating at an approximate altitude of 3,000 feet above sea level. Increased altitude tends to produce a rich mixture—thus, as the altitude increases a smaller jet is required.

Machines permanently operating at altitudes between 3,000 to 6,000 feet above sea level reduces the main jet size to the extent of five per cent.

Dismantling the carburetter (see Figure 48).

1. Remove the two screws (3) securing the mixing chamber top cap, take out the throttle and air slide with needle attached.
2. Remove the needle clip (29) to release the needle. The slides can now be taken off the control cables. Use an air line to clear choked jets.
3. Remove the two screws (3) securing the float chamber body.

Assembling the carburetter

Use care to locate the float needle (18) in the forked extension for the float, also to correctly locate the gasket (20). When fitting the slides, make sure the throttle needle (9) enters the jet tube.

Warning

The throttle needles 622/124, the needle jets 622/122 and jet holder 622/128 are of a new type—first fitted to Commando models. The new type needle can be identified by two circular rings at the top end of the needle (the old type had three rings).

The new needle jet has the orifice at the bottom of the jet together with a small "bleed" hole. The new jet holder is longer than the early type.

If any of the above parts are replaced it is vital that correct replacements are used.

Synchronising the carburetters

When the two throttle control cables, from the junction box to the carburetters, vary in length—due to the outer casing contracting or the inner wires stretching—this results in an uneven movement of the throttle slides when the twist grip is operated.

To synchronise:—
1. Remove two bolts clamping air filter plate.
2. Remove air filter element downwards and out.
3. Unscrew as far as possible the two throttle stop adjusting screws (26).
4. Fully close the twist grip control.
5. Release the cable adjuster lock nuts (2), screw down the two cable adjusters (1).
6. Insert the index finger of one hand through one of the carburetter intakes and press on the throttle slide—to prevent the slide from moving.
7. Slowly unscrew the cable adjuster until all play has been taken up. Tighten the adjuster lock nut.
8. Deal with the second carburetter in a similar manner. Put back the air filter element.

Start the engine and adjust the throttle stop adjusting screw to get the correct idling speed. It may be necessary to manipulate the pilot air adjusting screw (27) to obtain positive idling. Each cylinder can be dealt with individually by taking off one of the spark plug leads and caps.

Air filter

The air filter element should be cleaned or renewed at periodic intervals, particularly when the machine is operating in a dust laden atmosphere.

Electrical Equipment

The capacitor

The 2 MC is an electrolytic POLARISED unit, which can be irreparably damaged if incorrectly connected. The capacitor *must* be positioned with the terminals pointing downwards.

Terminal identification

Looking at the terminal end of the unit, two Lucar terminals of different sizes will be observed. The small ($\frac{3}{16}$") terminal is the POSITIVE earth (ground) terminal; for identification the rivet for this terminal has a red spot. The double ($\frac{1}{4}$") Lucar terminal is the NEGATIVE connection.

Running with the battery removed

After disconnecting the two battery terminals—before running the engine—it is essential to insulate the NEGATIVE battery terminal with insulating tape to prevent a short circuit, should the terminal make contact with the frame.

Checking the capacitor

A defective capacitor will not be apparent with the battery in circuit. Periodically check the unit by disconnecting the battery to determine if the engine will start; also there is full lighting whilst the engine is running.

Motorcycle Alternator Model RM 21
(Positive Earth)

Description

The alternator produces an alternating current (a/c) by means of a six-pole permanent-magnet rotor which rotates within a stationary six-pole laminated-iron stator assembly.

The rotor is attached to the engine crankshaft, which revolves at engine speed. The stator sub-assembly, comprising the windings and laminations, is attached to the primary chaincase.

The full generated a/c output of the alternator is externally connected to a separate bridge-type full-wave rectifier which converts the alternating current to a direct current (d/c) for battery charging.

Maintenance

The alternator and associated equipment requires no maintenance except for an occasional check to ensure that all the external cable connections are clean and tight. The rectifier securing nut should make good electrical contact. If it should be necessary to remove the alternator rotor from the engine crankshaft, the use of magnetic keepers is not necessary, but keep the rotor away from magnetically-attracted metal foreign matter.

Testing the alternator charging system in situ

Note: The effectiveness of the charging system depends upon the battery being able to accept and hold a state of charge. A battery having an internal fault such as a shorted cell, or sulphated plates, can cause high or low confusing ammeter readings respectively. For this reason, before suspecting the charging system, first ensure that the battery is in fact satisfactory. If, because of a fault in the charging system, the battery is in a low state of charge, independently recharge the battery or alternatively fit a substitute battery before carrying out the following tests:—

ELIMINATING THE ZENER DIODE AND THE EMERGENCY-START CAPACITOR AS A CAUSE OF THE CHARGING SYSTEM FAILURE.

1. Leaving the cable connections to the rectifier undisturbed, connect the negative (black) connection of a moving coil d/c voltmeter of 0-20 volt range to the centre terminal of the rectifier, and connect the other voltmeter connection to a good earth point on the engine or frame. Providing the battery to rectifier circuit is in order the voltmeter will read battery voltage.
2. Start the engine and run it at approximately 3,000 rev./min. The voltmeter should register 14.4-16.4 volts.
3. If the voltmeter reading is as stated this confirms that the alternator, rectifier, emergency-start capacitor and the Zener diode are working satisfactorily and the fault is obviously confined to the circuit between the rectifier (voltmeter connection) and the battery, including the ammeter and battery earth connection. Check the cable connections in this portion of the circuit.
4. If, however, the voltmeter reading remains unchanged (at battery voltage) or rises to a voltage below or above the limits quoted, proceed to test in accordance with paragraph 5.
5. An incorrect voltage reading at the centre terminal of the rectifier could be due to one of the following causes:—

(A) A zero reading, or low reading:
Unsatisfactory alternator-rectifier output, faulty Zener diode, or emergency-start capacitor.
(B) A higher than normal reading:
Faulty Zener diode.

In the case of the preceding paragraph (A):—

Disconnect the Zener diode, and with the voltmeter connected between the centre terminal of the rectifier and earth, start the engine and slowly raise its speed. The voltmeter reading should quickly exceed the Zener diode regulated voltage of 14.4-16.4 volts. If so, the alternator and rectifier and the emergency-start capacitor are all satisfactory, and the Zener diode must be suspected of having a premature operating voltage. Prove the Zener diode by substitution.

If, however, a zero or low voltage is still registered (with the Zener diode disconnected) the cause could be unsatisfactory output from either the rectifier or the alternator or a faulty emergency-start capacitor.

Disconnect the emergency-start capacitor and retest.

If a rising voltage can now be obtained, the capacitor is faulty and must be replaced.

If a rising voltage still cannot be obtained, either the rectifier or alternator is unsatisfactory.

Checking the alternator voltage (a/c) output

Remove the two alternator cables (usually green/yellow and white/green) from the rectifier outer terminals (see Figure 51).

Connect between these two cable-ends, a 1 ohm load resistor and an a/c moving-coil voltmeter (the resistor and voltmeter being in parallel with each other).

With the engine running at 3,000 rev./min. the voltmeter should register 9.0 volts (min.).

If the alternator output voltage is satisfactory, and if the charging circuit between the centre terminal of the rectifier and the battery earth connection is also satisfactory, a failure in the charging system can only be due to the rectifier unit. Check the rectifier fixing point (earth) and if this is found to be satisfactory, the rectifier can be assumed to be faulty and must be proved by substitution.

If, however, the alternator output voltage is not satisfactory, with either a zero or low voltage voltmeter reading, the cause could be either a faulty rotor or stator winding assembly.

Rotor: This may have become partially de-magnetised, the loss of magnetic energy having been caused either by misuse, or a faulty rectifier. In either case the only practical way to test the rotor is by substitution. After fitting the replacement rotor, ensure that the rectifier is also satisfactory.

Stator-winding assembly: If the encapsulated windings develop an insulation fault, the stator assembly will have to be replaced.

A short circuit between any part of the stator windings and the stator lamination pack is confirmed if the bulb lights when a 110 volt a/c 15 watt test lamp circuit is connected between either of the stator cable terminal ends and the stator laminations.

It is not possible to easily carry out a winding open-circuit test and a suspect stator assembly must be tested by substitution.

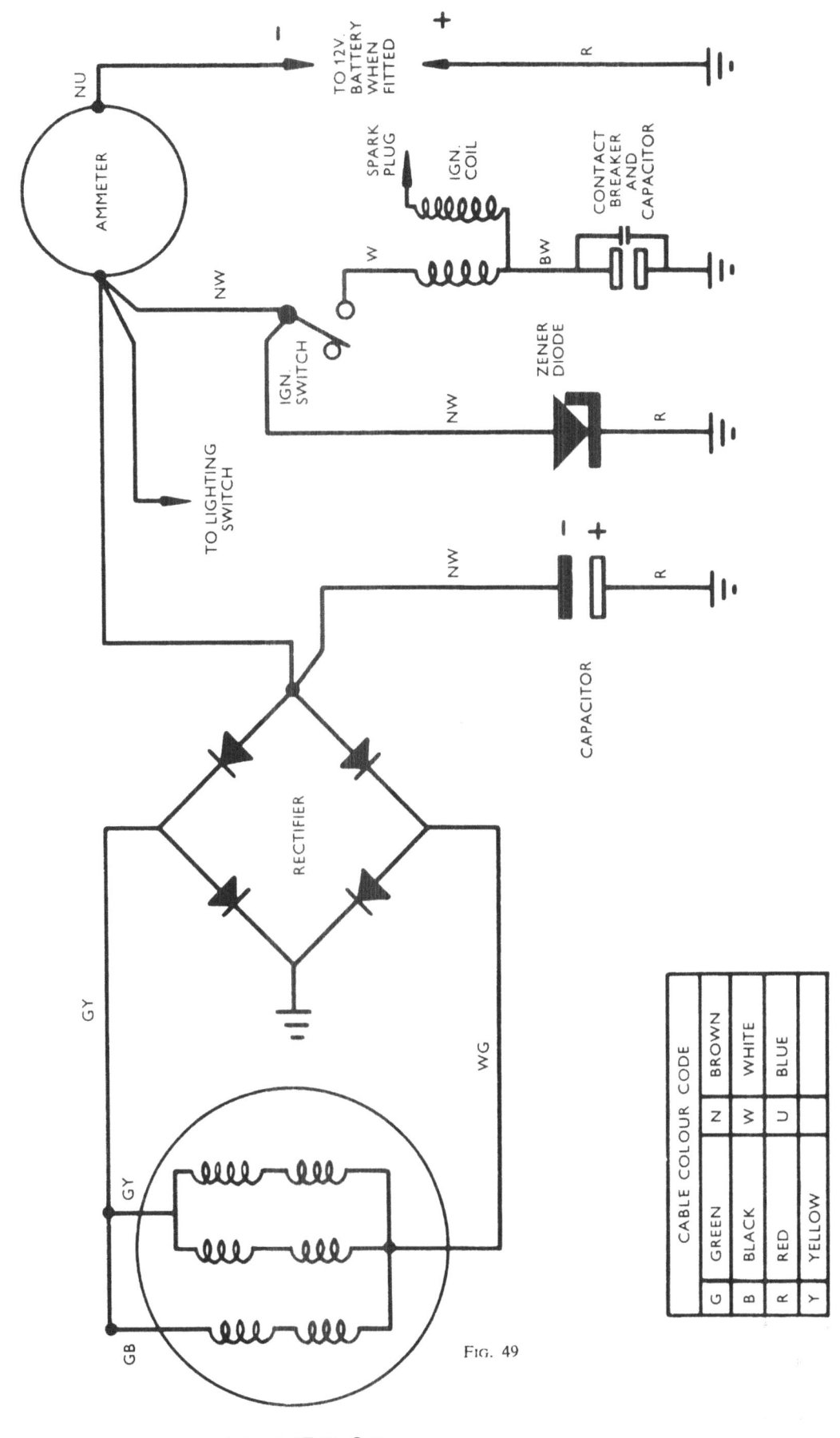

Fig. 49

Zener Diode Charge Control
(Serial No. 49345)

As the battery becomes recharged its terminal voltage rises, and when it reaches approximately 14 volts the Zener diode, which up to this point has opposed the passage of current, becomes partially conductive and thus provides an alternative path for a small part of the alternator output. Further small rises in battery voltage result in large increases in diode conductivity until, at approximately 15 volts (the on-charge voltage of a fully charged 12 volt battery), the bulk of the alternator output is by-passed and the system off-load voltage is stabilized.

If, now, an electrical load such as the headlamp is switched on, the system voltage will fall below 15 volts and less current will flow through the diode, the balance being diverted to feed the load. In the event of the load being heavy enough to depress the system voltage below 14 volts, the Zener diode will revert to its high-resistance state of virtual non-conductivity and all of the generated output from the alternator will go to meeting the current demands of the battery and equipment.

Test procedure

Disconnect the lead from the Zener diode and connect ammeter (in series) between the diode Lucar terminal and lead previously disconnected. The ammeter red or positive lead must connect to the diode terminal.

Connect d/c voltmeter across Zener diode and heat-sink. The red or positive lead must connect to the heat-sink which is earthed to the machine frame by its fixing bolts and a separate earth lead. The black lead connects to the Lucar terminal.

Ensure that all lights are "off", start the engine, and gradually increase engine speed, while at the same time observing both meters.

Note: It is essential that the batteries are in a good condition and in a reasonably good state of charge. If battery condition is uncertain, it should be temporarily replaced by a good battery for this test.

1. When the voltage across the Zener diode reaches 12.75 volts, the Zener current ammeter must indicate zero.
2. Increase engine speed until a Zener current of 2 amperes is indicated on the ammeter. At this value a satisfactory Zener diode should cause a reading on the voltmeter of between 14.4-16.4 volts.

Test conclusions

If the ammeter in test (1) registers any current at all before the voltmeter indicates that the voltage across the Zener is 12.75 volts, then a replacement Zener diode must be fitted.

If test (1) proves satisfactory, but in test (2) a higher voltage than that stated is registered on the voltmeter, before the ammeter registers 2 amperes, then a replacement Zener diode must be fitted. Torque the fixing nut to 28 in./lbs.

The Contact Breaker 6CA

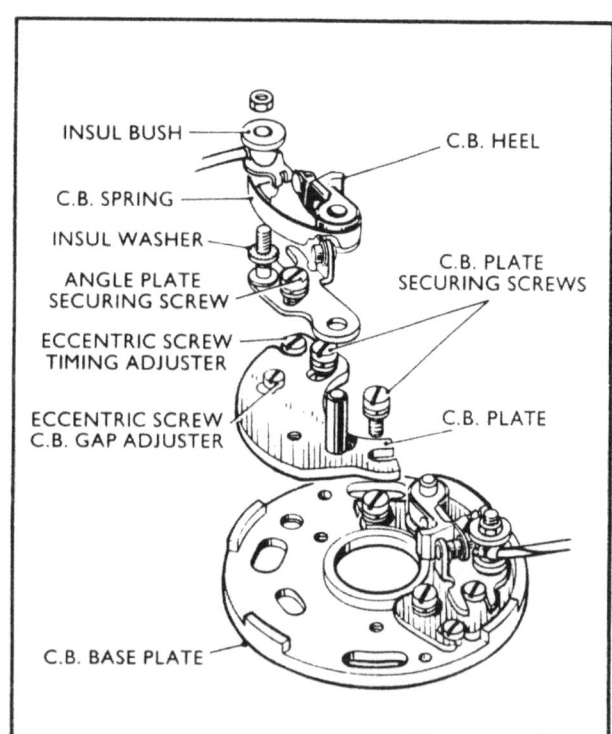

Adjustment for the contact breaker is described in paragraph "Setting ignition timing". A breakdown of the contact breaker is shown in Figure 50. The condensor pack is remotely mounted in the battery carrier compartment.

Specification

Contact breaker gap	0.014″-0.016″ (0.35mm-0.4mm)
Contact breaker spring load (measured at contacts)	18 oz. F - 24 oz. F.
Extractor thread	$\frac{5}{16}$″ UNF

Maintenance

1. After the first 500 miles (800 km) of a new contact breaker or new contact set:
   (A) Turn the engine until one of the contact breakers is open to maximum distance.
   (B) Insert a 0.015″ (0.38mm) flat feeler gauge between the contacts.
   (C) If the gap is correct the gauge will be a sliding fit. If adjustment is necessary, maintain the position giving maximum opening of the contacts and slacken the fixed contact (angle plate) locking screw. Rotate the fixed contact eccentric screw adjuster until the gauge can be inserted as a sliding fit. Tighten the locking screw and recheck the gap.

FIG. 50 *Part exploded view of model 6CA Contact Breaker*

(D) Repeat the above operation on the other contact breaker.
2. Every 6,000 miles (9,650 km):
(A) Examine the contact breaker. Contacts that are burnt, blackened or showing evidence of pitting and piling should be cleaned with a fine carborundum stone or emery cloth. Cleaning is best carried out with the contacts removed (see "Dismantling").
(B) After cleaning, remove grease and metal dust with a petrol-moistened cloth.
(C) Before reassembly, smear the contact breaker heel pivot post with Mobilgrease No. 1.
(D) Check and set the contact breaker gaps as described under 1 (C).
(E) Rotate the engine until one of the contact breaker's heel is in the middle portion of the cam that provides the open period of the contacts.
(F) Smear the cam either side of this heel with Shell Retinax A or equivalent grease.
(G) Rotate the engine and check that a small amount of grease is being carried by the leading edge of each contact breaker heel.

Dismantling
1. Unscrew and remove the nut securing the contact breaker spring to the anchor post.
2. Lift off the spring and heel together with the insul bush, capacitor lead and contact breaker lead terminations.
3. Unscrew and remove the fixed contact (angle plate) securing screw and lift off the fixed contact.

Reassembly
Contacts
It should be noted that the contact breaker lead termination and the capacitor lead termination should be positioned with both tags inside the curve of the spring. This is important as fouling of the contacts may occur if placed in any other position.

Automatic advance unit
The correct manner of assembly will be apparent on inspection. However, two points should be carefully noted.
1. Each spring has a tapered loop at one end. This end should be attached to the cam pin.
2. The cam has two weight location pins and the longest of these pins is designed to fit into the radiused range slot.

The rectifier
The full-wave rectifier with coloured connections is shown in Figure 51. Maintenance is confined to checking the central bolt for security.

The ignition coils
The two coils, in tandem, are secured to the frame by two bolts with double clips. During engine service, when the petrol tank is removed, check all the coil connections for security.

Stop lamp switch
The switch is attached to the rear brake pedal. The switch bracket is slotted for adjustment, when the brake pedal position is altered.

The rear lamp
The lamp is secured by two bolts. To remove the lens for access to the stop lamp bulb, take out the two lens fixing screws.

The headlamp
To change the main bulb, release the screw on top of the lamp body, the light unit can then be removed. Press down the cap for the bulb compartment—turn anti-clockwise—the cap can be removed. The main bulb can now be removed.

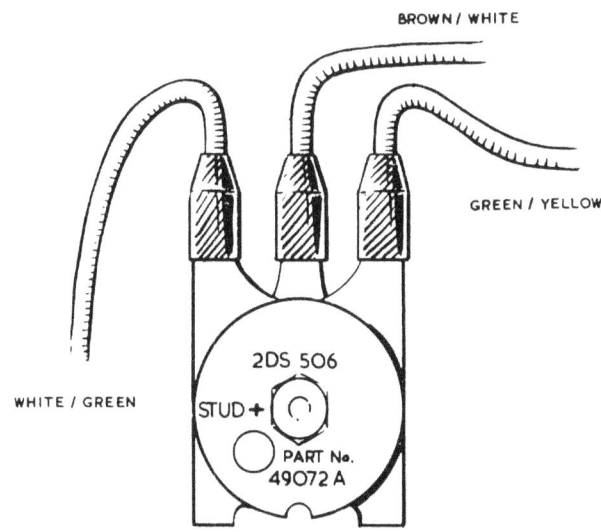

FIG. 51

FULL-WAVE RECTIFIER

The Battery

Lucas lead-acid batteries Model PUZ5A (12 volt)

The battery has a moulded translucent case, through which the electrolyte level can be seen. A coloured line on the side of the battery indicates the correct level at which the electrolyte should be maintained.

While the battery is being charged, water is lost due to gassing and evaporation. This makes it necessary to frequently (preferably each week) check the level of electrolyte and, if necessary, replace the loss of distilled water. It is normal for the level of electrolyte to rise whilst the battery is being charged and for this reason, to avoid any tendency to over-filling of the battery, it is important to check the level of electrolyte and top-up the battery only during off-charge periods.

To take a hydrometer reading, tilt the battery to bring sufficient electrolyte above the separator guard. If the level of the electrolyte is so low that a hydrometer reading cannot be taken, no attempt should be made to take a reading after adding distilled water until the battery has been on charge for at least 30 minutes.

Measure the specific gravity of the acid in each cell in turn. The reading given by each cell should be approximately the same; if one cell differs appreciably from the others, an internal fault in that cell is indicated.

The appearance of the electrolyte drawn into the hydrometer when taking a reading gives a useful indication of the state of the plates: If it is very dirty, or contains small particles in suspension, it is possible that the plates are in a bad condition.

The battery must not be subjected to a heavy discharge test.

Maintenance: Occasionally wipe away all dirt and moisture from the top of the battery and ensure that the connections are kept clean and tight.

If the motorcycle is to be out of use for a considerable time, the battery should be removed and maintained in a good state of charge, by applying a short freshening charge approximately every two weeks.

The specific gravity of a fully charged battery is 1.270-1.290 at 60° for climates normally below 80° F. (27° C.) and 1.210-1.230 at 60° F. for climates above 80° F. (27° C.).

The recharge rate of a PUZ5A battery is 1.0 amp.

Fig. 52 *Battery model PUZ5A*

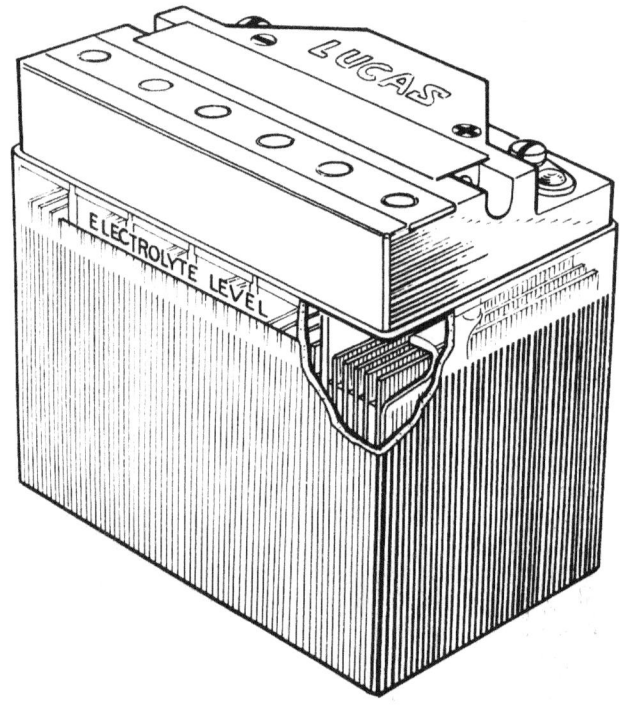

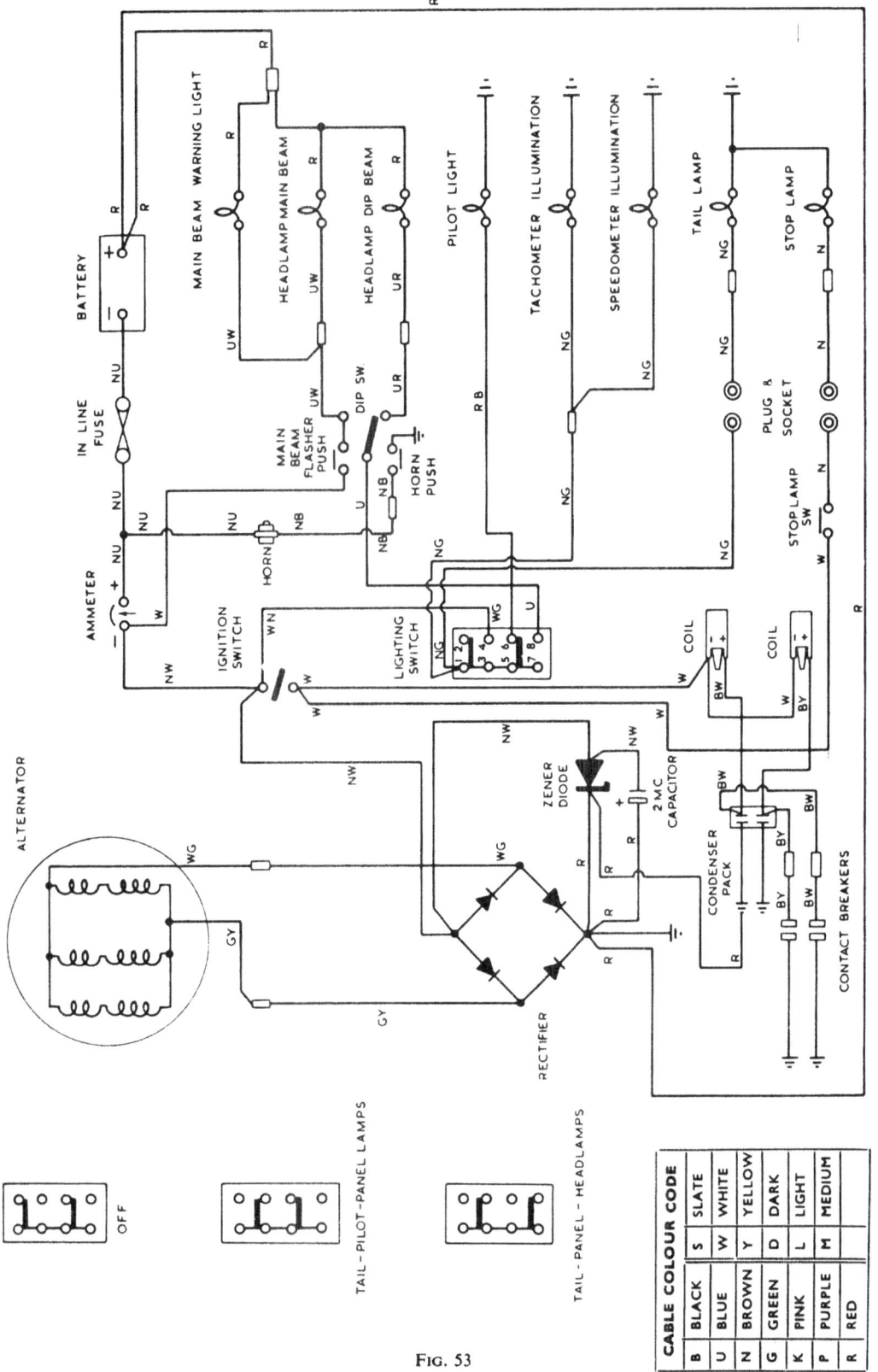

Fig. 53

Models after Engine No. 131257
March 1969 onwards - with camshaft driven contact breaker points

Engine Camshaft Chain

To examine, or adjust the camshaft chain, on engines where the contact breaker is actuated by the engine camshaft, the timing cover must be removed by:

Disconnect the rocker box oil feed pipe union nut from the timing cover.

Remove cap for contact breaker (two screws).

Remove contact breaker base plate (two hexagon bolts and washers) with the wires attached.

Remove auto advance unit central bolt.

Insert withdrawal bolt 06-0934, gently tighten this bolt to separate the unit from the camshaft. Take out timing cover screws (12). Note location—three different lengths are used—then remove the timing cover.

With the cover removed, oil will seep from the oil drilling adjacent to the oil pipe junction block. Use a timing cover screw to temporarily blank off seepage.

Adjust the camshaft chain as described in Paragraph 11, page 26.

Contact Breaker Oil Seal

An oil seal, Part No. 034053, is housed in the timing cover, which encircles the plain portion of the camshaft, to prevent oil entering the contact breaker compartment.

When refitting the timing cover, to prevent damage to the oil seal as it passes over the camshaft, a guide bush, Part No. 06-1359, must be used.

To use the guide bush, the threaded portion is screwed onto the camshaft as far as it will go. A little oil used on the outside diameter of the guide bush will facilitate assembly.

Removing the Oil Seal

Prise the seal out of its housing with a sharp pointed tool.

Fitting the Oil Seal

Warm the timing cover, press the seal into position, with the metal backing facing the contact breaker compartment.

Setting Ignition Timing

Before refitting the auto advance unit:

Remove cap on primary chain case to expose the indicator plate.

Position the engine on the drive side cylinder so that the mark on the rotor registers with 28° on the indicator plate.

Insert the auto advance unit with the rivets for the bobweights in line with the two screw holes for the contact cover—the slot in the cam face should now be at approximately 9 o'clock.

Fit the contact breaker base plate—the yellow and black ead is for the drive side cylinder.

Finally check and adjust the timing as described on page 27.

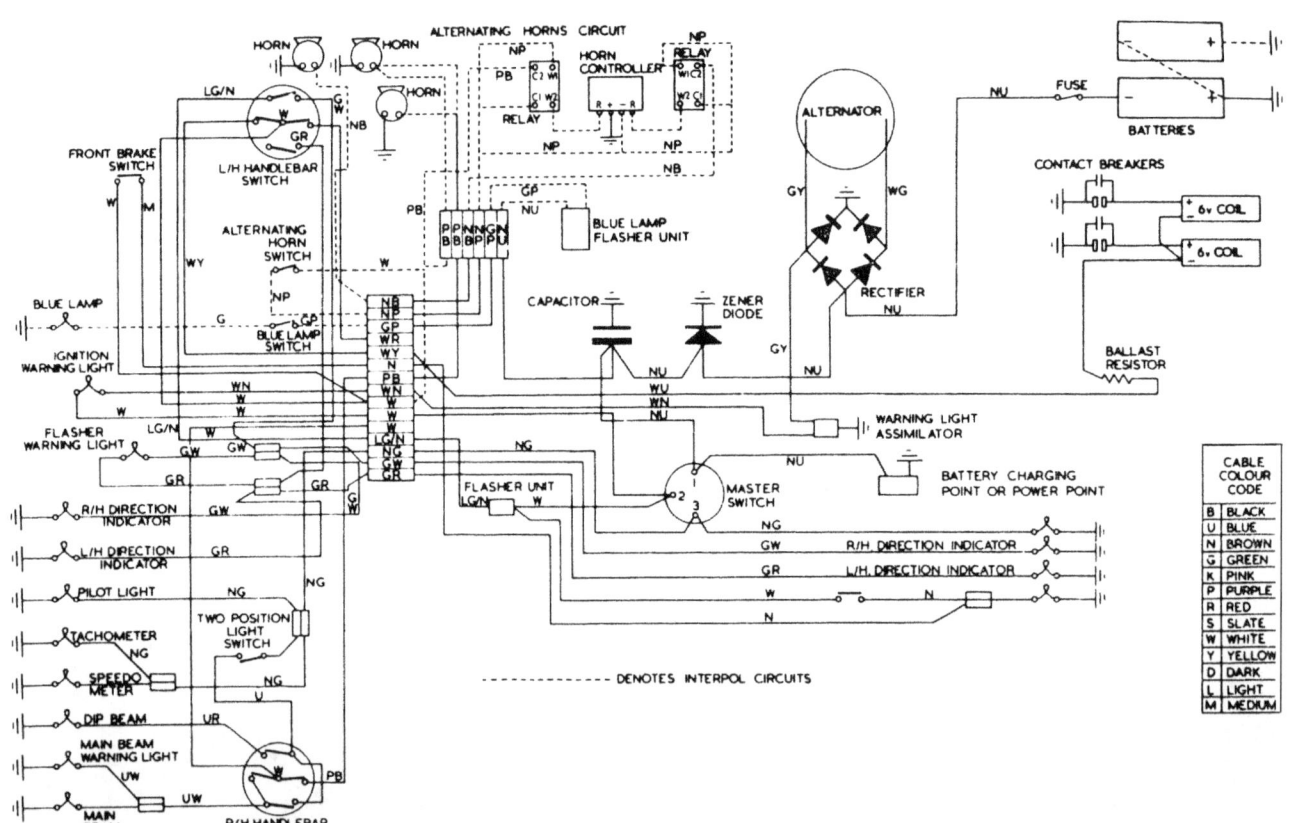

NORTON COMMANDO 1971 (ALL MODELS)

VELOCEPRESS MANUALS - MOTORCYCLE

1930'S BRITISH MOTORCYCLE CARBS & ELEC COMPONENTS (BOOK OF)
1930'S BRITISH MOTORCYCLE ENGINES (OVERHAUL & MAINTENANCE)
1930'S BRITISH MOTORCYCLE GEARBOXES & CLUTCHES (BOOK OF)
AJS 1932-1948 SINGLES & TWINS 250cc THRU 1000cc (BOOK OF)
AJS 1945-1960 SINGLES 350cc & 500cc MODELS 16 & 18 (BOOK OF)
AJS 1955-1965 SINGLES 350cc & 500cc (BOOK OF)
ARIEL UP TO 1932 (BOOK OF)
ARIEL 1932-1939 PREWAR MODELS (BOOK OF)
ARIEL 1933-1951 (WORKSHOP MANUAL)
ARIEL 1939-1960 4 STROKE SINGLES (BOOK OF)
ARIEL 1958-1964 LEADER & ARROW (BOOK OF)
BMW R26 R27 (1956-1967) FACTORY WORKSHOP MANUAL
BMW R50 R50S R60 R69S (1955-1969) FACTORY WORKSHOP MANUAL
BRIDGESTONE 90 SERIES FACTORY WSM & PARTS CATALOGUE
BRIDGESTONE 175 SERIES FACTORY WSM & PARTS CATALOGUE
BRIDGESTONE 350 SERIES FACTORY WSM & PARTS CATALOGUES
BSA BANTAM ALL MODELS FROM 1948 ONWARDS (BOOK OF)
BSA SINGLES & V-TWINS UP TO 1927 (BOOK OF)
BSA SINGLES & V-TWINS UP TO 1930 (BOOK OF)
BSA SINGLES & V-TWINS UP TO 1935 (BOOK OF)
BSA SINGLES & V-TWINS 1936-1939 (BOOK OF)
BSA OHV & SV SINGLES 250-600cc 1945-1959 (BOOK OF)
BSA OHV & SV SINGLES 250cc (ONLY) 1954-1970 (BOOK OF)
BSA OHV SINGLES 350 & 500cc 1955-1967 (BOOK OF)
BSA TWINS 1948-1962 (BOOK OF)
BSA TWINS 1962-1969 (SECOND BOOK OF)
CYCLEMOTOR (BOOK OF)
DOUGLAS 1929-1939 PREWAR ALL MODELS (BOOK OF)
DOUGLAS 1948-1957 POSTWAR ALL MODELS FACTORY SHOP MANUAL
DUCATI 160cc, 250cc & 350cc OHC MODELS FACTORY SHOP MANUAL
HONDA 50 ALL MODELS UP TO 1970 INC MONKEY & TRAIL (BOOK OF)
HONDA 90 ALL MODELS UP TO 1966 (BOOK OF)
HONDA 125-150cc TWINS C/CS/CB/CA FACTORY WORKSHOP MANUAL
HONDA 250-305 TWINS C/CS/CB FACTORY WORKSHOP MANUAL
HONDA 450 CB/CL 1965-1974 K0 TO K7 WORKSHOP MANUAL
HONDA C100 SUPER CUB FACTORY WORKSHOP MANUAL
HONDA C110 SPORT CUB 1962-1969 FACTORY WORKSHOP MANUAL
HONDA TWINS & SINGLES 50cc THRU 305cc 1960-1966 (BOOK OF)
HONDA TWINS ALL MODELS 125cc THRU 450cc UP TO 1968 (BOOK OF)
INDIAN PONYBIKE, BOY RACER & PAPOOSE ILL PARTS LIST & SALES LIT
J.A.P. ENGINES 1927-1952 & MOTORCYCLES 1934-1952 (BOOK OF)
LAMBRETTA 1947-1957 ALL 125 & 150cc MODELS (BOOK OF)
LAMBRETTA 1957-1970 LI & TV MODELS (SECOND BOOK OF)
MATCHLESS 1931-1939 ALL MODELS 250cc THRU 990cc (BOOK OF)
MATCHLESS 1945-1956 350 & 500cc SINGLES (BOOK OF)
MATCHLESS 1955-1966 350 & 500cc SINGLES (BOOK OF)
NEW IMPERIAL ALL SV & OHV FROM 1935 ONWARDS (BOOK OF)
NORTON 1932-1939 PREWAR MODELS (BOOK OF)
NORTON 1932-1947 (BOOK OF)
NORTON 1938-1956 (BOOK OF)
NORTON 1955-1963 MODELS 19, 50 & ES2 (BOOK OF)
NORTON 1955-1965 DOMINATOR TWINS (BOOK OF)
NORTON 1960-1970 TWIN CYLINDER FACTORY WORKSHOP MANUAL
NSU PRIMA 1956-1964 ALL MODELS (BOOK OF)
NSU QUICKLY 1953-1963 ALL MODELS (BOOK OF)
PANTHER 1932-1958 LIGHTWEIGHT MODELS 250 & 350cc (BOOK OF)
PANTHER 1938-1966 HEAVYWEIGHT MODELS 600 & 650cc (BOOK OF)
RALEIGH MOPEDS 1960-1969 (BOOK OF)
RALEIGH MOTORCYCLES 1919-1933 (BOOK OF)
ROYAL ENFIELD 1934-1946 SINGLES & V TWINS (BOOK OF)
ROYAL ENFIELD 1937-1953 SINGLES & V TWINS (BOOK OF)
ROYAL ENFIELD 1946-1962 SINGLES (BOOK OF)
ROYAL ENFIELD 1958-1966 250cc & 350cc SINGLES (SECOND BOOK OF)
ROYAL ENFIELD 736cc INTERCEPTOR FACTORY WORKSHOP MANUAL
RUDGE 1933-1939 (BOOK OF)
SUNBEAM 1928-1939 (BOOK OF)
SUNBEAM 1946-1957 S7 & S8 (BOOK OF)
SUZUKI 50cc & 80cc UP TO 1966 (BOOK OF)
SUZUKI T10 1963-1967 FACTORY WORKSHOP MANUAL
SUZUKI T20 & T200 1965-1969 FACTORY WORKSHOP MANUAL
SUZUKI TWINS 1962 ONWARDS 125-500cc WORKSHOP MANUAL
TRIUMPH 1935-1939 PREWAR MODELS (BOOK OF)
TRIUMPH 1935-1949 (BOOK OF)
TRIUMPH 1937-1951 (WORKSHOP MANUAL)
TRIUMPH 1945-1955 FACTORY WORKSHOP MANUAL
TRIUMPH 1945-1958 TWINS (BOOK OF)
TRIUMPH 1956-1969 TWINS (BOOK OF)
VELOCETTE 1925-1970 ALL SINGLES & TWINS (BOOK OF)
VESPA 1951-1961 (BOOK OF)
VESPA 1955-1963 125 & 150cc & GS MODELS (SECOND BOOK OF)
VESPA 1955-1968 GS & SS (BOOK OF)
VESPA 1963-1972 90, 125 & 150cc (THIRD BOOK OF)
VILLIERS ENGINE UP TO 1959 INC. 3 WHEELERS (BOOK OF)
VILLIERS ENGINE UP TO 1969 (BOOK OF)
VINCENT 1935-1955 (WORKSHOP MANUAL)
YAMAHA 1961-1967 YA5 & YA6 (WORKSHOP MANUAL & ILL PARTS LIST)
YAMAHA 1971-1972 JT1& JT2 (WORKSHOP MANUAL & ILL PARTS LIST)

VELOCEPRESS TECHNICAL BOOKS – MOTORCYCLE

CATALOG OF BRITISH MOTORCYCLES (1951 MODELS)
LUCAS ELECTRONICS BRITISH M/CYCLES REPAIR & PARTS (1950-1977)
MOTORCYCLE ENGINEERING (P.E. Irving)
MOTORCYCLE ROAD TESTS 1949-1953 (Motor Cycle Magazine UK)
SPEED AND HOW TO OBTAIN IT (Motor Cycle Magazine UK)
TUNING FOR SPEED (P.E. Irving)

VELOCEPRESS MANUALS - THREE WHEELER'S

BSA THREE WHEELER (BOOK OF)
VINTAGE MORGAN THREE WHEELER (BOOK OF)

VELOCEPRESS MANUALS - AUTOMOBILE

ALFA ROMEO GIULIA WORKSHOP MANUAL 1300 TO 2000cc 1962-1975
ALFA ROMEO GIULIA TECH MANUAL CARBURETED CARS FROM 1962
ALFA ROMEO GIULIA TECH MANUAL FUEL INJECTED CARS FROM 1969
ALFA ROMEO GIULIETTA & GIULIA 750 & 101 SERIES 1955-1965 WSM
AUSTIN-HEALEY SPRITE & MG MIDGET WORKSHOP MANUAL 1958-1971
BMW 600 LIMOUSINE FACTORY WORKSHOP MANUAL
BMW 600 LIMOUSINE OWNERS HAND BOOK & SERVICE MANUAL
BMW 2000 & 2002 1966-1976 WORKSHOP MANUAL
BMW ISETTA FACTORY WORKSHOP MANUAL
CORVAIR 1960-1969 WORKSHOP MANUAL
CORVETTE V8 1955-1962 WORKSHOP MANUAL
FIAT 500 FACTORY WORKSHOP MANUAL 1957-1973
FIAT 600, 600D & MULTIPLA FACTORY WORKSHOP MANUAL 1955-1969
JAGUAR E-TYPE 3.8 & 4.2 SERIES 1 & 2 WORKSHOP MANUAL
JAGUAR MK 7, 8, 9 & XK120, 140, 150 WORKSHOP MANUAL 1948-1961
METROPOLITAN FACTORY WORKSHOP MANUAL
MGA & MGB OWNERS HANDBOOK & WORKSHOP MANUAL
MG MIDGET TC, TD, TF & TF1500 WORKSHOP MANUAL
PORSCHE 356 1948-1965 WORKSHOP MANUAL
PORSCHE 911 2.0, 2.2, 2.4 LITRE 1964-1973 WORKSHOP MANUAL
PORSCHE 911 2.7, 3.0, 3.2 LITRE 1973-1989 WORKSHOP MANUAL
PORSCHE 912 WORKSHOP MANUAL
TRIUMPH TR2, TR3, TR4 1953-1965 WORKSHOP MANUAL
VOLKSWAGEN TRANSPORTER, TRUCKS & WAGONS 1950-1979 WSM
VOLVO 1944-1968 ALL MODELS WORKSHOP MANUAL

VELOCEPRESS TECHNICAL BOOKS - AUTOMOBILE

FERRARI 250/GT SERVICE AND MAINTENANCE
FERRARI GUIDE TO PERFORMANCE
FERRARI OWNER'S HANDBOOK
FERRARI TUNING TIPS & MAINTENANCE TECHNIQUES
HOW TO BUILD A FIBERGLASS CAR
HOW TO BUILD A RACING CAR
HOW TO RESTORE THE MODEL 'A' FORD
MASERATI OWNER'S HANDBOOK
OBERT'S FIAT GUIDE
PERFORMANCE TUNING THE SUNBEAM TIGER
SOUPING THE VOLKSWAGEN
SOLEX CARBURETORS (EMPHASIS ON UK & EU AUTOMOBILES)
SU CARBURETORS (EMPHASIS ON UK AUTOMOBILES)
WEBER CARBURETORS (EMPHASIS ON ALFA & FIAT)

VELOCEPRESS BOOKS & GUIDES - AUTOMOBILE

ABARTH BUYERS GUIDE
COMPLETE CATALOG OF JAPANESE MOTOR VEHICLES
FERRARI 308 SERIES BUYER'S AND OWNER'S GUIDE
FERRARI BERLINETTA LUSSO
FERRARI BROCHURES AND SALES LITERATURE 1946-1967
FERRARI BROCHURES AND SALES LITERATURE 1968-1989
FERRARI OPP, MAINTENANCE & SERVICE H/BOOKS 1948-1963
FERRARI SERIAL NUMBERS PART I - ODD NUMBERS TO 21399
FERRARI SERIAL NUMBERS PART II - EVEN NUMBERS TO 1050
FERRARI SPYDER CALIFORNIA
HENRY'S FABULOUS MODEL "A" FORD
MASERATI BROCHURES AND SALES LITERATURE

VELOCEPRESS BOOKS – RACING

CARRERA PANAMERICANA - MEXICAN ROAD RACE (BOOK OF)
DIALED IN - THE JAN OPPERMAN STORY
IF HEMINGWAY HAD WRITTEN A RACING NOVEL
VEDA ORR'S NEW REVISED HOT ROD PICTORIAL

AUTOBOOKS WORKSHOP MANUALS & BROOKLANDS ROAD TEST PORTFOLIOS

FOR A COMPLETE LISTING OF THE AUTOBOOKS & BROOKLANDS TITLES THAT WE CURRENTLY HAVE AVAILABLE, PLEASE VISIT OUR WEBSITE.

www.VelocePress.com

NOTES

www.ingramcontent.com/pod-product-compliance
Lightning Source LLC
Chambersburg PA
CBHW060255240426
43673CB00047B/1931